A MEMOIR OF
THE WARSAW
UPRISING

Miron Bialoszewski

edited and translated by
Madeline Levine

ardis / ann arbor

Memoir of the Warsaw Uprising

Pamietnik z Powstania Warszawskiego
originally published by: Panstwowy Instytut
Wydawniczy, Warszawa 1970.

Published by Ardis, 2901 Heatherway, Ann Arbor,
Michigan, 48104.

Library of Congress Catalog Card Number
ISBN 0-88233-275-9 (cloth), 0-88233-276-7 (paperback).

Publication of this book was made possible in part by a grant from the University of North Carolina at Chapel Hill.

CONTENTS

Frontispiece — Miron Bialoszewski in 1970.

A GUIDE TO THE PRONUNCIATION OF POLISH NAMES

As a rule, Polish names are stressed on the penultimate syllable.

Polish letters	English equivalents
c	ts
cz	ch
j	y
rz	zh
sz	sh
w	v
a	ah
e	eh
i	ee
o	oh; sometimes oo
u	oo (as in soon)
y	i (as in if)

Diacritical marks have been omitted in this translation.

TRANSLATOR'S INTRODUCTION

Miron Bialoszewski's *Memoir of the Warsaw Uprising*[1] has been both welcomed in Poland as a major literary event and condemned as a blasphemous mockery of a revered moment in national history. The functional prosaic title of the book appears to promise a work of unambiguous content: a recounting of a major historical event--the Warsaw Uprising of 1944--as recollected by a participant in that event. But Bialoszewski's memoir is not as straightforward as its simple title suggests.

If we can divide memoir literature into two basic categories—one, the public figure's review of events in the public domain, often written with an eye to perpetuating a particular interpretation of those events, and the other, the more private self-revelations of the memoirist who seeks in the past a clue to his own personality and career—then we can say that Bialoszewski's memoir partakes of qualities from each of these categories. His subject is a major historical event, but he was not a public figure when he participated in it. When he came to write his memoir some twenty years after the fact his fame was as a private man of letters, yet his return to the past is not primarily a search for self-knowledge nor an effort to reveal to the public the sources of his art. Rather, Bialoszewski's *Memoir of the Warsaw Uprising* is a nonfictional work of literature which is deeply revisionist both in its presentation of the Warsaw Uprising and in its approach to the memoir genre.

The author of this controversial memoir was born in Warsaw in 1922 and has made his home there ever since. Bialoszewski was

17 years old when the Germans invaded Poland on September 1, 1939 and 22 years old during the Warsaw Uprising. He began to write during the German occupation. These bare biographical facts are shared by a generation of Polish writers who were born during the 1920s and who came to maturity during the Second World War. They grew up during Poland's short-lived era of independence which spanned the years between the Versailles Treaty and the Nazi invasion. The spirit of national revival during the early years of the Polish Republic had faltered under the anxious uncertainty of the 1930s and collapsed during the more than five years of occupation.

The crucial experience in the lives of the generation to which Bialoszewski belongs was the traumatic loss of a normal youth during a period when violent death was an ever-present possibility. Old enough to have absorbed the traditional Polish-Catholic patriotism, members of this generation emerged from the war distrusting the tradition-sanctioned slogans and philosophies they had been raised on, substituting for positive beliefs an attitude of moral relativism. The grim experiences of their young adulthood have left an indelible mark on the literary output of this generation, which includes such well-known writers as Tadeusz Rozewicz and Tadeusz Borowski. Bialoszewski bears a family resemblance to these authors in that, like them, he is obsessed with the fragility of civilization and displays little if any faith in the durability of cultural and moral codes. Like them, he expresses his disaffection by rejecting the traditional standards of aesthetics in order to seek a more appropriate style for his fundamental scepticism.

Throughout Bialoszewski's poetry and prose[2] (the boundaries between these two categories are often blurred) there is a consistent thematic concentration on simple objects and personal events which are outside the mainstream of traditional poetic subject matter. His poems in praise of such domestic articles as slotted spoons, stoves, chairs and quilts are typical of this attitude. His poetic iconoclasm, manifested by a disdain for conventional language as well as subject matter, has aroused highly partisan feelings among Polish critics.

The language of his poems, like that of his memoir, is unpolished, abrupt, colloquial; the syntax is fragmentary and distorted. Bialoszewski plays with language, not it would seem, with the positive aim of renewing the poetic medium, but out of an abiding lack of faith in the received literary language. His poetics and the outlook which it expresses are minimalist, demanding no overarching traditions or philosophy—nothing, indeed, beyond the concrete realities of daily life and speech. The following poem, in Czeslaw Milosz' translation, is characteristic[3]:

And Even, Even If They Take Away My Stove

    My Inexhaustible Ode to Joy

    I have a stove
    similar to a triumphal arch!

    They take away my stove
    similar to a triumphal arch!!

    Give me back my stove
    similar to a triumphal arch!!!

    They took it away.
    What remains is
    a grey
        naked
            hole.

    And this is enough for me;
    grey naked hole.
    grey naked hole.
    greynakedhole.

During the years when he was beginning to achieve fame as a poet Bialoszewski was well known in Warsaw as the director of a small avant-garde theater which was housed in his two-room apartment in that city. There is a striking description of this Teatr Osobny (Private Theater) by the American columnist, Joseph Alsop, who visited Bialoszewski in the spring of 1959[4]:

Nothing quite like this apartment exists anywhere else in the world. Every single piece of furniture has been gravely maimed

11

or wounded at some time in the past. Abstract paintings, strange and menacing constructions of wire and masking tape, great numbers of fragments of Polish baroque church-sculpture, two damaged but still magical Polish-Byzantine ikons, the remnants of a beautifully tender late Gothic altar piece— all these and many other objects are hung or strewn about.

This museum of crippled objects which Alsop portrays has its literary counterpart in Bialoszewski's reconstruction of the Warsaw Uprising, with its careful attention to the artifacts of life under siege. Similarly, Bialoszewski's rejection of literary tradition in his poetry and his refusal to limit himself to conventional and so-called "tasteful" subject matter also finds its expression in his unorthodox treatment of this singular event in contemporary Polish history. Paradoxically, this poet of banality has chosen to address himself to a historical event of great moment, although he has done so in order to assert the primacy of the ordinary demands of life even in a situation of extraordinary horror.

The Warsaw Uprising broke out on August 1, 1944 as the war in Europe was drawing to a close. During the summer of 1944, while the Western Allies pushed eastward into France, the Soviet Red Army crossed the pre-1939 Soviet-Polish border into the territory which the secret protocol of the Molotov-Ribbentrop Pact had awarded to Russia. In July 1944, in the city of Lublin, the Russians set up a provisional Communist government for Poland. It was designed to contest the authority of the London-based anti-Communist government-in-exile which disputed Soviet claims to Poland's eastern territories. By the end of July, Red Army detachments had reached the east bank of the Vistula and were encamped in the working-class suburb of Praga, directly across the river from Warsaw.

At this juncture, the underground Home Army, encouraged and directed by the London government-in-exile, and assisted by other partisan groups, spearheaded the uprising in the capital. The leadership hoped that by liberating Warsaw they could seize the initiative in the coming struggle for power with Moscow's puppet provisional government. Moreover, for many of the participants, the uprising was to be a demonstration of Polish pride and vigor. Poles would not stand by passively to be "liberated" from the

German yoke by the detested Russians.

The uprising did not succeed, however. The German forces in the city were not as weakened as had been thought and, most importantly, the Soviet forces refrained from coming to the aid of the embattled capital until the uprising was practically defeated. The people of Warsaw were left to fight and die by themselves. By the end of the uprising in early October over 200,000 Poles had been killed in the fighting and bombings. After the forced evacuation of the surviving population in mid-October the Germans completed the physical destruction of the city, burning and bombing the few remaining buildings. When it was all over, Warsaw had been virtually obliterated. The clearing of the rubble and slow reconstruction of the city took many years and even today there are areas in Warsaw which still bear the scars of devastation from the 1944 uprising as well as from the doomed Warsaw Ghetto Uprising of Polish Jews in April 1943.

Bialoszewski was one of the survivors. In his memoir he speaks of the uprising as "the greatest experience of my life." Perhaps because of the centrality of this experience, he waited almost a quarter of a century before attempting to shape his memories into some kind of literary form. As he tells us in the memoir, it was precisely the question of *form* over which he hesitated:

> *For twenty years I could not write about this. Although I wanted to very much. I would talk. About the uprising. To so many people. All sorts of people. So many times. And all along I was thinking that I must describe the uprising, somehow or other* describe *it. And I didn't even know that those twenty years of talking (I have been talking about it for twenty years, because it is the greatest experience of my life —a closed experience), precisely that talking, is the only suitable way to describe the uprising.*

The form which Bialoszewski finally selected as least likely to distort the truth of his experience is a rambling monologue which wanders from incident to incident, with frequent digressions from a basically chronological structure. Bialoszewski rejects the diary form, which preserves the order of events as they occurred and

13

which presents the diarist's assessment without benefit of hindsight; he also rejects the retrospective narrative of memoirs in which events have been recollected, re-interpreted and then marshalled prior to writing to form a coherent progression. Instead, Bialoszewski adopts the pose of a racconteur and preserves, by a variety of structural and linguistic devices, the illusion of a spoken, off-the-cuff narration.

One of the most important narrative devices is the yielding to free association in utter disregard of the chronological havoc wreaked by this approach. The reader will confront this stylistic device from the very first pages of the memoir. Bialoszewski moves freely amidst a multiplicity of time levels in his narrative. These include the present time of writing; the past of the uprising which is recreated as though it were the present; the elapsed time between these levels seen variously as past or present, depending on the perspective from which it is viewed; and what we may call the "historical past" of the years before the uprising.

Although a breathless outpouring of recollections is the basic narrative style of the memoir, it is by no means the only voice in which Bialoszewski speaks. Bialoszewski frequently agonizes over the accuracy of his memories, but on occasion he speaks with the authority of a reporter as, for example, when he describes the post-war exhumations of the hastily buried dead at which he was present as a journalist. Occasionally, he yields to an emotional outburst, but even the deepest of emotions is expressed in a muted tone. This emotional understatement is effective because the horror which he describes is so overwhelming that any attempts at a sophisticated rhetoric would be both ludicrous and offensive in contrast. As Julian Przybos, a major Polish poet, once wrote, "It is impossible either to speak or to keep silent about this."

Bialoszewski strengthens the illusion of an unpolished spoken narrative by using colloquial language and ignoring the rules of grammar in favor of the intonations of the spoken idiom. This makes it very difficult to render the full flavor of the memoir in English translation. Since Polish syntax is more flexible than ours, I have been forced at times to opt for a more "normal" English than is strictly called for, rather than run the risk of making the text appear utterly bizarre—which it certainly is not in the original.

Although Bialoszewski preserves throughout his memoir the appearance of a spoken narrative whose development is determined primarily by the vagaries of free association and memories, the whole is actually carefully calculated to present a thorough picture of what the author calls the "topography" of the action. The text is densely aural and visual. We *see* Warsaw in the process of disintegration—not just the quick change from wholeness to ruins as the result of a direct hit but the multiple stages of metamorphosis of particular lovingly described churches and other buildings of the Old City (Stare Miasto, Starowka) as their contours and facades are slowly eaten away. We *hear* the unusual sounds of the city. Bialoszewski uses onomatopoeic devices to mimic the varied noises of the artillery, the guns, the minethrowers. We also hear, in one of the most majestic scenes in the memoir, a hymn which is being sung by thousands in a labyrinthine bomb shelter. Hymns, psalms, litanies, snatches of popular songs and sayings are all introduced by Bialoszewski and blended into his memoir along with information which he has gathered from newspapers, from his friends, his father and other sources. Because Bialoszewski defines the function of memoirist as that of witness, he is not content to rely on his own observations alone, though he is too distrustful to accept unquestioningly other versions of the event.

Bialoszewski does not, however, see himself as a witness participant of a great event such as the historians have defined it, but rather of the greater event of human suffering and brute survival against all odds. For the most part, the people portrayed in the memoir are little people—the objects, not the subjects, of history— heroic only insofar as survival against all odds is an act of heroism. The narrative point of view adopted in the memoir is designed to avoid the distortions which literary conventions might impose. The narrator of this memoir, Bialoszewski's "I," is a naive observer-victim. He does not actually reject such abstract concepts as "heroism," "military strategy," "international posture"; rather, they are simply outside his normal categories of thought. Bialoszewski presents himself as quite ordinary—a non-hero who occasionally has a "heroic" impulse and even less frequently feels an impulse towards evil. An ordinary citizen, he had been trapped by history in a moment of great drama and terror.

Bialoszewski eschews the historians' attempt to create a pattern out of, or impose a meaning on, the random incidents which are for him the only reality of the uprising. His memoir boldly asserts the importance of the trivial in the record of a great historical occurrence. Through his eyes we see the uprising as a series of sometimes humorous but more often exceedingly painful vignettes

15

as the besieged population of Warsaw attempts to cope with the basic human needs of finding shelter, food and water in a city which is being consumed by explosions and flames before their very eyes. Bialoszewski tells the story of the uprising as he saw it, literally from underground Warsaw—from the shelters and cellars and sewers in which he and his small circle of companions hid as the city collapsed and burned above their heads. His is a civilian victim's view of a military and political debacle:

> *So, what was it all?*
> *A pile of ruins? Of bombed-out cellars? And a pile of corpses?*
> *There's no need for me to play the sage. Others have long since made history of this, have drawn their conclusions and publicized them. It's well known. I am speaking for myself—a layman. And for others. Also laymen. Inasmuch as we have the right to speak, because we were there. Laymen and nonlaymen. All condemned together to a single history.*

Bialoszewski begins from the Stendhalian/Tolstoyan assumption that no participant can have an overview of a military operation and limits his reconstruction of the Warsaw Uprising to events which he or a few trusted individuals actually observed. But the Tolstoyan rejection of the overview in favor of the distancing achieved through individual observation presumes the integrity of the individual observer. Bialoszewski undermines even this premise by questioning the validity of his own perceptions and recollections. Memory is not a simple process, and he is careful to insist repeatedly on the shakiness of his recollections. Indeed, Bialoszewski is obsessed with the problems of remembering: the difficulty of fixing an event in time; the inevitable fusing of distinct memories into a single image; or, conversely, the fragmenting of a single incident into several disjointed images; the near impossibility of freeing one's personal recollections from accepted interpretations and the numerous literary and cinematic depictions of a celebrated event. Time and again the narrative stops as Bialoszewski suddenly hesitates over a particular detail.

The obvious effect of this concern with the accuracy of memory—the yielding to flashbacks, the overlaying of memories from different moments—is to increase the warping of the book's chronological skeleton which is, as I have mentioned, also distorted by the related principle of free association. The reader is constantly being thrown off balance; the irritability which Bialoszewski's method induces in the reader is a calculated device for conveying the terror which prevailed throughout the uprising.

Several Polish critics have commented on the prominence in the memoir of the verb "latac" and its derivative forms. "Latac," literally "to fly," but meaning in colloquial speech "to run," or "to scurry," appears with various directional prefixes and sometimes in nominal forms approximately 250 times in this non-literal meaning alone. This astonishingly high frequency of occurrence is the verbal expression of the chaos in Warsaw, where people were in a constant state of running as fast as they could from barricade to barricade, from one seeming shelter to another. A translator who has to find English equivalents for it is also struck by the equally high frequency of the word "chyba," an elastic term whose function is to cast doubt on the accuracy of the statement in which it occurs. (It has been rendered here variously as "perhaps," "it seems," "most likely," "I think.") Not counting its appearances in recorded dialogue, "chyba," too, occurs in the memoir about 250 times. If we add in other words of hesitancy such as "moze" ("perhaps"), "nie jestem pewien" ("I'm not sure"), "nie wiem" ("I don't know"), "nie pamietam" ("I don't remember"), "zdaje mi sie" ("it seems to me")—the count soars to well over 400. Clearly, the question of *how* one remembers, the reliability of one's own observations and memories, is a second and equally important subject of this memoir.

These two colloquial words, "latac" and "chyba," stand as symbols of Bialoszewski's revisionism. "Latanie"—the scurrying about of civilians and partisans alike in response to the natural instinct to flee in the face of overwhelming danger—is a far cry from the pictures of dignified purposefulness and heroic martyrdom which more pious studies of the Warsaw Uprising have presented as a matter of course. Bialoszewski's pervasive scepticism about the previously assumed "truths" of the uprising and about the possibility of ever getting at any truths through a narrative memoir is similarly embodied in the word "chyba." It is, paradoxically, this thorough-going rejection of historical and literary assumptions which transforms Bialoszewski's rough-hewn narrative into an astonishingly moving tribute to the city of Warsaw and the endurance of its civilian population.

This memoir, which insists on the importance of every re-membered detail, however trivial, may at times appear tedious. But the cumulative effect of Bialoszewski's preoccupation with the minutiae of life under extreme wartime conditions is extremely moving. The lingering descriptions of architectural monuments in the process of disintegration unite to form a prose poem in memory of a beloved city—a work redeemed for literature by its very crudity.

Memoir of the Warsaw Uprising is not an inspirational book. It offers no comforting conclusions about individual heroism or historical necessity. There are no lessons to be drawn from the tragedy of Warsaw, no higher meaning to redeem the city's suffer-ing. We are left with the simple fact that human beings are infi-nitely vulnerable and are offered no suggestion that this can ever be otherwise.

Madeline G. Levine
Chapel Hill, N.C.

NOTES

1. First published as *Pamietnik z powstania warszawskiego* (Warsaw: PIW, 1970).

2. Bialoszewski has published the following volumes of poetry and small prose narratives: *Obroty rzeczy* (1956); *Rachunek zachciankowy* (1959); *Mylne wzruszenia* (1961); *Bylo i bylo* (1965); *Donosy rzeczywistosci* (1973); *Wiersze* (1975).

3. In Czeslaw Milosz, ed. and trans., *Post-War Polish Poetry* (Harmondsworth: Penguin, 1970).

4. "Boguslaw Sent Me," *The Boston Globe*, June 6, 1959.

Tuesday, August 1, 1944, was cloudy, humid, not too warm. It must have been about noon when I stepped out into Chlodna Street (my street at that time, number 40); and I remember that there were many trolleys, cars, and people and that right after I reached the corner of Zelazna Street, I realized what day it was (the first of August) and I thought to myself, more or less in these words:

"August 1 is Sunflower Day."

I remember facing Chlodna Street in the direction of Kercelak. But why that association with sunflowers? Because that's when they're in full bloom and even beginning to fade already; because that's when they are ripening. . . . And because at that time I was more naive and sentimental; I hadn't been made cunning yet; because the times themselves were also naive, primitive, rather carefree, romantic, conspiratorial, wartime. . . . Thus (that yellow color must have been in something) the light of inclement weather with the sunlight struggling to break through (it did) on the trolleys painted red as they are in Warsaw.

Recollecting my distant self in small facts I shall be frank, perhaps too detailed, but on the other hand I shall write only the truth. It is twenty-three years later; I am forty-five years old now; I am lying here on my couch uninjured, alive, free, in good health and spirits; it is October, nighttime, 1967; Warsaw once again has 1,300,000 inhabitants. Once, I was seventeen and I went to bed and for the first time in my life heard artillery fire. That was the front. Most likely it was September 2, 1939. I was right to be terrified. Five years later the all too familiar Germans were walking the streets in their uniforms.

I am using the term "Germans" here and elsewhere because any other usage will seem artificial. Just as at that time the Vlasovites often were thought of as Ukrainians. We knew that the Germans weren't the only Hitlerites. We even saw it. I remember the Latvians after the liquidation of the little ghetto in 1942. With rifles. All in black. They were posted up and down Sienna Street. Close together. On the Aryan sidewalk. And for whole days and nights they scanned the windows on the Jewish side of Sienna. The remains of windowpanes covered with drapes, stuffed with quilts. Corpselike goose-down. Along the street—that one street—from Zelazna to Sosnowa stretched not a wall but barbed wire. Along its entire length. The roadway, the cobblestones, (on the other side tall reeds and goosefoot were already growing), had turned gray and shriveled up into charcoal. And they would crouch down. That's how they took aim. And I remember that one of them would fire from time to time. At those windows.

Well, that August 1, at about two in the afternoon, Mama said that I should go get some bread from Teik's cousin on Staszic Street; evidently, there wasn't enough bread and they had worked something out. I went. And I remember that when I returned there were a great many people and there was a commotion already. And people were saying, "Two Germans have been killed on Ogrodowa Street."

It seems to me that I didn't go the way I should have because they were rounding up people, but somehow it also seems that I really did take Ogrodowa Street. The commotion I saw in Wola may have been only local because right afterwards I ran into Staszek P., the composer, and later Staszek laughed, "And my mother said that today was such a peaceful day!"

Staszek himself had seen many "tigers." "Tanks as big as apartment houses." They were cruising around. Someone had seen one thousand people (ours) on horseback, riding up to no. 11 Mazowiecka Street. Various things were going on. And it wasn't even five o'clock, or "W" hour, yet. Staszek and I had to go to 24 Chlodna Street to see Irena P., my colleague at the secret university. (Our Polonistics department was located on the corner of Svietokrzyska Street and Jasna, on the second floor; we sat on school benches; it was given out that this was Tynelski's school of commercial studies.) Well, we were supposed to be at her place by five (I had a date at seven with Halina, who was living with Zocha and my father at 32 Chmielna Street), but since it was early we walked along Chlodna from Zelazna to Walicow and back. The sacristan had spread a carpet on the church steps and set out potted green trees for a formal wedding. Suddenly, we saw that the sacristan was cleaning up everything, rolling up the carpet, carrying in the potted trees, rushing to get it done, and this surprised us. (Actually, the day before—July 31, that is—Roman Z. had dropped in to say goodbye to us. The Soviet front could be heard distinctly; explosions and simultaneously the planes with their bombs in the German districts.) Well, we went to Irena's. It was before five. We were all talking; suddenly we heard shooting. Then, it seems, heavier weapons. We could hear cannons. And all sorts of guns. Finally a shout, "Hurrahhh. . . ."

"The uprising," we told each other at once, like everyone else in Warsaw. Astounding. Because no one had ever used that word

20

before in his life. Only in history, in books. It was a bore. But now, all of a sudden . . . it exists, and that's why there are those "hurrahs" and the thundering of the crowd. Those "hurrahs" and that thundering were the taking of the Courthouse on Ogrodowa Street. It was raining. We watched intently whatever we could see. Irena's window looked out onto a courtyard with a low red wall at the end, and beyond this wall was another courtyard which extended all the way to Ogrodowa Street and housed a sawmill, a shed, a pile of boards, and wagons. We're standing there watching and then someone in a German tankist's uniform, I think, wearing a forage cap and an armband, leaps across that low red wall from the other courtyard into ours. He jumps down onto our garbage shed. From the shed onto a stool. From the stool onto the asphalt.

"The first partisan!" we shout.

"You know what, Mironek, I could give myself to him," Irena tells me enthusiastically through the curtain.

Right away people started running into that courtyard from Ogrodowa Street and grabbed the wagons and boards to use them for barricades.

Then, I remember, after Staszek had cooked some *kluski** and we had eaten, we played a game, thumbed through Rabelais' *Gargantua* (my first contact with him). Then we went to sleep. Of course, it wasn't quiet. Throughout the night. Only the large caliber guns, which became so familiar later on, quieted down a little. Well, Irena went to sleep in her room. And Staszek and I lay down on her mother's bed in her mother's room, for of course she had not returned from the center. It was raining. Drizzling. It was cold. We could hear the stuttering of the machine guns. First quite close, then farther off. And the rocket flares. Every so often. In the sky. We fell asleep to their noise, I think.

Most likely it was 1935 when, for the first time in my life, I heard about bombardments. When the Italian fascists attacked Abyssinia. Lame Mania was visiting us, listening to the radio through earphones, and suddenly she announced, "They're bombing Addis Ababa."

I had a vision of Aunt Natka's house on Wronia (I don't know why that one precisely), the fifth floor, and that we were there on the landing between the fourth and fifth floors. And that we started collapsing together with those floors. Then right away I thought that that was probably impossible. But then, what was it really like? . . .

21

What happened on the second day of August 1944? Since June the Allied offensive in the West had been moving through France, Belgium, Holland. From Italy, too. The Russian front had stopped at the Vistula. Warsaw was entering the second day of the uprising. Explosions woke us up. It was raining.

People began organizing. Block leaders. Duty tours. Digging cellars. Tunneling underground passageways. All night long. Barricades. At first people thought they could be made out of anything, such as the boards from the sawmill and the wagons on Ogrodowa Street. Ogrodowa (we looked out on it) was covered with Polish flags—a strange holiday! Meetings and conferences in the courtyards. Assignments: who, what. It seems there was a news sheet already. Of the uprising. And partisans. Showed up. In German cast-offs—whatever they could find: a helmet, boots, with anything at all in their hands, as long as it could shoot. We looked out at Chlodna Street. And it was true: a front had formed. Throughout Warsaw. On the spot. Or rather, several fronts. Which the first night had created. And the day began to force back. This was reported in the news sheets. There were explosions. All sorts. From cannons. Bombs. Machine guns. Was it the front? The real one? The German-Russian front? It was moving from somewhere in Modlina towards Warsaw (our great hope). Nothing dreadful yet from Wola. But Chlodna Street was in trouble. It seemed to be ours. Already decked in flags, I think. But on the corner of Walicow and Chlodna Streets there was a "Wache." There was a second "Wache" (the house with the columns) on the corner of Zelazna and Chlodna Streets. "Wache" meant a building which was held by the Germans, and that meant shooting from above (from all five floors). Machine guns. Grenades. Every so often a single shot from the roof, from behind the chimney, someone wounded, someone killed. It was men in hiding who were doing the shooting.

"Pigeon fanciers," they were called. People chased them, hunted them, but it was useless. They would shoot from our houses. Then they would be caught. What a lot of them there were. All the time. To the very end. It seems they would walk behind the tanks as they rode past and would jump through the gates. Shells hurtled in from the German districts, from Wola, from the Freight Station or the tracks, from the armored train, from the Saxon Gardens. Planes flew overhead and dropped bombs. Every now and then. Frequently. Sometimes every half hour. Even more frequently. And tanks. From Hale Mirowskie. From Wola too. They wanted to conquer, or rather, to clear the line. Chlodna Street. The first barricades, temporary, wooden, weren't worth anything. The tanks rode right over them. Shells set them on fire in an instant. Or incendiary bombs. I remember people throwing down tables, chairs, wardrobes onto the street from the second floor of the house on the far corner of Chlodna and Zelazna, and other people grabbing them for the barricades. And those tanks rode over them, immediately.

So people started tearing up the concrete slabs from the sidewalks, the cobblestones from the streets. They had tools for this. The trolley drivers had prepared iron crowbars and pickaxes for the uprising. They handed them out to the people. And with these the cobblestones were broken into pieces, the concrete slabs were dug up, the hard ground was broken. But those two "Wachen" were a terrible nuisance. I know that my mother suddenly showed up at number 24, in Irena's backyard. She was worried about me. She'd run over from beyond Zelazna Street, from 40 Chlodna. She brought me something to eat. I preferred to stay here at Irena's with Staszek. I walked Mother to the corner. The one near the "Wache." We separated for the time being, going in opposite directions. Everything was done stealthily, at a run, under cover of the barricades. At the intersection the trolley wires were torn and twisted from the crossfire; someone had hung a portrait of Hitler on them and this infuriated the Germans. They were shooting at that intersection. The "pigeon fanciers" were shooting.

I can't recall exactly what happened on the second and what on the third of August (on Wednesday and Thursday). Both days were cloudy and drizzly. There were already fires, bombs. Both days there was racing downstairs.

"To the shelter!" or rather, to ordinary cellars. To the yard for discussions, duty tours, to work at digging, building barricades. But now we sat in the foyer, or better yet in the kitchen, within the innermost walls, because the shells were pouring in. We slept on couches set up in the foyers. Once Irena and I ran down without our shoes on because of an air raid and bombs. Staszek was in the w.c. at that moment. Then the bombs fell. Somehow, nothing hit us. A few minutes later Staszek came down and said, "You know, while I was sitting on the toilet the entire floor and the whole w.c. with me in it caved in. . . . And how. . . ."

Anyway, we didn't go out into Chlodna Street right away. Which was good. The gate, like all the others, was barricaded. We decided to hang out a flag. It was slipped through the iron grating.

"Attention!" and "Poland hasn't died yet."

The Germans began shooting. At the flag. At the gate. Someone got something in his finger. Probably the lieutenant who hung out the flag. Or maybe the commandant of the Antiaircraft Defense for this house? I don't remember. Once there was a sudden dreadful explosion. Which made everyone jump. We dashed downstairs.

"The Germans were blown up in their Wache on the corner of Walicow!" people were shouting.

"Five apartment houses blew up with them!"

We ran out into Chlodna. The street was covered with clouds. Rust-colored and dark brown. From the bricks, from the smoke. When it settled we could see a terrifying transformation. A reddish-gray dust was covering everything. Trees. Leaves. Probably a centimeter thick. One Wache less. But at what a cost. Finally things began to change. To instability. And always for the worse. Visually too. From Zelazna Brama Square, from Bank Square, from Elektoralna Street along our side of Chlodna, a stream of people was fleeing beneath the wall—all bent down, gray, covered with some kind of powder. I remember that the sun was setting. Fires were burning. The people ran on and on. In a stream. From the bombed-out houses. They disappeared into Wola.

The next day, around sunset, Staszek and I were instructed to carry concrete paving stones. To the other side of the street. Staszek grabbed a slab and carried it across. I was amazed. Suddenly, we hear shells. One hits a wooden fire barricade behind the church on Chlodna Street. It bursts into flames. Right afterwards something hits Hale Mirowskie. It catches fire. Burns with a vivid flame. Tomato-colored. The sun is setting. The weather is fair for the first time. On our side of Chlodna Street people are running beneath the wall to Elektoralna and beyond. Just like yesterday. The same people. They are fleeing from Wola.

"The Ukrainians are on the march from Wola and butchering people. And burning them on pyres!"

The fifth day, Saturday, August 5. A lot of prolonged roaring. I run out the gate.

"The Wache is taken!" I race upstairs. With that joyous news. To Ircna and Staszek. Chlodna was free. All decked in flags in a minute. Crowds formed instantaneously. To make barricades. Everyone. Women. Old men. I remember. Salesladies in white aprons.

24

And an old woman who quickly passed me bricks with one hand because she was holding her purse in the other. I passed the bricks to a salesgirl in her white apron. And so on.

People were shouting, "A bucket brigade! A bucket brigade!" The bricks were gathered from the blown-up houses on the corner of Walicow. Suddenly, we hear airplanes. We run to the steps of a secession-style stone house at number 20 or 22. Bombs. We run down to the cellar. It was the house of Mr. Henneberg, I think, an engineer, one of the Henneberg brothers and the father of my three schoolmates and scouting friends. I used to visit there before the war. I remember that whenever I visited them in those days the house was full of people, the door to the balcony was open and there was a terrific noise from the street, as if people were actually riding through the apartment. This morning or the day before, Mr. Henneberg had climbed the trolley mast and cut the wires and then thrown them down so that the tanks would get all tangled up in them; and he'd cursed out loud at the Germans. Not long ago, just this year in fact, I read in *Stolica* that one of the younger Henneberg brothers, one of my schoolmates, that is, had died in the uprising. The other one also perished. I remember their mother from my school days, when she was in mourning; she had very blonde hair. We could hear the tanks. They were on the way already. All or nothing. We had to escape.

In the cellar of this building there was one old gentleman.

"Where are you from?" I asked him.

"From Krakowskie Przedmiescie."

He described how the Germans were arresting people and herding them in front of the tanks against the partisans, so that the partisans would shoot them.

"And the whole street has been burned down. . . ."

"Which street?" I asked.

"Krakowskie Przedmiescie," he said very sadly.

I remember that I was surprised then, first of all at hearing someone call Krakowskie Przedmiescie a street and secondly, at the old man's being so terribly upset about it. Now I am not surprised.

After the bombardment we went outside. We were summoned to the next barricade, the one right before Zelazna Street. They needed men. I ran over. They handed out picks and crowbars. For the cobblestones and sidewalks. At last, parts of the trenches were dug up. I saw for the first time what a tangle of pipes and conduits there is underground. They warned us to dig carefully. On the fourth corner of Zelazna a cigarette kiosk was overturned as a barrier; the cigarettes spilled out. One guy started gathering them up.

"Hey, mister, at such a time!" And other people also began yelling at him. He was embarrassed, stopped, went on digging with us. Suddenly people with wheelbarrows were carrying out the corpses of those Germans from the Wache. Stripped to the waist. Barefoot. Their green soles sticking out. Bare. And I remember the belly of one or was it two Germans protruding from the wheelbarrows. There were several of them in each wheelbarrow. They had to be buried. On the square in front of the church of Saint Boromeusz. And no cross was to be placed there. But a circle was to be marked out in the earth (which was done, I saw, at dusk).

I am picked to be a helper. I am ashamed to refuse. But I wish for an air raid right at that moment, so that others will have to do it instead of me. And there is one. Quickly, quietly. They fly over. Already the bombs are falling! So the men with the wheelbarrows just drop them, the German corpses sail into the trenches, into the excavations, strike the pipes, the cables and remain somewhere deep down there. With the result that some people had to dig them out afterwards, but by then it was other people who had to do it. After the bombs. I ran two houses away. Just as fast as I could.

Then I went back to Irena. We decided to separate. Because we really had to go back to our mothers. Irena remained here, in her own house. I was supposed to go back to my house, to 40 Chlodna Street. Staszek to his. 17 Sienna Street. But people were running from that direction and screaming, "Panska Street's being bombed! They're bombing Prosta!"

We said goodbye between Walicow and Zelazna. I ran off towards Zelazna. People, things, ruins, changes, commotions. A crowd. Flight. Pigeon fanciers. I remember. I see: a line of what looks like boy scouts in green uniforms is making its way from Chlodna Street into Zelazna near the arcades in those various blind alleys. They're holding bottles of gasoline. They turn into Zelazna. The weather's fine. Saturday. Sunny. I rush into our house. Mama's there. And besides Mama:

"Baba Stefa!" because she really was sitting there in an armchair. In the living room. Just like that. I called her Baba Stefa because I was reading Rabinandrath Tagore then, in which Panu Babu is a character. Stefa, a Jew, was our boarder until the spring of 1944.

Almost one of our family. Before that she'd lived with my father's second wife (common law, Zocha), at 32 Chmielna Street, with Zocha, my father and Halina. I don't know if there were some other reasons or if they simply had quarreled, but one day in 1942, after we'd gotten hold of this apartment on Chlodna Street which had been vacated by Jews (because up to that time the ghetto had been here, the wall of the ghetto crossed Chlodna between Wronia and Towarowa Streets; they had constricted the ghetto somewhat; they were always constricting the ghetto, so that several apartments were vacant; Father managed to get this one, 40 Chlodna; well, it was not so much that these apartments were destroyed as that they had a certain peculiar look: dried-up feces, obviously human ones, lay in the center of our kitchen), Stefa made herself at home right there in the kitchen, concealing herself behind a green drape whenever someone came to see us, although she often showed herself later on because she knew several of our friends and relatives, trusted them, and anyway very little was known about her. So I cry out, "Where have you come from! . . ." and we are delighted, we greet each other, shout in amazement, what a coincidence! Probably, I was more excited than she. "Baba Stefa, can it be. . . . Are you really here?"

"Oy, what hasn't happened to me. . . ."

The armchair in which Stefa was sitting was also left by a Jew, not from this house but from an apartment house which I think is standing to this day; either it was never damaged or it was rebuilt; in a blind alley, literally blind, which led from Zelazna Street right into Chlodna on the left side, the one nearer the Vistula. They were holding an auction there. Of Jewish furniture. Father rushed into our house. He shouted at me to follow him. Swen was there, so he came along to keep me company. Although I didn't want to go. There. But it was hard to say no because of Father. The gate of this apartment house where the Jewish auction was being held was filled with a heap of junk. Rubbish. A racket. Human. Father grabbed several chairs, each one from a different village so that each had its own weight and size, and off they all went to 40 Chlodna Street. That's how, in 1942, Father brought Stefa to us from 32 Chmielna, at first supposedly for one night, for two, and so she stayed on for two years. He made up documents for her in the name of Zosia Romanowska. Because Zosia Romanowska had gone to Grochow to see her sister and brother-in-law on September 8, 1939 and had taken her sister-in-law with her—only to have

27

the door there slam closed so that no one could get it open; when the planes flew over, and before anything could be done, they had already fallen through to the cellar. Only one person survived (up above, under the ruins): Zosia's other sister-in-law who was holding by the hand her neighbor's little daughter, already dead; she herself was buried alive in the ruins and when later she lived next door to us on Leszno Street with Nanka (when we had already lost the apartment in Srodmiescie), that is, when she was living in the room Zosia had left vacant, she was afraid, I know, to cover herself to the neck with her quilt. Because as she drifted off and lost her awareness of the quilt it would seem to her that she was buried up to her neck in ruins. Well, Stefa had identity papers in Zosia's name; a little older than she, but as if Stefa were faded, not really ruddy but giving the impression of ruddiness, resembling a Jewish woman more or less, so that it was lucky that the Germans weren't aware of these things and even more lucky that Stefa had great courage and a saving self-assurance; as soon as she saw Germans on the road—for she walked along various roads from Sluzewiec down to Wilanow or Augustowka with her so-called petty wares, very petty, safety pins, Czech jewelry, in order to have something to live on and a bit of money to spare—well, as soon as she saw some Germans she would walk up to them herself and ask, "*Wie spät ist?*" and she always came back by trolley on the "*Nur für Deutsche*" platform. Once, when she met me in the city and we were going to go home together, she said, "Why don't you ride with me; I'll teach you a lesson." And actually, not only did she get on at the "*Nur für Deutsche*" platform but she shoved her way to the front end of the car which was separated from the rest of the car and the crowd by a chain (it was empty here); I followed her, standing there rather stupidly; she sat down and began arguing with a Volksdeutsch woman, who, she said, was crowding her.

So, Father brought over the chairs after he'd brought Stefa. Two Jewish matters. Which were separated after a short time. And reunited once again.

In 1943, I think, we held one of our so-called "soirées" in the house where the chairs had been auctioned, or perhaps in the one directly across from it; at any rate, in the blind alley of Zelazna. Swen, Halina, Irena, Staszek and I. In the apartment of whomever it was who lived there. A patriotic-literary soirée, with theatrical performances; Swen performed, playing Nike, and I, as a walk-on, played the king. Out of timidity, woodenness, I sat stiffly the whole time and spoke the same way. My colleague in the secret university, Wojtek, who perished in the uprising, in Zoliborz, said that he'd really enjoyed it. I told him why I acted that way. "It doesn't matter; it was very nice."

I remember that we performed an excerpt from Wyspianski's *The Wedding*.* Swen played Stanczyk, wearing the national flag which he carelessly had brought over either in his briefcase or in a little bundle.

In his own way, Father had the most unusual business projects. Once, he dragged a whole bushel of potatoes from Kercelak to Leszno Street, to the fourth floor, at that. Rotten ones. Frozen. But even so they were priceless. Nanka, Father, Mama and Sabina remembered from the last war that you could make potato pancakes from such frozen potatoes. They made some for us and they were good. Another time Father bought an icebox at an auction. Mama and Stefa kept wondering why. Since it was broken. And once, he arrived at Chlodna with a whole coatful of fish, very tiny ones. Just like that. In the skirt of his coat. They were slipping out all over the place. He told Mama that she should make croquettes out of them. She did. There were so many of them! Enough to line all the windowsills. And we had four windows then. Once, on Christmas Eve of '42 or '43, the door opened and Father came in carrying a Christmas tree—a skinny pine. Mama was astounded. So was I. Father acted as if it were perfectly natural. We ought to begin decorating it. I got started. It was strange hanging the decorations on those pine branches. In general, a pine isn't a tree, if you ask me. It was like decorating a pine in Otwock. It had nothing in common with a Christmas tree, or so it seemed to me then. An entirely different species. None of the fragrance. Nor the prickliness.

Among Father's many ideas was that of profiting from the dead, one example of which I've already given. But there were more. We received marmalade, bread and various other foods on the basis of ration cards in the names of about four deceased persons. Relatives, of course. But such things were done in those days. What wasn't done then?

Let me explain Stefa's case, at last. Stefa would have lived with us until the end. But one day in Spring 1944 I came back from the city and Mama (she used to sew clothes for women so that she and I might have something to live on, or rather, she remade them over, because these were clothes made from already made-over clothes, what we called *fatalachy*; if you started tacking

29

fur trim onto a coat or a pelisse, you used rabbit fur; you knew it would shed, like cats in springtime, but what else could you do). . . . Anyway, Mama, who sewed for our janitress too, said to me at the door, "You can't imagine how scared to death I was today. The janitress shows up for that rag of hers and says to me, 'That lady who's your boarder, well, when she walks across the yard she twists her head like this and walks somehow sideways; you can tell she's a Jew from a mile away'."

So Stefa had to move out. As it turned out, the janitress hadn't made that remark out of malice, but who could tell. We had to assume the cat was out of the bag, as they say. Anyway, one warm day, in May I think, after Stefa had moved out, I woke up at 6 a.m. and I could hear a real commotion. Downstairs. I was struck by it at once. I rushed to the window in my shirt. There, on every landing, was a German with a rifle. And they were going over all the landings and checking everyone. No one knew why. In our apartment, at least, it didn't go any farther than a check of identity cards, and my *Ausweis*, and then they left. One German and his Polish-speaking aide in a white coat. Maybe nothing would have happened. To Stefa. If she'd still been there. Perhaps she would have passed as Zofia Romanowska. But who knows who that guy in the white coat was.

Well, on August 5, 1944, Stefa was sitting there in that chair, the Jewish one, with which she had been reunited, a turban on her head, because turbans and wooden shoes were fashionable out of necessity throughout Europe, it seems, but for some reason you could recognize German women in particular by those turbans and Stefa, after all, was pretending to be German. So, Stefa was sitting in that chair and saying, "Where haven't I been. I'm riding the trolley. A commotion. I look at my basket. And then someone throws me an armband. They stop the trolley, take us to Gesiowka. There we are, the partisans drive us back, we run through Krasinski Gardens, across Bielanska and then through the Saxon Gardens; the Germans are there, so we double back; Zelazna Brama, people are on their knees, they're going to shoot us. I'm telling you, Miron, it was a miracle we escaped."

"But you made it back here?"

"Ech, what it was like. . . ."

It seems Aunt Jozia showed up right afterwards. Her house (49 Ogrodowa Street) adjoined ours (40 Chlodna). Its third courtyard (the rear wall) had a hole in it and that was the passageway into our long courtyard. I was happy that there were more of us. Though, to be honest, Aunt Jozia returned to her house. But Stefa stayed on; it wasn't gloomy. And also, she'd survived. But suddenly, after various setbacks and news bulletins, such disastrous deterioration and such hell set in, that one lost interest in everything. The attack against Chlodna, against Ogrodowa was in progress. People had been shot to death, burned on pyres on Gorczewska Street, on Bem, on Mlynarska, on Wolska. Those who were stubbornly defending the lines of the Polish front kept finding the stairways and exits cut off; they lay on roofs, on the fourth and fifth floors; the roofs caught fire, burned through, and the men caved in together with the roofs. An inferno, as in the ghetto on Easter night of 1943.

Rescuing, digging out, extinguishing fires, helping—it was difficult, but people did it. And it was made impossible by new bombs falling all the time, more fires being set. Or rather, it was hopeless. A vicious circle. At someone's cry, "Planes!" we rush to a cellar, a shallow crawl space housing a workshop for glass cylinders and bombs. A crush. Panic. Prayer. Explosions. The rumbling, bursting of bombs. Groans and fear. Again they fly low. An explosion, they're probably bombing the front, we crouch down. Nearby an old woman beats her breast, "Sacred heart of Jesus, have mercy on us. . . ."

The howl of planes, bombs.

"Sacred heart. . . ."

And suddenly something rocks our house. Window frames, doors, glass panes are blown out. Explosions. The end? Still more crashes. Even more explosions. We go outside for a while. The yard is changed, it's black, covered with dust, gone gray, the windows are empty, the glass smashed to smithereens. In front of the gate is a crater half the length of the street. We look out from our second-floor window. At that scene. Crowds in the courtyard. Hell —nothing less—and without end. It's bad. The crowds panic. With packages, bundles. They run about. Some towards the gate. Others, away from the gate. Some through the hole towards Ogrodowa Street. Others towards us from Ogrodowa Street. Suddenly, an uproar. A horrifying scream. A kind of humming from the crowd. They're carrying something. Someone. . . . They put it down. Corpses? A scream. . . . Whose?

"That's Mrs. Gorska. Her son's been killed in the school on Leszno Street."

They bring in the corpses. A whole school bombed. Number 100-something Leszno, 111 or 113. Where once I went to see a Christmas pageant. Long before the war, of course. During one of the acts the curtains in the left corner of the stage were torn. The wings were suddenly exposed. It was a catastrophe, because a crowd of angels, kings and others were awaiting their turn there. With a squeal they rushed into a corner, huddled together, formed a triangle. The angels huddled together, pressed close to each other, covered their faces with their hands and squealed. How painful it was for me now in this courtyard.

(Mrs. Gorska, her son and her daughter-in-law, were patriots. Baptists. They used to come and do their sewing at my Mother's. The two women. When Mother would ask them, "Wouldn't you give up your faith?" they'd answer, "I? Never. I was raised in this faith and I'll die in it.")

I decided to drop in on Irena for a while, at 24 Chlodna. I found them all in the cellar already. Depressed. But it was quieter here and there were fewer people.

Two women were sitting opposite them. One was worrying about her children because she had left them at Wedel's in Praga. The other, a little younger, was with her. They sat there, slumping. In that passageway. Which, in normal times, was intended to be used occasionally for fetching potatoes or coal.

"Like owls," Staszek said slowly and, characteristically, in an awfully audible whisper.

I remember the calm. And the relief. After my house. We passed the night here. Because I know that on the next day it was sunnny, warm, the sixth of August. The owls (the older one was Henka; the younger, what was her name?—I know she could tell fortunes from cards) said, "Today is the Transfiguration of Our Lord. Perhaps the good Lord will change something for the better."

And suddenly the news erupted, "The uprising has failed."

"My God," the cellar, stairs, women, crowds jumped up, "so much effort and all for nothing, my Lord? It can't be possible."

"And yet. . . ."

"My God." People wrung their hands, raced about the court-yards. After the first complaints there was discipline, solidarity. Because there was despair.

And suddenly people came running up with a cry, with news sheets, with a declaration. It wasn't true.

The partisans themselves, I remember, had spoken of the defeat and initiated the despair; but now, what joy!

But Sunday had just begun. There was fear such as had not yet been experienced. It was then that we three decided to go our separate ways. Staszek would go to Sienna Street. Irena would remain here. I would go home once more. Sun, heat, smoke, fires, explosions; I raced home. It was probably that day that I found Aunt Jozia. In the afternoon the Germans, with the Vlasovites pushing ahead of them, began launching the final attack on Kercelak, on Towarowa, Okopowa. Kercelak fell. Our lines drew back. They were already near the barricades on the corners of Wronia. And they were shooting. But on the Towarowa-Kercelak-Okopowa line more streets were still to fall, no longer in Wola but in the direction of Srodmiescie. (Actually, those of us on Chlodna Street, right up to the Kercelak-Towarowa-Okopowa line, were really in Srodmiescie, not only in the traditional administrative Center but in the uprising's center, at least as it had been designated by the leadership when Warsaw was divided into districts before the outbreak of the uprising.) Meanwhile, the strip between Towarowa and Kercelak-Wronia was being defended. But the attack was proceeding not only along the streets, with infantry, tanks, artillery, machine guns, grenades, flame throwers, anti-tank guns, but also (and this was much worse) from the sky. Protected by all of these, the planes flew over in endless formations, turned and came back, and bombed apartment house after apartment house, outbuilding after outbuilding. Chlodna. Ogrodowa. Krochmalna. Leszno. Grzybowska. Lucka. And so on. They collapsed and burned. Suddenly a shout, "Let's dig out the buried."

I report. We wait by the gate. We're released.

"They're gone already. Others."

But right away there's another shout, "39 Chlodna is on fire! Who'll put it out?"

We run over. It's right across the way. The whole building is burning. Probably three stories. There's no water. No, there is water, but buckets have to be used in addition to the pump. Through the hole in the wall. There is also sand for firefighting. Women run over and help. Heat. Flames. These means of extinguishing fire are practically useless. The walls are already in flames. On the third floor smoke is coming from behind some of the doors. But they're locked. We hurl ourselves against them. No use. We break them down with axes. We dash in. A wall is on fire. A bare

33

wall. We run over with those pails. For water. We go back. We pour it on. Whatever good that does. We run downstairs.

The women are yelling, "Use sand! Use the sand!"

We dash upstairs again. Now the planes come. They scatter bombs. And bomblets. Incendiary.

"Put out the bombs!"

We rush over. Pour sand on the bomblets. There are about twenty of them. Maybe thirty. In a pile. At the entrance. More on the third floor. They're smoldering and hissing. And the wall is already on fire from them. Sand does a wonderful job. We hope. We pour it on. Will it help? After all, they're bursting one after another. It does help. But now the right and the left walls. Are aflame. Already. We race downstairs. Pass each other. It's good there are several of us. And those women. They give us the buckets filled with sand (I can't remember if we lost the water all of a sudden). They pass them to us through a hole in the wall, so that we won't have to run across unnecessarily. They carry them over to the stairs. Then we grab them. Run inside. I remember that I chased those bomblets. That I stamped on them. Because there was no alternative. They were extinguished on the run. While they were smoldering. The whole pile. Better yet: the flames on the walls were becoming fewer and fewer. Unbelievable. After someone sprinkled sand the fire curled up and disappeared. A miracle! We've put it out! In this hell! Our job is done. We go back.

The attack is getting worse. The bombardment is becoming heavier by the minute. Those who are rescued, more or less conscious, uninjured, rush into our cellars. Terrible panic. In the courtyard too. We ourselves are panicky. We move to Aunt Jozia's. Through the hole. To 49 Ogrodowa Street. There are some women in the yard near the stoves, in the smoke, and some guys are out there fighting with axes. They chase each other. Throw the axes. The axes sail through the air. I am not exaggerating. We go to my aunt's apartment on the fourth floor. But we can't remain there longer than two minutes. With Aunt Jozia's boarder (an old lady) and her brother (also grayhaired) we rush downstairs to someone's apartment on a lower floor carrying bundles of their clothing and ours. Into someone's kitchen. We sit down. Aunt Jozia's boarder gives something to her gray-haired brother:

"Here, have some bread with sugar." He takes it, eats.

"Would you like some more bread and sugar?"

He nods his head.

34

I couldn't eat anything for two days.

Suddenly, such explosions, crashes, that we run downstairs.

The arrival of the bombed. Everyone is gray. From the ruins. Covered with smoke. Aunt Jozia, Stefa, Mama observe that the cellar is weak, the house made of boards, plaster-covered laths and bricks. But the neighboring cellar—at number 51, with its Klein vaulting, is new, the building not yet covered with stucco. We quickly move there through the holes, the underground passageways. There are crowds there. They are sitting on the concrete floor. It's damp. In the corners are carbide lamps. Mama, Aunt Jozia and Stefa take out their crumpled linen, spread it out on a free bit of floor. In that crowd. Chaos. Explosions, shells, bombs . . . unbearable. But the worst is that the Ukrainians are coming. And butchering. Everyone. People talk about it non-stop. People. Twenty years later—right now, in 1964 and 1965—exact figures have been offered by witnesses on both sides. Our newspapers have printed estimates of how many people were massacred in Wola just on Saturday and Sunday, August 5 and 6. Several tens of thousands. Some who were not shot to death were burned together with those who were supposed dead. They were thrown on common pyres. From St. Stanislaus Hospital on the corner of Wolska and Mlynarska Streets (now the Hospital for Infectious Diseases No. 1) patients were shot to death or thrown out of the windows alive into the courtyard below. The Ukrainians set fire to everything as they passed. Living or not. People were buried on the spot. Just like that. In 1946 I was sent to the exhumations as a reporter. I went there with a news photographer. We entered that courtyard. Three or four rows of freshly exhumed, shapeless clumps covered with earth. I had various associations. With cutlets in rolls covered with some sauce. I remember one in particular with a single bone sticking out. The rest was a sodden mass.

Suddenly a woman orderly rushed into our shelter. "Who will help carry a wounded man?"

And suddenly, after the uproar and despite the explosions, there was silence.

"Will no one help?"

There were several hundred women there. And probably as many men. Everyone froze.

"No one at all?"

"I'll go." I stood up.

No one moved. I jumped up after the orderly. Up the stairs.

And out into the street. Ogrodowa.

"Over here! Over here!" I snatched up the front end of a stretcher. We got moving. We joined a procession of stretchers. In front of us. Behind us. Towards Zelazna Street and further on, in the direction of the Courthouse, since the hospital for the uprising was located there. The whole winding procession moved on toward the Courthouse, toward the center of the city. It was Sunday afternoon, four or five o'clock; there was heat, rising smoke mixed with dust; either there was a fire nearby or something was just smoldering; explosions, cobblestones underfoot, we walked rapidly, now looking down at our feet, now forward again, now backwards, now at the houses and the sky: people rushing past, tall apartment houses, now and then barricades across the road, cornices. Also, I want to add, pigeons. But it seems either there weren't any pigeons by then or they were kept so that they wouldn't fly about; or perhaps they really were there and did fly up and wheel around and it was only the cornices and the window frames which had produced that smoke and dust. But the reason I don't trust my memory is that most likely I didn't really know what was what at that time, because it has seemed the same at other times and in other places. Right after the war, when I was living on Poznanska Street and it was Easter night with an early morning mass of the resurrection, those pigeons—this time real ones—fluttered about and cooed among the cornices after each explosion. Anyway, we went on at a trot. The shells were also bursting against the gates—traditional gates with a driveway leading into a courtyard, with wrought-iron St. Nicholases on the sides or in niches. Barricades. The walls. Before we reached Zelazna Street we had to squeeze through a narrow passageway (there were narrow passageways everywhere between the barricades and the walls as a security measure). After we crossed Zelazna too. It seems two of them were near each other. Because the barricades were close together. Everywhere. And soldiers were lying down on Zelazna and firing their rifles. Ordinary ones. In the direction of Kercelak. There was panic. Civilians in flight. A desperate defense. News of those burnings, firing squads, shootings, circulated; facts circulated, came at us, ever nearer. Once, twice we ran past with those stretchers. The orderly and I were carrying a woman. Covered with ashes. On her hair. And her face. In convulsions. Her clothing was shredded. She'd been buried. On Chlodna Street. Right behind us, although the person's (a man's) hands and legs were thickly bandaged, the blood was flowing so profusely that it was pouring off the stretcher. I no longer know what else happened.

The Courthouse. We rush through the gate. People are standing there inside the gate, just some people, ordinary people, one of them our neighbor from 40 Chlodna. She begins to cry at the sight of all this. I think a general convulsive sobbing began. Throughout the entire courtyard. I was told to set down the woman who had been buried. To leave her there. Because this was the hospital. I think we set the stretcher down. We ran to get the next one. And already this one was being carried inside.

I ran away. I wanted to go home. On the way I dropped in at 24 Chlodna, to Irena's cellar, by the back way behind the sawmill. I found Irena there and those two Owls, and Mr. Malinowski, as block leader, wearing an Antiaircraft Defense armband. It was quiet here, more peaceful than anywhere else. At least in the second outbuilding. It didn't face the front. Farther on, you could hear everything. And it was bad. But the peace in that cellar! Just an ordinary cellar. Twisting corridors, a maze of little rooms. Darkness. At most, a gray light fell inside there. It was nothing. I didn't feel like going any farther. I told them. What I had seen. What was on the other side of Zelazna Street. Because they asked. I hung around. Until it was evening. They suggested I stay. Here. For the night. Why make your way across Zelazna? Perhaps it's even worse now than it was before, perhaps they're already moving in? From here you can escape. It's closer to Starowka. Almost everyone planned to go to Starowka as soon as they were ready. I talked more and more with those two Owls on this theme. The elder, Henka, her hair combed in an upsweep, was still worrying out loud about her children because they had remained in Praga at Wedel's. The younger, Jadzka I think, started telling our fortunes. I told them I had a friend on Rybaki Street. Swen. That actually he'd been living in Wola for the past few months, on Szlenkierow Street. That for some reason I think he's on Rybaki now. Because his mother had remained there. Obviously, I had no proof. Intuition, at best. And what is called wishful thinking. On the whole I simply ignored the fact that first Teik and Swen had broken off relations with each other over an insignificant matter, that I had then broken off relations with Teik out of solidarity with Swen, and finally I had broken off relations with Swen and made up with Teik (let me remind you—Teik from Staszic Street). Furthermore, I came up with the idea of swimming the Vistula. They grasped at that as

37

an obvious plan. I said that Rybaki Street was just the same as Wybrzeze Gdanskie. Because of the apartment blocks. Also red. Poured concrete. Unfinished. Big. (Something of a "shelter for the homeless" during the war; Swen had lived there until recently although he'd been working for a long time as a social worker in the Parysow district.) So, those apartment blocks faced Rybaki. The Vistula was behind them. All three of us could swim, we agreed. And from there we could walk stealthily at night towards Zeran, Jablonna. The Russians were already at Jablonna. I don't know how we imagined ourselves swimming to the other shore which was also held by the Germans and, what is more, crossing the front. And such a front at that—a front such as probably never had existed in the history of the world before this war. Probably we just assumed that since it was a question of Warsaw and Zeran everything would somehow take care of itself.

We stayed on there. Till night. The attack had ceased. There were the normal small explosions, noises. Perhaps it was completely silent. Everyone came out into the yard. Discussions. Gossip. News sheets. More tunneling. Of cellars, passageways. Mr. Malinowski proposes that Irena and I should sleep in his apartment. After all, how can we go up to the third floor? And they have a large apartment on the ground floor, in the first courtyard. We go with him. I am given a room. My own. A bed. A quilt. I undress. I fold back the quilt in order to crawl under it. And then . . . a shell hits the corner of the house! Then a second, a third, a fourth; nothing else, only shells. And flames. Everyone jumps up. Dashes into the courtyard. Waves of people are pouring into the courtyard from Ogrodowa Street. With suitcases, children, knapsacks. Some are leaving already. Others are gathering here. A crowd. Explosions. Discussions. Moving about from one group to another. Irena is standing there with a haversack. We consult. With Mr. Malinowski. And the whole group. We are standing near the wooden gate into Ogrodowa Street. Irena is hesitant for some reason. But I think it's high time. I consult the Owls. They're ready.

"I'll just run over and bring the keys to Mama, since I took them from the apartment."

I really had taken the keys when we walked out of the house during the panic. Now they're always jangling in my pocket. I run over to Zelazna Street. The partisans are lying down on Zelazna again, firing in the direction of Wronia, worn out, sweaty, amidst a pile of rubbish.

"Where are you going?"

"I've got to. 40 Chlodna."

"What? You can't."

"But my mother. I took the keys."

"Listen! You won't be of any help. The keys are useless, and anyway...."

"But...."

"The Germans are already there."

I backed away. I ran into Irena's courtyard. Henka and Jadzka were ready. Once again I asked Irena if she'd made up her mind. But she was still standing there near the gate, with the same people, the haversack still hanging from her arm, and what I was saying wasn't getting through to her at all. So Henka, Jadzka and I rushed out into Ogrodowa Street, this time to the right. At a run....

One of them said, "Let's just take off our shoes so they won't hear us."

We take them off. We run. Barefoot. Along Ogrodowa Street. A barricade. We squeeze past. To Solna. Something's burning. Explosions. Beams are sailing through the air. Noise. They fall into the fire. With a thud. We dash along Solna. To Elektoralna. A barricade. We squeeze through. Onwards. Along Elektoralna. To Bank Square (where Dzierzynski Square is today, only smaller and triangular). Something's burning on the right. An entire house in a single flame. We race past. Somewhere beyond Orla Street a whole house is on fire on the left. Actually, it's being consumed by flames. There are hardly any ceilings left. Or walls. Just one huge fire about three stories high. Again the beams groan, collapse. It's hot. That's probably the Office of Weights and Measures. Night. It's quieter here. Maybe the attack is letting up? We are not the only ones in flight. A whole stream of people is moving in the direction of Starowka. We run left, following a group of people. Into the rear courtyard of the Club or rather the Rotunda, the former Ministry of Finance and the Leszczynski Palace. There's more space here. It's less crowded. Isolated explosions can be heard from Bank Square. The cornices, again. But not as gray. Yellow. Which means in this dawn (it was barely dawn) they seemed to be covered with gold leaf. Perhaps this is where I saw the pigeons. The ones which flew up. Or just those cornices. In a different style. With little Corazzi angels. With garlands. Tympanums. The courtyard fronts on Leszno Street. Suddenly it is really dawn. We are detained at a barricade until more people arrive. There are even some

Jews with their womenfolk. One of them is holding a bundle under her arm. The barricade straddled Leszno near where it now crosses the East-West artery. But Rymarska Street was on the right side then, branching off from Bank Square. And to the left was Przejazd with a view, just as today, of the Mostowski Palace. They check the Jews' papers. They are detained. For further questioning. We are let through. All of us. We race past the Leszno barricades. To Przejazd. A long stretch there. And a turn to the right. Past the barricade. Dluga. The sound of explosions. On the left, on a gentle curve on Dluga Street, is the Palace of the Four Winds. The whole building is on fire. It's already destroyed. The flames are howling in the outbuildings, in front. The beams groan, collapse. The tympanum, with its bas reliefs, is still standing. The twinkling medallions. The carved gates of the inner courtyard. And those Four Winds. On the pillars of the gate. They have gilded wings. They gambol, shine. They seem to be dancing even more gaily than usual. We run on.

Starowka, at last. You can see it. At the end of Dluga Street, past several barricades, a bluegreen ball on the belltower of the Church of the Dominicans is glinting. How strange. The remains of a burnt tin spire? Perhaps. We rush on, no longer barefoot (we had put on our shoes at the corner of Leszno and Przejazd, I think); we run along Dluga, down Mostowa Street to Rybaki. It's daytime already. And silence. Stare Miasto is quiet as can be. On a bend in Rybaki Street, beyond Prochownia, children are playing on the grass among the cobblestones near the wall of the housing estate. The rear of Prochownia faced the Vistula, as did the rear of every building on Rybaki Street. That wall which I have just mentioned was very old. It had two shell-shaped, rococo gates. An old inn. As soon as we'd passed it I said to Henka and Jadzia, "Right here."

14/16 Rybaki Street. A pair of two-story brick housing blocks, without stucco, on a concrete foundation, with a third block added on, which struck me as being less imposing. Those two housing blocks stood crosswise between Rybaki Street and the Vistula. Between them was a large courtyard. From Rybaki all the way to Wybrzeze. We entered the courtyard through a latticework gate. And walked along the left side against the wall (because the center was taken up with garden plots and overgrown) to the stairwell, the one leading to Swen's mother's apartment. (Would she be there? And Swen too? I felt an uneasy hope.) Their windows faced the Vistula so that stairwell was right near Wybrzeze. I took a look and right inside the entrance to that stairwell two guards were standing, from the night shift, wearing armbands; one with the red armband of the People's Army* (there was a large contingent of the People's Army here). And the other I knew from home and from Swen's office, Mr. Ad. . . .

"Is he in? Swen?" I asked. "Are they at home?"

"They're here. All of them. Swen and his fiancee. And his aunt and her son. And my wife and child."

"Where are they?"

Mr. Ad., smiling all the time, said, "In the shelter; they're still asleep."

We hurried down the stairs which smelled of cement and unstuccoed bricks into deep cellars with thick walls. Silence. And the smell of a steamy laundry room. It struck our ears and our noses. As for what struck our eyes—it's a shame even to talk about it.

A dusky abyss with flickering candles on a small altar which was adorned with a porcelain Mother of God; as for the rest—the strangest platforms, cramped, everyone asleep, snoring, depressing.

These platforms turned out to be groups of plank beds. Each group was made up of several beds. Each plank bed was made of two or four beds which were tied together. They were long; several people were lying on each of them. In the dim light broken pieces of furniture protruded among the groups of plank beds. And only a single main aisle from the door to the altar and around the room could be made out. In addition, there were cement pillars. The macabre aura of a chapel in the catacombs.

I sought out Swen's family's platform. I noticed them all lined up. They were asleep. I bent over Swen. And said something. I don't remember what. Swen stretched, look up at me, was surprised, was moved to tears, began greeting me. Immediately the rest of them, especially Swen's mother, stirred and began bustling about.

Aunt Uff. and Zbyszek were still asleep. I told them whom I was with. They said that was fine. They told us to find a spot. They welcomed us. Gave us some food. Celinka, Aunt Uff. and Zbyszek, on the neighboring pallet, and Mrs. Ad. and her tiny daughter woke up right after that. Other people too. They stirred. Half rose. Standing up, full length, was just not done. What for? Just to be all crowded together?

So, they stirred, stretched, dug about in their bundles without standing up. And it began: "Buzz-buzz-buzz"—what chattering!

Also, it seems, a morning prayer at the altar, or rather from the altar or to the altar. The morning or first prayer. There were many other prayers in addition to that one. And chants. As it turned out, there weren't that many that first week. Afterwards they became more frequent. And closer together. Until it reached the point that in all the cellars throughout Warsaw people were praying aloud in choruses and in chants, everywhere, and without interruption.

What else? A new, hideously long story of communal life against the background of the possibility of death began at that moment, from that entrance. What do I remember? Both a lot and a little, and not always in order or day by day. I may confuse the order of some things, the dates (even of events which were rather important, although I have several dates fixed in my mind), the positions of the fronts—ours, and the larger one.

I found out that the uprising had caught Aunt Uff. and Zbyszek in a shop on Freta Street. A couple of days before we came, life had been transferred to the shelters from upstairs. Along with everything which could be moved. A neighbor who was deaf but able to speak, a woman we called Baciakowa (which wasn't her real name), brought her sewing machine and her little son with his legs in a hip-high cast, and sewed on that machine in the cellar across from us and sang a lot (Swen smiled) because she could not hear the explosions. The entranceway (it was supposed to be a door but was only an opening by 1939) into Baciakowa's cellar was only one small unit of the labyrinth under 14/16 Rybaki Street. There was an endless number of corridors, cellar rooms with and without pillars, passageways, exits to the staircases, corners, separate vaults, storerooms, bins, sub-basements, passages leading to the boiler room with its many pipes and sewer mains. In addition, the two main blocks (A and B) had a connecting passageway, or what was called a tunnel, here. Under the garden plots with their pumpkins. And tomatoes. And probably potatoes which were so much in fashion throughout Warsaw during the occupation that not only the larger and smaller squares (from which in the winter of 1939 those who had been hastily buried in September were exhumed), not only the river banks, but even Aleje Jerozolimskie, were planted and blossomed with potatoes in July.

Our cellar "hall" appeared to be the main one for this block even though there were two or three others just like it under block B. After all, the altar was located here. And perhaps it really was the largest? Perhaps. Near the door—that is, near the entrance opening from the stairwell on the right—stood a barrel full of water, in case of fire. On August 7 the water was no longer very fresh. Later it produced a stench, quarreling, and the decision to change the water in the barrel by means of a bucket brigade. The door led to the corridors, half-cellars, passageways with goats, dogs, stoves, over which the women quarreled incessantly and the men were always ready to fight with axes. The second fight with axes in this uprising. From there, stairs led directly from the cement floor to the ground floor upstairs. Right to our left were the toilets (the plumbing was still functioning for the time being), everything was in working order, even the electricity. Here, dusty rays of sunlight shone in from above so that once they had entered early in the morning they shone like that for several hours every day, because the weather was always sunny. The most important comings and goings, meetings, discussions, my writing, and the time I spent sitting on a heap of bricks took place here.

The cellars began again across the way. A whole new chain of them started over there. Later, this was our famous walking trail. People would go for strolls over there. And it wasn't the same as on the surface. Here, after all, there were streets, squares, crowds, life, the making of friendships.

Let us return to that first day. Swen had fled here with Celinka the day before I had. At five o'clock on August 1 they'd been outdoors, near Chmielna Street. They had run with their arms raised among the tanks on Nowy Swiat, I think. Celinka had a room on Chmielna Street. And it was there that the living together of many people—entangled, yet separated from each other—commenced. Communal living en masse. But what was there to eat? How long would it last? For a couple of years Swen's mother, older, experienced, had been hiding rusks in sacks. So Swen brought Celinka over on Sunday. They crept through half of Srodmiescie along a circuitous route. Because there was no other way. Somehow or other they got to Zlota Street or Panska, then to Chlodna by way of Walicow, then along Ogrodowa to Solna, Elektoralna, across Bank Square, finally via Dluga Street to Mostowa—that is, by Staszek's route from Chlodna to Sienna and mine from Chlodna to Rybaki. The Palace of the Four Winds was already on fire. It was hell in Staszek's and my neighborhoods. Because of the onslaught from Wola. And they too had been struck by the silence on Rybaki Street. So they had run up to the second floor. It was empty. But there was that silence, the summer weather and the

Vistula, so Swen, figuring that his mother must be downstairs somewhere, went to look for her and told Celinka that she should just look out the window in the meantime. The window looked out directly on Praga. On the great trees of the Zoo. The beach. The railroad bridge, the old one on the left, near the citadel. To the right, the Kierbedz bridge with its lattice work. It was a good thing that there wasn't any firing from Praga then, because Celinka would have been in trouble. When the people in the shelters found out about her they wrung their hands. So Swen quickly ran upstairs to fetch her.

Swen asked me almost immediately whether I'd heard the latest hit song, "Do you remember the hot July nights. . . ." And I learned right away that Mr. and Mrs. Ad.'s tiny daughter was named Basia. And that they sang to her,

> *I have a puppet on a string,*
> *He leaps to the left, he leaps to the right,*
> *That is the greatest fun. . . .*

They sang that song to her over and over again throughout August. And when I remember it I become even sadder, because of that melody and those words. I don't know why. (The entire Ad. family, all three of them, survived; they are all alive, but I hadn't seen them for years until one beautiful June day several years ago Basia herself came to see me, introduced herself, told me who she is, that she is interested in my poetry and that it seems I knew her when she was a young child in the shelter; and from this a close friendship developed until Basia married an Italian Polonist; she is now living in Florence even though after we had left and they stayed on there on Rybaki Street her mother, Roza, had said to her, "Don't cry, you won't live anyway." They were even driven in front of a tank.)

Well, that day Jadzka and the other woman, Swen and Celinka (I think), and I ran over to Mostowa Street. Uphill. Past three or four barricades. Not the kind of barricades that were erected at the beginning, nor even the kind that we put up six days later on Ogrodowa Street; these were made of concrete slabs piled up to a great height, fortified with sand, bristling with metal rods which had been hammered into the earth. They were absolutely impregnable. It was only then that I looked at all of this with disbelief. Because it was here that the uprising began to look as if it came out of a book. The kind about a siege. From the Middle Ages. And about an exotic, steamy city. Where people start eating the bark from the trees, and the soles of their shoes. But here, after all, the danger was practically on top of us. We were encircled. There were storm attacks too. And when they happened . . . but more about that later. Also the sky. And the heat. And the crowds. I almost had vertigo from astonishment. I can remember that feeling to this day. Even to the burning in my nose.

Well, we ran uphill along Mostowa Street (there was the escarpment and those inclines). To the corner of Freta Street. To the store. Straight ahead. Unbelievable. The store was open. But in a strange sort of way. Practically split open (bent over). But they were selling. What? Kasha, I think. Bread? I think we bought those two items. In any case we bought something. For the first and last time. Because I didn't see any more stores either before or after that.

There was such congestion on the sidewalks that people were walking in the streets. They were crowded with refugees from all over Warsaw. Everyone who had fled from Wola was here. Stare Miasto was a famous redoubt. (Already famous.) Impregnable. Barricades. Serpentine streets. Not for tanks. Stare Miasto is strong. Its walls are solid. Thick. And also. . . . Tradition.

Chance meetings. Passing Irena P. with her haversack. She had joined the Home Army.* Teik hurring into action at the head of a squad, which was walking rapidly in Indian file, over the cobblestones of Mostowa Street near Stara and either he didn't notice us or it made no difference to him, so occupied was he and they with what they were approaching. Actually, I don't know if I met him twice on Mostowa in August or if the first time was at the corner of Chlodna and Zelazna Streets when I was returning home on Saturday from Irena's. Probably on Rybaki Street (those two times —with an interval between them). Because otherwise I wouldn't keep getting those people in single file, his uniformed soldiers, confused with those boy scouts in uniform. But enough of that for now. I have a feeling that Teik's meeting with Swen came later, so there'll be more about it later on.

There was something else from that walk—something triumphant and disastrous—which reminded me for some reason of the mood in 1939 because it was also summertime. I'd like to talk about Dluga Street. Dluga was the most important street in that section of Warsaw. Also the widest. And the most elegant. At that

45

time, at least. Because, according to what I heard then, the most important offices were located there, even the headquarters of the People's Army. I have already mentioned that Dluga Street had two roadways between Krasinski Square and Freta. Between these roadways was a series of two or three small plazas. Which lent it chic. Like a boulevard. There was also some sort of grass growing there. Loudspeakers were blaring on both sides of the street. And there was talking. Flags were hanging in every doorway. Large numbers of people were sitting on the iron balconies. I remember that. And I remember an elegant automobile with the Polish national flag on it squeezing through the crowds of people.

In the evening, Henka and Jadzka were in our cellar, not in our corner but in theirs (they had found a corner for themselves)—plank beds agains a wall near a pillar in another nave. . . . Jadzka, on her plank bed, told Swen's and my fortunes from cards. She even divined some significant details. About life.

What else? Prayer. I'm sure Swen had begun to lead the prayers by then. No. Not yet. That's right. It was still some woman. Swen started two or three days later. He refused. He read the news sheets out loud (I pass directly to that because it was an identical liturgy); he stood right in the center of everything, in the main isle of the nave (since we've already blundered into such a comparison); that is correct, since there were three naves. He always stood near the right side of the aisle, close to the entrance, near the plank beds and, I think, a pillar, but perhaps I'm adding that detail from my imagination. Two women would take two candles from the altar to illuminate the latest news. Not necessarily once a day. Just as with prayer. In the morning and the evening, too. At least. So, the women would take the candles from the altar. And light them. They would draw close to Swen as if for the recitation of the Gospels and stand on either side of him. Deaconnesses. I was the subdeacon or sacristan. The rest of our family sat close by on the plank beds. Swen stood at the center of our circle and of the larger circle of the pressing crowd which first would be sitting or squatting and then would stand as he read. But they always listened intently. To what was reported. Because it was important. Everyone grew quiet then. Right from the start. Yes, it was truly very pious. The reading, that is. There were several news sheets or placards, of assorted sizes, published by various editorial committees—either by the Home Army or the People's Army or the Civil Defense. The reading would be accompanied by mass scowling,

46

complaints, wringing of hands or outbursts of joy.

Let's move on. For a certain number of days I'll be getting things confused. Until August 15. Except that on the 12th (I've recalled what took place then), something happened. And something else happened on the 13th. Something well known. Here's what I've recalled: a trolley driver and his girl on the plank bed across the way, practically beside the barrel. Somehow they were also near the door, the unfinished door to the stairwell, but also somehow near the pillar, although a moment ago it seemed to me they were near the wall. In any case, they were close to us, within earshot. They had a carbide lamp. And they were using it. But I can remember many such lamps in the darkness. The concrete darkness. Or the darkness behind the pillar. Or perhaps it's because they changed places later. Though it was also close by. Or that everything was in darkness. That's it, I'm sure. They said they were a couple. Not married. He was rawboned. In a navy-blue trolley-driver's uniform. She. . . . For some reason I remember her mostly from above—her disheveled hair, bushy, tangled. Against the background of the carbide lamp. That hair. She too was rawboned. She wore a suit of sorts or, rather, a jacket. A gray check or a salt-and-pepper pattern. They were relatively young, fairly good-looking and pleasant, and through all this they were in love. We got to know them. Or rather it happened like this: on one side, the one near the altar, we became friendly with the Ads., and on the other side (the side with the barrel and the exit) with the trolley-driver couple.

I'm going back for a while to August 7, to that first day in Stare Miasto. What else did I learn? Right at the beginning? In general, that swimming across the Vistula would be. . . . Well, I didn't ask about it right away because I was embarrassed. I sensed immediately that it wasn't right to inquire about it right off. After a while I screwed up my courage and asked, in a half-whisper at that; Swen shrugged his shoulders and burst out laughing. "Whaat? . . . Go take a look. . . . The shore is covered with barbed wire, the tanks are out, and at night the searchlights keep raking the Vistula and the shores."

Naturally, that convinced me immediately, since I'd really been convinced from the very first moment we entered that terrain and that shelter. Jadzka and Henka also heard him. And gave up just as I did. Anyway, they were blind instincts. First you wanted to go here. Then there. In Wola there was the dread of

47

mass shootings and burnings. So a person wanted to escape from that hell by some miracle. But then something else popped into his head. A new mood. All over again. And I know, just as surely as I know myself and every average Warsawite, that I would have wanted to return immediately from that miraculous salvation outside of Warsaw to this hell. After all, in 1939 my parents and I had fled as far away as Zdolbunow, so that I wasn't even in Warsaw after September 5, and throughout September I was disconsolate at not being here. And when people told me what had happened, and wrung their hands, and mentioned September 23, 24, 25, I wanted to know about those days in particular. Throughout the entire occupation I regretted that I hadn't been there on September 25 during that famous bombardment from eight in the morning until eight at night. When Nanka, Sabina and Michal were on Ogrodowa Street at the corner of Wronia in Olek's ground floor aparment. (Olek was the brother of Zosia Romanowska—the woman who perished in Grochow.) Well, according to what Sabina told me, Nanka stayed there, not moving an inch the entire time, huddled over and clutching at her liver. So now I had what I'd wanted. Yet I wanted to flee. But had I fled, I repeat, I would have regretted not having experienced what I was about to experience. That's why I feel so sorry for those who died in the bombardment. The joy of experience passed them by. That one might not survive—that's another question entirely. But I don't want to be bothered now with such considerations. There will be more and more of them anyway. Not because I suddenly have a craving for them. But because in that life they were the very stuff of life. Imagining what might take place or what would definitely take place a moment later accounted for at least half one's thoughts. The rest were devoted to taking care of various immediate needs—food, shelter, clothing. It was summertime and hot, so there wasn't any particular difficulty with the latter, because one could get along with nothing, just a fairly threadbare suit with clumps of dirt on the pants legs, and slippers with holes in them—in other words, we worried about the immediate needs of bare subsistence, what touched our skins, and finally, about that threat from the Vistula and, even worse, from the sky. Memory has forced the rest back. It is difficult to say "memories" in the strict sense of the word. Because there are memories from the day before yesterday. And memories from an hour ago. Memories from Wola and others fresh from Mostowa Street. They're all muddled. Intertwined. With possibilities, with what might have been. Against the background of what was happening. Obviously, there must have been a break for talking too. And a rather long one at that. Especially since talk was focused precisely on those themes. By and large.

And I also found out . . . something. That Celinka (Swen laughed uncontrollably as he told me this) was still going to work on Miodowa Street every day. To the Health Center. But her Health Center was in Parysow. She went to the local one with a girlfriend whom she'd met here. Swen didn't go. "So they planned to go there and work in the office every day until today when they got there there was no more Center!" And Swen doubled up with laughter. And so did I. Celinka too. "They were on duty for a long time!"

During those first days we used to walk to the corner of Mostowa and Stara Streets, or rather, past the corner along Stara itself, to the right of Mostowa, to get free dinners from some nuns. I don't remember what kind of nuns they were. Stara ran along the embankment from Mostowa Street so that it was relatively high and became even higher towards Nowe Miasto, towards the Market itself. These nuns who provided our dinners were located across from the rear of the Church of the Dominicans. But the garden of the Dominicans stretched all the way to Rybaki Street. Or rather, their grounds were intersected by Stara Street and perhaps by those nuns too; they spread out along the escarpment to the very end, at the base of the cliff all the way to Rybaki Street, and were separated from Rybaki by an ancient, utterly old-fashioned wall, white, with a gate over which was carved (in metal, so it was like a real one) a monstrance, the symbol of Saint Jacek Odrowaz, our Polish holy man of the Middle Ages, from Stare Miasto, a Dominican, the patron saint of the church of the Dominicans, which actually was called Saint Jacek's. The church at the fork in Dluga Street whose bell tower spire had burned until it shone green. So, that wall (white, thick and white!), on the left side of Rybak Street as one walked from Mostowa, from the escarpment at Swen's house, began not so very far past the corner, past the apartment house, at the courtyard, and right afterwards there was that gate with the monstrance in a bend in the sidewalk, only not paved with concrete slabs but with cobblestones, a triangle like the one directly opposite it, the one past the Powder House where those children were playing in the grass early in the morning (because there was definitely grass growing there). I even think I remember that beneath the Dominican monstrance a kind of braided grass was growing with leaves on drooping stalks, and camomile I think, the common variety, low, the kind that likes to grow between cobblestones. The garden (it was a fruit and vegetable garden to feed the Dominicans and their students and wards [they had several]) stretched out in length and breadth and was visible as you walked uphill. And further on in the direction of Koscielna Street it bordered on the apartment houses on Rybaki Street and on the gardens of the Sisters of the Sacrament, who also were situated on the escarpment and also provided food. Anyway, a lot more will be said about this. And in more detail. Because this terrain will be very important.

For various reasons. Well, people would stand in line at this convent on Stara Street for the thin soup I have mentioned. I don't say "thin soup" at all disparagingly because it was a real luxury at that time and a sign of good will to serve soup, especially if it was good and thick. People stood with their large pots on the street and along the stairs leading into the red building. The one across from the white Dominicans. The monastery. Massive, baroque, situated high up on the escarpment, practically on its summit. And everything was white because they loved that color. They also wear white habits, though with black trim, it's true, and the Polish Dominicans even use a thick red sash as a belt; they have been granted that privilege because the Tatars once slaughtered the Dominicans in Sandomierz, which probably won't be of any interest to you until you see the display cases in Sandomierz, in the church, with the recently exhumed skulls of those Dominicans, split by Tatar hatchets; a hatchet is even still buried in one skull (after it sank in it couldn't be pulled out). The whiteness remains all the more firmly engraved in my memory because of the heat, August, and the smoke, and because sometimes the sky was white from smoke and from the scorching heat, and the Powder House was white like that, and the Sisters of the Sacrament were white, that is, their high church which was also visible from below, with its sky-blue cupola, so that it was also linked with the sky. In addition, there were Paulist Fathers (Paulists have been in Poland only in the twentieth century). Paulists are dressed entirely in white—although it's true their church building was here without them because in the nineteenth century the Tsar dissolved the Paulists and the Dominicans and the Benonites (who were in Nowe Miasto behind the Sisters of the Sacrament) and changed their church into Bienkowski's knife factory; that is, the Tsar approved the change and so it remained until the uprising. More about that later because it is also significant in the action. But there were definitely some representatives of those orders. There was a priest from Saint Jacek's and there were the Paulist Fathers whose church was across from the Dominicans so that it fronted on Nowomiejska and Mostowa, just as the Dominicans across from them were at the intersection with Dluga Street, as I have already explained. But the Paulist Fathers had two towers, baroque, which had not burned but were still intact, and they had a double stairway leading up to the main doors. Against the background of all the goldenness created by the gold leaf stood the Mother of God surrounded by lamps. And all this could be seen from below, from the corner of Mostowa and Rybaki Streets, and the Mother of God stood at the end of a long, long uphill climb, steep, over cobblestones. In connection with this I recall that Mostowa had an extension leading to the Vistula. Only it was called something else. Bolesc. The left side of Bolesc Street as you walk from the escarpment was the same as the Powder House from the side. Bolesc Street led all the way to Wybrzeze, just as it does to this day, as it did then and as it had for centuries past, when it had been important, when the bridge—still just a low, pontoon bridge—ran not from Bernardarska Street but rather from Mostowa itself. Actually, when you walked along it towards Praga, then in addition to the trees which were already very large during the uprising (though perhaps in the past they once were small), straight ahead, in addition to those trees, was the center of Praga. With the *ratusz*.* Ratuszowa Street began at the place where Mostowa would have been had it continued across the Vistula. And the Church of the Mother of God of Loreto. Baroque. A so-called church within a church. Perhaps I am speaking too much about these monuments. But they were important. Because they perished with us. We could see Praga. The escarpment and everything which I've described was above us. And the fact that they were holy places is also not irrelevant. Stare Miasto was the seat of the People's Army. And also the concentration of our holy places and of the clergy. I am writing about this sympathetically. Because there is much that is good to be said about the clergy. After all, it was precisely those thin soups which were the beginning. Of my astonishment, I mean. Not only weren't they refusing people, but they were even urging them. To eat whatever was served. The wait in line was quickly over with. Waiting

51

itself didn't take long. People weren't impatient. Just as with every-thing then. We didn't grow impatient. After all, we were standing there with companions. Family, friends, or new acquaintances. Eve-ryone would be talking right off. Everyone knew everyone else. Friends. It was even pleasant. As I remember it. Only there were those airplanes. We would flee somewhere into the shadows. And then once more move to those steps. Holding our messkits. I re-member having something which jangled and was lightweight. And I think we ate on the spot, right away, on those cobblestones, in the gutter. How long did that last? Not so long, I think. The daily trips. That means those poor nuns just cooked and cooked. What I want to say is that what had happened to the institution on Mio-dowa Street suddenly happened to them too. Just as it did to eve-rything else. Anyway, some time around August 13 it was all over with those thin soups. Standing on Stara Street, with its view, standing on the escarpment, just being outdoors, became impos-sible. And now I recall that it was while we were going for soup one afternoon, I think, that I saw Teik climbing uphill rapidly, fol-lowed by a line of people in battle dress. So, it seems as if once he was connected with that shop. And a second time, with the soup. But the time on Chlodna Street was probably a hallucination.

All of this is like one prolonged hallucination. A terribly ba-nal tale. But it suits me. It fits what I felt then. Because you didn't have to be a poet to have things multiplying in your head. If I write very little about my impressions. And everything is in ordi-nary language, as if nothing happened. Or if I hardly every look in-side myself, or seem to be superficial. It is only because it can't be done any other way. After all, that is how we experienced things. And, generally speaking, that is the only device, not an artificially constructed one, but the only completely natural device. To con-vey all of this. For twenty years I could not write about this. Al-though I wanted to very much. I would talk. About the uprising. To so many people. All sorts of people. So many times. And all along I was thinking that I must describe the uprising, somehow or other *describe* it. And I didn't even know that those twenty years of talking (I have been talking about it for twenty years, because it is the greatest experience of my life—a closed experience), pre-cisely that talking, is the only proper way to describe the uprising.

Let us return to our story. About August 13. Bombs had fal-len. On Stare Miasto. It goes without saying that they had already fallen on Miodowa Street. But in those days Miodowa wasn't as clearly included within Stare Miasto as it was later when it was completely cut off from the rest of Warsaw along with Stare Miasto; just like all of Dluga Street and even Bielanska and Przejazd—they were all Stare Miasto. We didn't think of them as belonging anywhere else. And perhaps that whole business is reflected to this day. That it is Stare Miasto. Later on, I shall give other examples of such topographic redefinitions. All the same, the bombs fell on Muranow too. The street which leads from Bonifraterska to the Vistula. That is, to be more precise, from Stare Miasto to Nowe Miasto. And people began to call it, too, Stare Miasto. And it has remained Stare Miasto to this day. Or Nowe Miasto. I am not confusing these two entities because Nowe Miasto is a part of Stare Miasto. Well, the bombs were falling on Muranow, on Zakroczymska, and they struck a huge fuel storage area. There was a tremendous explosion. A number of people died. It became known as the Muranow incident. Among us. I remember that the first bombs which were dropped on Stare Miasto landed on the corner of Mostowa and Nowomiejska Streets. Where today—(if I'm not Mistaken) —the "Nowomiejski" dairy bar is located. Between the walls and Mostowa Street. The present walls. Because at that time there were no walls on that side of Mostowa and Nowomiejska as you face the Vistula. They just came to an end on Nowomiejska Street. There wasn't a Barbican either. Because it was immured in the Gdansk Cellar. In a stone building by that name. Well, the bombs landed somewhere—on the house in which the shop was situated (the shop where we had bought something on that first day), or on the house across the street from it. And it was then that I understood that it had finally begun. That there was nothing we could count on anymore. Not even half a day of peace. That my Stare Miasto vacation was finished. But actually the difference was that *it* had finally begun. It was no longer just a premonition. It *was*. When we reached Stara Street all of a sudden it was nothing but a heap of red bricks, dust and the steps. Perhaps the first bombs were already falling then on the Sisters of the Sacrament. Perhaps they'd already begun to burn. Because they did burn down to the ground. By stages. Whatever they had there. Something also happened to the Dominicans, I think.

A gunboat was patrolling the Vistula and shelling us. And on the far shore the Germans seemed to be sitting in those tall trees watching us through binoculars. It was said that they saw and heard everything. Tanks thundered along Wybrzeze and occasionally strayed into Koscielna Street, up to the first barricade. I don't know exactly what happened to those tanks. Because by then a saying with which people frightened themselves had already become popular, "Be quiet! There's a tank on the other side of the wall." And the entire shelter would repeat, "Quiet! There's a tank outside the wall. . . ."

Even the gentlemen with the red armbands liked to say that out loud. Swen would laugh uproariously at that. But the tank outside the wall was really there a few times, it seems. Because once (I was looking out) way up there in a little red window in a tiny cellar a partisan was waiting, squatting, bent over, with a bottle of kerosene in his hand. But that was probably later on.

What else happened in those first four or five days on Rybaki Street? A pumpkin expedition. I think it was around that time. In that courtyard. Which means that in the course of two or three days things had changed so drastically that dashing at full speed into the yard to pick two pumpkins and rushing back with them into the stairwell entrance had become terribly risky. We cut up the pumpkin into sections and ate it immediately with our so-called family. The food situation was becoming difficult. Now, when the districts within the fortress were being destroyed, how many people could have found sufficient food? And also, how could we dig when shells and bombs were falling here? For the time being, Stare Miasto and a part of Muranow and Stawki Streets, that is, the storehouses on Stawki, lived off those storehouses. There were continuous battles to keep them in our hands. Just as there were battles for the electric works on Powisle. We lost the reservoirs more quickly. That was the first catastrophe: no water. The second, a little later: we lost the electric works—no light. The third, a local catastrophe for Stare Miasto: the loss of Stawki Street—and hunger. The Sisters of the Sacrament were still saving people then as best they could. But more about that later.

But what was it really like? As we already know, Wola had fallen. Mokotow was holding out. Zoliborz too. Czerniakow. Powisle. Most of Srodmiescie. They were all ours. Of course, not literally all of Mokotow or all of Zoliborz or Czerniakow. That's an important point—that they weren't ours entirely. Surface communication was becoming more difficult all the time. Soon the news reached us that communication was established with Czerniakow, Zoliborz, Mokotow, but only via the sewers. Plus the fact that, as people said, you would have to walk part of the way to

Czerniakow on your knees. A storm sewer (on Krasinski Street, I think) made communication with Zoliborz even more complicated: the Hitlerites would open the manholes there from time to time and toss grenades into the sewer or (this I know from films) would bar the exits with barbed wire and hang grenades on it.

Despite this, communication was uninterrupted. (People were dying above ground too. What difference did it make!) The couriers were mainly girls or young boys. Surface communication was maintained with Powisle for a longer time. That is, between Srodmiescie and Powisle. And for the time being we had surface communication with Srodmiescie too. Though admittedly it was most uncertain. And probably very costly.

What did people do in the shelters?

They talked. Sometimes I would walk through the corridor to the central cellar, the one with the wing where sunlight entered from above, and I would sit there and write. There were many prayer sessions in which people could participate. At that time I was still something of a believer. (No doubt, some people will look upon this skeptically or ironically. Or they will refer to it mockingly, which infuriates me, although I won't say anything because I simply have an emotional tie with it.) People waited for the news sheets. Which arrived several times a day. Because there were many printing presses. The Home Army's. The People's Army's. The People's Party's. I don't know if the Civil Defense had its own. Right-wing sheets also appeared (the "Warszawianka," for example). We didn't discriminate among them then as we should have. We thought, if they were Polish, they were Polish. Anyway, the fascistic ones didn't appear in Stare Miasto. The Home Army and the People's Army were there. They accepted each other. And the people accepted both of them. After some initial sparring, as I recall, they simply grew accustomed to each other. And there was agreement.

More about our occupations. We started taking strolls. Swen and I. A stroll consisted of our linking arms and walking through all the cellars of our block in turn. At the end of the chain of our block B there was a tunnel. A long one. Covered with cement. Under the courtyard. Under those potatoes and pumpkins. And we frequently went through this tunnel on an inspection tour of the second chain of shelters, beneath block A. To be precise I should add (later I will be talking not only about specific details but about our life in this terrain) that two additional lateral blocks also belonged to block B, smaller ones, which actually formed a single unit with our block, although one of them had its own triangular courtyard. So, that is where we took our strolls. They lasted a long time. Because there were many people in each cellar. In the corridors and the narrow passageways, too. And there were also little cellars along the way. Without doors. Just open compartments. We had new acquaintances in one of them. A young couple. We used to go there to gossip and to listen to their cricket. Because there was a cricket in the wall there. Actually, there were other crickets too. But this one was the loudest. In one of the farthest of the large cellars we found an acquaintance—Leonard. He was usually sitting on some bundles, probably not his own. He was alone. Or perhaps he sat on some small bricks? Skinny. With glasses. And he had on a white coat. That's right. Leonard lived on Rybaki Street. At number 23 I think. In a four-story apartment house on the other side of Rybaki. Facing the escarpment. I shall write more about Leonard's house, which was still standing then. (Either Leonard came here earlier in search of a safer place since our buildings, after all, were made of reinforced concrete, or I have placed various events about a week too early.) A split-level apartment house which was traversed by the Nowomiejska route, at first one of two in all Starowka and later the only one to remain until the very end. Leonard definitely dropped in on us at times, too. But I remember him more often in his own cellar. In the bright illumination of an electric bulb. Perhaps it only seemed bright then. Because there was so much darkness. Underground. Against the background of the red walls. The same, after all, as ours. However, I think they didn't have cement pillars there. I think Leonard was very sad at our last meetings. Undecided. About where he should go. When his home no longer existed. He was trying to decide, like us, whether he should go up to the Sisters of the Sacrament. Finally one day he told us he was going there. I think. On our next walk we didn't see him. Later, there was no way we could meet him. Only after the war and after our return to Warsaw did we find out that that's what he had done. That he had gone to the Sisters of the Sacrament. And that he was buried there with the rest of the people. Then, in 1946 or so, someone else said that he'd been buried alive at the Sisters of the Sacrament but that he'd made his way to a small window, had dug himself out and that, it seems, he'd just walked away from there. But then someone else said, I think, that that was probably not true. Especially since neither we nor anyone else at all has seen Leonard again since the uprising. Nor even heard about him being alive since the uprising.

People had settled in the tunnel although there was also the most traffic and occasionally a draft there—a terrible draft at any hour of the day and night, despite the heat. In fact, it eventually became cold there. Once, when we were wandering about the cellars during a terrible bombardment of our blocks we were driven by blind, dumb instinct in the direction of block A. Through the tunnel. Naturally. The whole family with all our bundles. After all, on one of our walks there we had found my distant relative, Aunt Trocinska, Aunt Jozia's sister-in-law. I might not even have recognized her. But she tugged at my sleeve joyfully. She had been living in block A during the occupation. So she was under her own house. And after her first shelter had become unbearable, she'd moved to the tunnel. She was alone. She had only a few belongings. I remember that she lived right beside the door which led from block A. She insisted that we move there. Swen and I quickly returned to our family, to the first cellar. And in the evening, probably quite late, almost at night, we enthusiastically marshalled our entire family, which trudged along after us through the tunnel, to a wall near the same door as Aunt Trocinska. There were still only a few people in the tunnel. Just those drafts, the slamming of doors and people rushing through with or without bundles, more and more quickly; one probably can't even speak about slowness in relation to the uprising. That same night, I think, many more people settled down near us in the tunnel. In the morning the tunnel was already congested. We remained there not more than thirty-six hours. Perhaps not even that long. We weren't frightened away by the people. Just by the drafts. During the first night we were already freezing. And probably the second night drove us out. Right at the beginning. There wasn't very much to cover ourselves with, after all. Why have such hopeless luxuries when it was summertime? And when it smelled of heat and fires everywhere? But I've run ahead again.

We recognized an engineer in the cellars of block A. Later, when Swen was leading the prayers in front of our altar, we collaborated on writing a real litany. I remember from this litany:

> *From bombs and airplanes—protect us, Oh Lord,*
> *From tanks and Goliaths*—protect us, Oh Lord,*
> *From shells and grenades—protect us, Oh Lord,*

From fires and being burned alive—protect us, Oh Lord,
From being shot to death—protect us, Oh Lord
From being buried—protect us, Oh Lord. . . .

The litany was rather long. We recited it one evening. Aloud. It caught on immediately. The other cellars began reciting it, too. I remember that we wrote it down for the engineer. The next evening that engineer met us and said, "Do you know, at this moment 1,500 people in my block are reciting your litany."

There were at least 3,000 of us at that one address. There were 300 or 350 partisans alone. They kept coming in. Just like the civilians. From other bombed-out houses. Just like Leonard.

Swen's recitation of prayers stemmed more from his acting ability than from piety. Before that the prayers were rather monotonous. They became interesting when Swen took over. And more sensible. In addition to his acting ability, Swen had a sense of what was vital or, rather, of the most urgent needs. After one evening prayer, I think it was the day when the men were fighting with axes near the entrance to the little shelter (they really hadn't done any harm to each other, in the final analysis), Swen turned from the altar to face everyone.

"Please, let us swear to each other that we will not quarrel."

"We swear it. . . ," the whole crowd repeated obediently.

And it actually helped. At least for a while. Then Swen repeated it. And again the shelter obediently swore. Again it helped for a while. So it wasn't just words.

I am returning now to the course of events. To the trolley couple we had made friends with. The date, August 12, is connected with them.

On August 12 a few people left our shelter, as was common during the daytime, to run some errands, I don't know for what exactly—for food, water, to do rescue work, perhaps for a duty tour on the barricades—and the trolley driver was among them. For the time being, we had become accustomed to the shells. To the bombardment. From Praga. From the gunboat on the Vistula. And from the armored train on the tracks of the Gdansk Station. These shellings weren't as frequent yet as they were to become a little later. In any case, August 12 itself was a turning point. In the afternoon, when they were gone, Stare Miasto suddenly shook from several repeated explosions and strong wind blasts. It was something entirely new, like a typhoon. It seemed clear to us that the upper stories all over lower Starowka had been torn off. At any rate, people said that all the roofs had been ripped off. An unknown weapon. And people did have a feel for the varieties of weapons. They rushed out to check. And returned with that news about the roofs. That it was something really bad. Some sort of "V." Panic erupted. What could it be? But not for long. Because shortly afterwards the same thing was repeated. Until then the nights had been peaceful. There were no planes during the night. There were sudden artillery attacks. And other things. Such as tanks. But from then on this new weapon—mine throwers—began to stalk us, especially at night and, all the more frequently, several times a night.

There were also flame-throwers. We didn't know what they looked like. Either of them. At first you could only hear three to six creaking screeches and right afterwards just as many explosions and wind blasts. People used to say when they heard those screeches, "They're cranking up the nickelodeon again. . . ."

And right away a humorous verse about the cranking up of the nickelodeon appeared, and we even read it in the newspaper.

Throwers—that was a proper name. Because those wind blasts threw us and the walls about.

But let us return to the trolley driver's girlfriend. She waited for him till evening. He didn't return. She didn't sleep that night. She cried. He didn't return in the morning. We consoled her. I think we stopped consoling her several hours later. Because there was no longer any reason to. At this moment I'm no longer so certain that that was on the 12th. But maybe it was. The next day was the 13th. The famous day of the explosion of the "Goliath" on Dluga Street. So perhaps I'm right after all. Even before the "Goliath," on the morning or the afternoon of the 13th, the trolley driver's girlfriend asked us, "Could you help me search for him in the hospitals?"

"Of course!"

And the three of us—she, Swen, and I—rushed into the city.

Or perhaps it was the 14th after all? Because the 13th was a Sunday. After all, which of the eywitnesses has ever associated the explosion of the "Goliath" with Sunday? That's probably proof enough.

That a short period of time appeared long is no cause for wonder. Every day people would say, "It's already the twelfth day of the uprising. . . ." "It's the thirteenth day of the uprising already. . . ."

It seemed as if we already had entire years of this behind us, and what was there ahead of us? As if there never had been, nor would there ever be anything else—only the uprising. Which it was impossible to endure much longer. Each day it was impossible to endure it much longer. Then each night. Then every two hours. Then every fifteen minutes. Yes. People kept track of time incessantly. They listened to the air or felt the ground to see whether it was trembling or not. Where are they? The Eastern front? Somewhere beyond the Vistula, or where? In Wisniew? In Piekielko? People listened to the radio or to those who listened to the radio, which is to say, to what was happening in the West. There too (since June) a front was on the move. French cities were being liberated. Belgian cities. And us? There were parachute drops. Arms. They flew over more than once. First those from the West. The Allies. Mostly they were Poles in those planes. Mostly or exclusively. Someone told a story about how once a whole fleet of those airplanes flying from somewhere in England or Africa with supplies for us struck a cold air front over the Alps (I think). All the motors froze. And all of them crashed on the spot. Once at night an airplane from the Union of South Africa crashed right in front of our eyes. Into Praga. Another crashed on Miodowa Street. Where it joins Krasinski Place. Right onto the barricade which already had a trolleycar on top of it. The fliers were pulled out. I happened to meet them—by chance—on August 13. They were Poles. Also. Or perhaps they weren't from that plane?

Where Dluga Street intersects Kilinski near the Garrison Church, on the side facing the Vistula of course, new hospitals had been set up in various cellars. Organized on the spot. Mainly because of the "Goliath." According to a version I heard recently from an acquaintance of mine, a teacher who was there, on August 13, on that incomprehensible Sunday, late in the day, probably after sundown, a "Goliath" released by the Germans turned into Freta Street from Swietojerska. Just a little tank. Or, rather, a robot tank. At first no one knew that it had been released. Or, rather, set loose. Allowed to come closer. And it was captured by Poles. At once crowds of people rushed up to cheer. They followed the trophy, walking alongside of it. They turned from Freta into Dluga. And somewhere near the foot of Kilinski Street, when the euphoria had reached its peak and the balconies were jammed with people, a catastrophe occurred. The timing mechanism went off. The balconies were left with lots of figures draped over the iron railings. The majority of the corpses, pieces of legs, hands, guts, clothing were found in the garden plots at the center. Those new hospitals came into being that night. My teacher friend had two brothers who were taking part in the action. One, the elder, perished in a skirmish. The other, just a boy, was helping with something over there. He was always rushing about. That's what he was doing then, too. They, my friend and her mother, that is (they had escaped from Wola), were sitting in the cellar when the younger brother was on Dluga. His sister (my friend) rushed outside. She searched for him. After the explosion. Because someone had told her that the kid had been there. And in the garden, grassless at that time, on the bare earth, she found a piece of his leg with his shoe still on it. Someone said, however, that her kid brother was alive and no doubt was in the new hospital. She wanted to go inside. But they wouldn't let her in. Because they were just setting it up. By the next day the hospital had already been bombed. Irena P., when I saw her again during the uprising in Starowka, I think, said (she too had been there then) that they had had to shovel up the guts.

When we rushed out with the trolley driver's girlfriend onto Rybaki Street we first checked the hospital on the corner of Rybaki and Bolesc. On Prochownia. There was a hospital there on the ground floor. The trolley driver wasn't there. They told us that if the wounded man wasn't from the military, more likely he'd be somewhere on Dluga.

Rybaki Street already looked different from what it had been like at the beginning. Every few steps there were barricades of earth, steel rails, paving stones and concrete with narrow little crannies near the wall. The walls of the old driveway and the two shell-like gates of chipped plaster were pockmarked. The houses were already losing their normal contours. Their height. The lines of their facades.

From the corner of Bolesc we turned back a short way in the direction from which we had come (Koscielna). Right at the bend, as has already been described, was the wall at which the gardens of the Dominicans, dropping down from the hill and intersected by Stara Street, came to an end. In this wall, described several pages back, was the gate which has also been described already, that same gate with the monstrance which marked the beginning of the Staromiejski route from lower to upper Stare Miasto. After rushing through the gate you immediately made a sharp left turn. Then you ran to the garbage shed near the opposite wall. You jumped onto the table placed beside it. From the table onto the garbage shed. From the garbage shed (a bin of the old kind with a lid) through a hole in the wall. And you were on a slightly higher level, or rather, at the bottom of the courtyard from which you could scurry along a board through a window, from the window into someone's apartment, from that apartment through a hole in the wall into some other dark place which was at ground floor level at one end but, in the middle of the building, was a cellar. There you landed blindly amidst a crowd of people who were sitting or lying down, some of whom were even wounded. Some of them cried out, "Oh Jesus! . . . don't trample us . . . Jesus! . . ."

From there, you raced along various turnings in the dark up to some higher place, out into the courtyard. From that yard through a gate. Out to Mostowa Street. Here you ran across the street at an angle, stooping behind the barricade. Along the cobblestones. From there you could always see a bit of blue sky and the Vistula through a chink in the wall. The street runs downhill. And that barricade was considered both a lookout and a front. Often, partisans were lying on it and firing at Wybrzeze and Praga. Perhaps even at those legendary trees with the Germans and their binoculars. On the other side of Mostowa (there were houses there then) you hurried through the gate of the lower courtyard of the Gdansk Cellar. Or perhaps that wasn't the Gdansk Cellar but only part of a neighboring building. Somewhat lower down. It seems to me that the oldest hospital in Warsaw, Holy Lazarus (I remember its burnt-out walls were still standing, adhering to the ancient ramparts, when it was uncovered after the war; they dismantled the monument), stood, I think, directly opposite the entrance from Mostowa near that first lower courtyard. If there really were two courtyards there. And behind the hoardings, or the wall, at least behind the wide-open wooden gate, it seems there was a second courtyard. Also covered with cobblestones. And that was the one which housed the Gdansk Cellar. The Gdansk Cellar has always been a famous building. My grandmother lived in it. My father spent entire months there as a child around 1905. The Gdansk Cellar stood four stories above that courtyard with its cobblestones and gray cats always sitting in it, or, rather, it was four stories counting from below or two above the upper level, which faced Freta Street, or the front. The stairs were wooden. Also with cats

62

on them. I remember that from before the war. Only at that time no one knew either about the landmark value of Holy Lazarus (which had been reconstructed, after all, built onto, renovated, like the majority of such buildings in Warsaw, so that it was difficult to see it as a monument), nor did anyone know that the Gdansk Cellar, in addition to its elaborate construction, was a parasite on the remains of the Barbican. To continue. You rushed into a stairwell. Up to the second floor. And after racing through the passageway you realized that that was the ground floor on Freta Street. Then came the gate and then, right away, the street. The hill of Stare Miasto. On this route, in the Gdansk Cellar and its exit onto Freta, at the intersection of Dluga, Nowomiejska and Mostowa Streets, people were always passing by quickly, in crowds. They would walk past once or twice. Searching. Taking care of things. And they would rush on. Dluga was always the most central and important street.

One of the buildings, either the Gdansk Cellar or the one housing the baths near Mostowa, had a facade decorated with graying cream-colored tiles, which were fashionable in the nineteenth century. Come to think of it, there were similar tiles on the Cathedral on Koscielna Street. The colors of the town houses, however, were already beginning to turn burnt gray. One corner of Mostowa and Freta was in ruins. Perhaps even both corners. I know for a fact, from recent testimony, that the first bomb demolished the building on the right of Mostowa which faced the Vistula; and yet to this day I can picture the left corner. The one with the shops. A pile of red bricks. After all, those weren't the only ruins here. But still, that was only the beginning then. It is true that people may have been suffocated to death by flour in the cellar of the old market when the bomb fell. But the churches, convents and the Cathedral were still standing. There were still streets. It was incredibly strange how distant everything was then. Although now it is four times larger than it was then, Warsaw has never seemed so large and complicated, so endless. Space was chopped up. Layouts and divisions were multiplied, peeled away, excavated, overlapping in a fine network. Today, I am struck by the thought that I was at the intersection of Krucza, Piekna and Mokotowska while they were shooting from Politechnic Square, and that it all seemed and felt so very far away. Certainly, I could see neither men nor cannons. Against one's will one transposed the entire topography of the front. The Praga shore seemed to be located on some other map. The Hitlerites with their binoculars in the Zoo's tall trees and the Eastern front in Zeran seemed something which existed, it is true, but only as a second or third reality.

We rushed into the hospitals. All were located on the left side of the street. There were quite a few of them. I think some people were still struggling to live on the ground floors. But since it was dangerous (Miodowa was already quite shot up) the hospitals were in the basements. And since the basements were merely shelters, and since shelters beneath old houses were ordinary cellars for coal and potatoes, with narrow stalls and vaults, it is not surprising that even after all our experience we were overwhelmed once more. With astonishment. Signs were posted along the narrow corridors over the entranceways to the potato bins: Ward 5, Ward 6. And in the corridor itself, the one leading from the courtyard entrance, lay the wounded. That too was a ward. Some people were lying on the cellar floor. On what? On whatever blankets were available. And on wrapping paper too. And also under newsprint. Others were sitting. They half rose. There were yet others, swathed in bandages, with faces burned the color of a mahogany wardrobe, covered with strips of gauze bandages. Their arms were also swathed in gauze. And they were so connected by these twinings that they seemed to be supported (by something). They would walk into this ward or that. Like totem poles. They were constantly walking to and fro. Because it was crowded. They were practically marching through the place. And they held their bandaged arms, both of them, raised up symmetrically (that's where that "totem poles" comes from). Their mouths were open. They were breathing. They were walking about in a state of dreadful impatience. Because they couldn't sit still. Because they had been burned alive and still were living—living, but not alive. They were probably the airmen. From the plane. The men who had crashed onto the barricade with the trolley on Miodowa Street. We asked them a few questions. Nothing much. They nodded their heads about some things. But it wasn't really a conversation. They walked about. Only that. With those raised arms. With their breathing. With a slit for the nose and mouth in the bandages on their faces. The trolley driver wasn't here either. So our chances were dwindling. The trolley driver's girlfriend was crying. I think all three of us went home. After a while. What else was there to do?

I have already mentioned the small cellar near the entrance to the stairwell where there was a stove on which the women did the cooking. There were always several cauldrons on the stove, close together, so that they could barely fit. There were quarrels because of this, and even that incident with the axes. Once two neighbors quarrelled over whose turn it was. One of them was offended and went to her own apartment to cook. Upstairs, that is. Right afterwards, a shell landed and she was hit by shrapnel. I was near the stairs when they brought her down. There was a commotion. Someone cried out, "A stretcher!"

And already she had been placed on a stretcher. I don't know if I helped too. But I did become one of the stretcher-bearers right afterwards. At the feet, I think. She'd caught the shrapnel in her heel. And I remember that the blood just came pouring out. It wasn't bandaged because there probably wasn't anything to do it with and the hospital was nearby. On Prochownia.

Her children ran downstairs after us, howling. She was groaning. We reached the courtyard quickly. It was a bright day. Hot. Shells were falling. We ran into the street at a trot, carrying the stretcher. Rybaki Street was like a drum. Boom! Boom! The narrow passage near our barricade: we had to take the stretcher with that woman and her leg pouring blood sort of at a tilt and squeeze through. Further on, the driveway. The wall. Shells were striking the wall and those two niches. Whatever we passed went boom! And so it went till the corner. Till Prochownia.

There we set down the stretcher. In the center, on the ground floor (I don't know if there was room in the cellar). I remember the gray light. A crowd, poverty and grayness.

"Just a moment, citizen." I think that is how I was addressed. "We just have to transfer the wounded lieutenant, who has lost both his legs, from his bed (bed?) onto (onto something or other)."

"Very good." I waited, in shock. But no. They let me go after a few minutes. "It's not necessary. There's someone else by now."

The shells kept on striking. The drum. Up and down Rybaki Street. I went home. They were shooting. God, how they were shooting! But I got there. In one piece.

Sometimes the stove (or perhaps there was more than one, I don't remember) was not so crowded, however. Because Swen's mother would set her pot on it. That is, the food for all of us. Or sometimes Swen and I would bake pancakes on the stove top. From dark flour.

People were eating twice a day then. So it wasn't too bad. At times one might get something from the general allotment, too. But one day panic erupted: "We've lost the storehouses on Stawki!"

It was from just such a storehouse on Stawki that we had once gotten potato flakes. Generally speaking, we didn't even dream about potatoes. Throughout the entire uprising. So that was an exceptional occasion.

Another day Swen confided in me that his mother had confided in him that there was no longer very much flour left. In addition to what flour she still had there were also some rusks which Swen's mother, with her marvelous foresight, had managed to dry. But that "not much," for six people, wasn't very much at all. There was also ersatz coffee. But that was only something to drink. Of course, it wasn't sweetened—not even with saccharine.

So? What advice could one give in this situation? Something had to be done. And a way out was found. Once, as we were walking away from the altar a good woman who "lived" near the pillars on the other side of our shelter beckoned to us, "If you would be brave enough to go upstairs to my apartment for flour, because I have some up there but I'm afraid to go, you could bring me a little and take as much as you want for yourselves. . . ."

We didn't have any courage to spare on either the first or second day. It was no longer August 7 or 8. We had gone upstairs once, I don't remember if it was at the very beginning or a little later, but anyway it was during the days when there were still some peaceful moments. We went secretly. To the second floor. Why? To get rusks, I think. There must have been some important reason. There were still doors then. Because I remember opening one, going inside. And a couch. A green one. We used to sit on that couch staring out the window at the Vistula day and night. We had held our literary circle meetings here with Teik, Halina and Irena. Once I'd even written a story about us on that couch. And I had described it as "threadbare." For some reason Swen held that against me. Later, he laughed about it.

I had gone to Swen's for the first time one night and naturally, like most people who visited friends in those days, slept over. I was sitting on the window sill. Looking at the Vistula out of the corner of my eye. Swen and I were talking about something. At one point Swen lifted the seat of the couch and, squatting, he searched in it for something for a long time. I was amazed that he was so distracted. But later he explained to me that he'd been looking for pajamas for me and that he was embarrassed. Now the scene was being repeated. Swen squatted in front of the opened couch and hunted for something in it. I was standing near the door (the window was dangerous) and didn't see what he was looking for. (We had already found the rusks, if that's why we were up there.) Swen dug out some spoons, I think. I'm not sure. He told me later, so I learned what it was. But I no longer remember.

Probably on the third day, after a second prodding from the lady near the pillars, Swen and I agreed to go upstairs. We were terrified. We thought there might be a shelling, but we went on with it. I think we stopped first to take a look at Swen's apartment. Things had changed drastically. One couldn't even speak of opening the door. There was no door. The hall and the apartment were no longer divided. There wasn't even a wall. Everything was all jumbled together and perforated by the shells. I glanced in the direction of the couch. A piece of it could be seen. Completely buried under a piece of wall. We ran to the woman's apartment. We grabbed the flour quick as lightning. As much as we could. And quickly fled downstairs!

I was happy that the spectre of hunger was pushed off. For Swen's mother, Swen, me, Aunt Uff., Zbyszek and Celinka. It was also a question of honor. I had stopped being a parasite.

I'm having problems again with the sequence of events between August 12 and August 18. I know that for my readers it's not important exactly what happened when. But they shouldn't be surprised. It is important for me; that precision of dates and places (as I think I have already indicated) is my way of holding on to the grand design. I have also realized that in spite of myself I may carelessly mix up or lose my various distant, more distant and sometimes not quite so distant personae. But that's how it was. People lost each other as suddenly as they found each other. They'd be close for quite some time. Then others became close. Suddenly these were lost and new people became important. That was common. A matter of herd instinct. It didn't make any difference what herd you belonged to, as long as you were in a herd. Everyone was always flitting about, as happens (in any case) at such hours of death; people couldn't find a place for themselves. The people from one cellar went to the one next door, and the people from next door went over to the first. Just as the people from lower Stare Miasto moved uphill and the people from up on the escarpment moved below. Because anywhere else was better. And even if it entered someone's mind that it was all the same everywhere, that didn't help at all.

Let us return to the uprising. Of August. As we thought then. That it would be called the August Uprising forever. Throughout Poland. But even as near as Mlociny, as Wlochy, Warsaw was not Poland; Poland lived her own life. For Poland, the most important thing about Warsaw was that it was burning. That made an impression. Roma Oliwowa's father went to Siedlce to get some wood, came back and said, "Oho, Warsaw is burning."

Pilots flying over at night to help out with the airdrops for Warsaw had no difficulty taking aim. Warsaw was where it was red.

Well, to get back to Poland, . . . Warsaw was not Poland. And the uprising remained the Warsaw Uprising. So, let us return to the Warsaw uprising. One day or evening—it's hard to say which—the shelter was full of burning carbide lamps, a few candles (there was a lot of carbide everywhere; on Chlodna Street I saw people rolling large corrugated tin kegs along the sidewalk with a grating sound and with a smell (of carbide) from under their armpits). So even then it was hard to distinguish in that endless evening of the shelters, what was daytime and what not; in memory, it is even more difficult. . . . On one such seeming evening, suddenly, as sometimes happened, people came in, as usual without anything, this time from Wola. Not straight from Wola but after having stopped along the way in other shelters, which had been bombed, no doubt, or which struck them as being worse than ours. We became friendly with a fat woman with heavy arms and legs (she was waring only a flowered summer dress, with short sleeves) from Towarowa Street at the corner of Wolska. She had run away from there. In front of her eyes people had been stood up against the wall, mostly men of course, shot, set on fire. Like many others, in this confusion, burning, screaming and shouting, somehow or other she had fled. Our large brick shelter with the altar had already been jammed for many days. So she had no place to sleep. The plank beds were filled to capacity. She found a loose door for herself, one with louvered panels, perhaps from a cellar toilet, and somewhere near us, several beds beyond the Ads., closer to the altar and right beside the entranceway, she spent the first night on the door (laid flat) and when she awoke her fat arms and thighs were completely covered with furrows from the panels.

There was a crush. There was less and less space. Also, fewer buildings. Little by little, the territory of our Stare Miasto redoubt began to shrink; at times the barricades and trenches had to be moved back. The trenches were ordinary ones. Ditches. For running and shooting. Stretched out. Winding. As at a front.

Also, there were more and more bombardments. Artillery, the gunboat on the Vistula, the armored train on the belt railway tracks; in short, every conceivable sort of shell. That's just by the by. But the planes. That danger. Every day. And the days were long. The planes would fly over. Or rather, they would descend over the roofs. And then, when you could already hear that they were there . . . drrrr . . . that they were diving over our roofs, the roofs of our housing blocks or the buildings close by, then you knew that they also had bombs. And the whining of the bombs would be distinguished immediately from the roaring dive of the planes; you waited a moment, just an instant. That moment was the actual hit. After it came a thud, or rather, an explosion. And after that—a smashing, crashing, shattering of something,—the results of the hit. Luckily, there were an awful lot of duds. People said we owed that to the Czechs. That the bombs were manufactured over there and they purposely didn't assemble them properly. Well, as soon as that whining could be distinguished from the roar of the engines, the falling of the bomb, the hit and the silence, we began to count, quietly in the first days, then Swen and I together, then aloud in a family chorus: "One, two, three, four, five, six, seven, eight, nine, ten, eleven . . . twelve . . . (here we began looking at each other) thir-teen. . . ." And a gesture of disbelief, a shrug, a sigh: "A dud."

But soon the airplanes would fly over once more, roaring; there'd be that separation of the bombs, the whining, the silence, and . . . "One, two, three, four, five, six, seven, eight, nine, ten, eleven, twelve. . . ." And at this point it often suddenly exploded!

Most frequently they exploded at eight or nine. Yes. But the planes would be flying over once more and . . . "One, two, three, four, five, six, seven. . . ."

Crash!

Us? No. . . . And again that whining.

"One, two, three, four, five, six, seven, eight, nine. . . ."

Crash!

No, next door it seems; no, because we're still here. There was no other proof. And now they're flying over once more, whining. . . .

"One, two, three, four, five, six, seven, eight, nine, ten. . . ."

Crash!

And right away the next one.

"One, two, three, four, five, six, seven, eight, nine, ten, eleven ... twelve ... thir-teeen. ..."

"Oh. ..."

Then there might be a sudden lull. For half an hour. An hour. And. ...

"One, two, three, four, five, six, seven, eight, nine, ten. ..."

"sssss"

and immediately

"one, two, three, four, five, six, seven, eight, nine, ten, eleven, twelve ... thir-teen ... whew ..."

and already new ones were diving down

"one, two, three, four. ... My God! ..."

and after a while once more

"they're here already"

"oh Jesus"

and

"one, two, three, four, five, six, seven, eight, nine, ten, eleven, twelve ... thirteen ... whew!"

That was during the day. But at night. We are lying there. In a crowd. A flood. By the cellarful. And suddenly:

crash ... crash ... crash ... crash ... crash ... crash ...

Windblasts, fire and the buckling of walls. Six times, usually.

God, how those walls moved. ... Once, I'm watching them — and it seems they're moving a meter back and forth ... and back ... and forth ... are we taking off? ... no ... they were rocking up and down ... a little less, still less, and they settled down ... as they were before. I rubbed my eyes in amazement.

After every such "nickelodeon" there would be a buzz of conversation for a moment and then people would lie down at once, just as they were before they'd been awakened, and would fall asleep immediately.

And once again:

"whissh ... whissh ... whissh ..." Fires, windblasts, flying walls (red), people with children in their arms hurling themselves en masse in the direction of the water barrel, to the narrow passageway leading to the far cellars, and people from the far cellars rushing into our shelter.

All at the same time.

They collide, knock into each other. They come back. The "nickelodeon" quiets down. They flop down on the planks. They sleep. Until once again. An hour later. Two. Half an hour:

70

whissh . . . whissh . . . whissh . . .

And once again with their children in their arms, off to the passageway, the others towards us, collision, quiet, exhaustion, just as they're standing there, in suits, in coats . . . with the children, snoring. . . .

No. The nights after August 12 were not pleasant. I shall pass over the shells. The tanks. The stealthy approaches. Those were the "nickelodeons."

An expedition . . . for flour. We had done it once before. Successfully. We had given some to the woman. She had some. And we had some. But all of a sudden Swen had the bright idea that for --how many of us were there?--he, Mama, Celinka, Aunt Uff., Zbyszek and I--six! Well then, for six people who had to eat twice a day, or even once a day, and even taking into account the rest of the rusks (we still had some), there wasn't so very much flour left. So he said, "Let's go upstairs."

I followed him. The first time had been bad enough. Something had struck. Our block. In that area. But somehow or other. I kept myself under control. But now it was something smaller. On the first floor I yell to Swen, "Let's go back!"

He: "No!"

Suddenly a crash. A shell in the wall beside us.

Swen rushes higher.

I scream: "Let's go back! Swen! Swen!"

He doesn't say anything.

I scream (the shells are hitting) and I'm going back already, "I'm going down! Don't move!"

It didn't help. The shells were striking the stairs. Ours. I fled. I was chicken. Swen returned after a moment panting and smiling and with new flour.

I was all the more impressed since Swen had a bandaged knee; there was something wrong with his knee and (because it was like that from the beginning) he hadn't joined the fighting. Other men, without good reason, without explanations, crouched down, practically curled up behind the barrel, behind the pillars, under the plank beds. And didn't join.

But there were whole groups who did volunteer. At every call. For the wounded. For excavations. To the barricades. For relocations. Fortifications. Ditches. Firefighting. Et cetera.

I have already told of Swen's suggestions for self-improvement

71

which he'd announced at the altar and how everyone in the shelter smote his breast and repeated, "We swear." It wasn't always successful, but there would be breast-beating once more, reconciliations, and requests for forgiveness.

Once, when our entire red shelter was still snoring away and only the thin candles were sputtering, suddenly on the left side near the wall with the pillars an argument erupted.

"What's the matter with you, lady, are you nuts?"

Because someone had a child and someone else either took the chamberpot from the child and sprinkled chlorine from it along the passageway between the left side of the shelter and the left wall . . . or else it was about the chamberpot, but without any chlorine, and the figure of someone walking about and sprinkling something just came to me. I think it really was chlorine, and I think it was about the sharp odor . . . but enough about that.

Or else it was about the barrel. The one not so far from us, near the exit corridor.

"It stinks. What's that? Change it!"

"Ooh . . . so what . . . who gives a damn!"

Finally there came a moment when a decision was made about the barrel. It was already stinking halfway across the shelter.

"Change it."

"Change it; change it."

"But how? Who?"

"By a bucket brigade."

"Yes, yes."

"A bucket brigade! Please, everyone, line up and we will pass each other the dirty water . . . one to another . . . and so on and so on. . . ."

Just like the bricks on Chlodna Street for the barricade.

And so it went. To the bottom. First that old stinking water. Then new. First through the little corridor to the toilets (a stream of people). Then back through the little corridor to the barrel. We passed it along. From person to person. We cleaned it out. Filled it up. Changed it.

The days didn't differ from one another so very much. But it was suddenly decided to observe, to celebrate one holiday—August 15 (it fell on a Tuesday). Out of spite. From early morning.

That church holiday (now abolished) was at the same time as the anniversary of the so-called "miracle on the Vistula."* Which had never taken place. Nothing had happened aside from the

72

metaphor. But in the course of time the metaphor had become realized. But that was associated with pre-war days. This time people were also waiting for a miracle on the Vistula. Also involving them. On the other bank. And beyond Zeran. If only they'd come.

"If only they'd come."

"If only they'd arrive."

"If only they were here."

People listened to the front. Listened to the ground. They were advancing. Sometimes they stopped.

"The fifteenth day of the uprising. . . ."

"The fifteenth day."

It seems to me that I have placed certain facts before that date, the bursting out of hell. But I recall that August 15 came after many horrors, here, in Starowka. That morning, I don't remember how it began, obviously it was hot, smoky, something was burning there, which means there was a lot of smoke and live flames. . . . Well, that morning, or rather forenoon, there were a few hours of rest, peace, holiness after all those cataclysms.

A High Mass was supposed to be celebrated in the great hall with the pillars with the participation of five hundred (I think) partisans who were already quartered with us, and the entire population of blocks A, B, C and D. Candles and dishes were prepared; from somewhere or other a carpet, I think, perhaps even something else for decoration. What? I don't remember. I remember that we had begun to assemble. That it was hot, peaceful. That there was a crowd of civilians and a crowd of partisans in their German jump suits, pieces of uniforms, with rifles and helmets in their hands, taken from the Hitlerites. That the crowd was really enormous, that the candles were lit, that the priest entered in a green or maybe a white stole. And the mass began.

No one took into consideration the possibility of a commotion, of the disruption of our plans. Nor had anyone shaved for two weeks. The heat intensified, the mass continued. The people were standing and it was peaceful. It went on and on. At the end the priest began practically simultaneously with the partisans and the crowd, "God, Thou who Poland. . . ."

It was sung to the end. People went their separate ways. Everyone. To their cellars. The troops to their quarters. Or rather to their positions on the ground floor, in the windows, at the exit, at the barricades, and the rest with the civilians to the shelters. And it was then, I think, that the planes flew over. They dived down onto our roofs. And started dropping bomb after bomb. I think we didn't even keep count then. There were so many of them at one time. All aimed at our block. The people knew that the Germans were aware that a large number of partisans were here. But so what? Should they be angry? (Sometimes civilians were angry at the military and vice versa, but not that day.) I don't know if it was then that someone fired a rifle (sometimes people did that) at the pilots. And hit one. The plane fell. But the bomb also fell on us. On our cellar. An explosion. Darkness. A shock. And—it's amazing, but we are standing, thrown together, just as we were before. So it didn't land on us? Then there were the tanks. An attack. They hit us. Then artillery. And as soon as Swen and I—after a couple of hours—in the sunshine and the heat—dragged ourselves out into the courtyard we noticed that there was a hole behind the wall of our shelter and that people were digging out something white. And not just one thing. We all knew that when instead of a cellar or house there's a hole (open) and people are digging out something white and something else in white is lying there, then many people have perished. So they'd bombed through to the cellars after all. Of our nearest neighbors. But we hadn't caught it.

From that day the ongoing hell of Starowka continued without a respite. And, I think, day and night, also without a break, the Sisters of the Sacrament were burning. All their buildings by turns, those on the escarpment and those under the escarpment.

From then on people would say every day, "The Sisters of the Sacrament are burning."

Yes, the Sisters of the Sacrament were burning. And rushing about in their veils. White. And slaughtering pigs and cows. Daily. And distributing them to the people. And they were also receiving and caring for people. Ever larger hordes. Thousands. Those Sisters of the Sacrament who for hundreds of years, since their founding by Marysienka, had sung behind gratings and taken communion through gratings, suddenly became active, social, a heroic institution, the support of Nowe Miasto. They provisioned part of the troops too. The troops gave their portions to the civilians. Only, the same error was committed every day in a vicious circle. It was hot weather. And they didn't distribute the meat from the pigs and cows which had just been butchered but only those slaughtered yesterday or the day before yesterday. And the ones from yesterday or the day before were already stinking. And when the troops cooked it (because the troops did cook it), in the central shelters, in cauldrons, then the stench pervaded the entire cellar. Once we even tried to eat it. But Swen and I couldn't touch it. It stank unbearably. Although we were already very hungry.

In this stench I remember the partisans lying side by side under shared blankets with girl couriers and nurses after a nighttime action. Some of the women were offended, but only slightly, by the whispering and ogling. I think mainly they were surprised. That in such a situation a person could think about something like that. The rest were perfectly indifferent.

In general, relations with the partisans were good. Although I remember one painful scene on Freta Street in front of the Dominicans. Some women were cursing out some partisans who happened to be passing by. Because of what they had done. In another place (but this is only hearsay) partisans cursed some women. Because when the Germans announced that people could come out with white cloths or handkerchiefs and surrender on the Zoliborz viaduct, several women set out. Information about this incident varies. At any rate there was probably more than one such surrender. Or rather attempt. One, it seems, was lucky (for those women with the white handkerchiefs). Another time, it seems, the Germans shot at them. And maybe it was then that the women retreated in horror. To the nearest house. The partisans slammed the door in their faces, disgusted. Then, it seems, they cursed them but let them in at last. But some of the women were offended in turn. And went to another house.

The business of the key to our apartment (mine, Mother's and Stefa's) at 40 Chlodna Street kept haunting me. How could they have gone home—how had they gone out to the Germans—if they had no keys? And in general, how was Mother getting along? And Aunt Jozia and Stefa? I had the keys. But perhaps Aunt Limpcia and Granny Frania (my mother's aunt and her daughter) knew something? They lived at 16 Bielanska Street in the basement of an annex behind the Radziwill Palace. In their courtyard. With their whole family. They were surely there. So what prevents me from seeing them? Perhaps I'll succeed now in making my way further along Leszno to Zelazna? They say, anyway, that Leszno is in our hands—all the time. That you can walk for a kilometer along Leszno through cellars connected by breaking through the walls. Anyway, I just wanted to get away. And I did get away. Swen didn't want to. And Swen's mother said, "Don't go."

But I insisted.

I set out.

Rybaki Street. The familiar Staromiejski route. From the slope to the garbage shed, into the hole in the wall. The small courtyard. A leap up to the balcony. Someone's apartment. A courtyard. Rushing across a long board into the window of someone's apartment. People are sitting there. Women. People. A hole. Crawling through into the darkness amongst people lying there.

"Oh, Jesus. . . ." Those are the wounded.

From the cellar into the courtyard, the gate, a leap, across Mostowa Street, barricades, with partisans lying prone, firing their machine guns at Praga. An open wooden gate. The cobblestone courtyard. Dark brown. Large. Below the Gdansk Cellar. The House at the Sign of the Cats. Here—the second floor. There—the ground floor. Freta. And Dluga. Almost straight ahead. . . . I scurried across Dluga. It wasn't as bad as it might have been. Perhaps something was burning. It was then that I looked over the barricade at the end of Miodowa Street. With the trolley and the airplane. And I ran into Dluga Street. Onwards along its crooked, serpentine, uneven path. There was a barricade every so often. And it was a little more dangerous. People warned me. Because at the intersection of Dluga and Przejazd, opposite the Arsenal famous for the outbreak of the November uprising,* stood a seven-story building which was occupied by the Hitlerites. They had the whole neighborhood under fire. Dluga Street in particular. In front of the Arsenal, on the right of Dluga Street, was the intersection of Nalewki, and on the left, almost directly opposite, the end of Bielanska. In front of this intersection was a barricade. You ran along the right side as you came from the Vistula, because it was safer (more protection). And you ran right across Dluga behind the barricade. You rushed through a gate and into the courtyard of a house which almost bordered on or directly bordered on 16 Bielanska Street. Where Aunt Limpcia lived, or rather Olimpcia, or Olimpia. With her husband Stach, with Ryszek (my cousin), her brother Ceniek, and my Granny Franka, her mother, that is, who called her Olemka. I reached their courtyard through the passageway from Dluga Street. A strange, long yard. Paved with cobblestones. Stretching from the side of Bielanska (right after Tlomackie) and the side of the Radziwill Palace (the one which stands today on the center strip of the East-West Artery); winding between the picket-fence entrance gate and the apartment house at the front, 16 Bielanska, and the front of the palace, with its circular entranceway and its three pillars; further on, the courtyard twisted again, went around the palace from the other side and opposite it there was a long annex. At the end of this building, just beneath the garden wall at the rear of the palace, right there—I walked quickly, I think I flew, flew up to it and looked into their window, "Aunt!" I yelled, "Aunt Limpcia! Rysiek!"

Aunt Limpcia was preparing soup (barley soup); Rysiek ran out onto the stairs; I think Limpcia's husband was there too in an instant, my uncle, poor Stach; Stach's brother Joziek was definitely there also. They called to me. I ran down. To them. (They didn't need any other shelter.)

"And Granny Frania?" I asked.

"Oh," Aunt Limpcia was stirring the thick barley soup, she was unperturbed. "Granny's in the palace . . . in the corridor. It's crowded there, they have light. . . . Why don't you go over and see her; oh, when she sees you. . . ."

"And my mother, do you know anything? She stayed on Chlodna. I have the keys. I want to get through to Chlodna."

"We don't know a thing. How do you plan to go?"

"Well, I could try Leszno."

"Oh . . . don't even bother to talk about it. How? You won't get through. What do you think? That you'll get far? To Zelazna? And that there aren't any Germans at 40 Chlodna?"

"Well, yes. . . ." I agreed.

"Go along with Rysiek to Granny, he'll take you there, and I'll finish cooking the barley soup meanwhile. Do you want some? You'll get a big helping."

"Yes, I do. . . ."

"Then go, but Granny will burst out crying. . . ."

We walk over to the palace. We go inside. Across the driveway. Into a wide, semicircular, rococo hall, formerly a ballroom, which leads in two directions; now the light of electric bulbs is sparkling here . . . and there are people, people. And talking, noise, buzz . . . buzz . . . and garbage up to the ceiling. Along both sides— one heap of garbage beside another—and people, on it, under it, lower down, sitting, lying down, talking . . . and turning and turning . . . and so we walk on, twisting and turning all the time.

Until finally Rysiek points, "There!"

I look. She is sitting there.

She is sitting there. Granny Frania.

"Granny! Granny!"

She turns around on her stool, looks with red eyes. Grabs me around the neck, kisses me, and begins to cry.

"What's happened to your mother, what's happened to you, Lord have mercy, how worried I've been about you. How is Kazia?"

I tell her (Kazia is my mother).

We sat there for a while. Then we went back. I got some soup. Thick. Splendid. Lots of barley. Full. A huge, full bowl. I ate it all up.

"Would you like some more?"

"Please."

I got a second helping. Just the same. What happiness I felt then with those bowls, till I was full. I sat awhile. I had to go back. But just then a nasty fusillade got started against Dluga. From that seven-story building on Przejazd.

"How can you go home? How will you get through?"

"Beneath the barricade."

It seemed to be getting worse by the minute. I run outside. I can see that every few minutes, at the Dluga gate, right in the entranceway near the barricade, people are getting set, shoulders down, and racing across! I screw up my courage for a minute. But then I see a girl courier. She runs past and nothing happens to her so I snap to it, duck down, dash across—yes, just like that. And already I am racing along the other side of Dluga. Into the distance, into the distance. Near the smoldering ruins. Past the Four Winds. At last I pass the curve and the bend. Where you can already see Krasinski Square, farther along on Dluga. There on the left is a little street (after that bend in Dluga), a little, dead-end alley at the rear of the Krasinski Gardens. It was called Baroque Street. Officially. Before the war. The area was proud of that novelty. But people understood it as "Barrack Street" (which is what they used to say). (I confess that until 1946 I too thought it was Barrack Street.)

All of a sudden—bombers. They are diving at the rooftops, scattering their bombs. Now they're gone. Now they're back again. Farther. Nearer. Now they're flying into Baroque Street. We do too. They fly blindly. We too. We is I. And someone else. Like me. We. Two of us. Here. Only. Neither here nor there. Because now. They're here! We run. Into some one-storied what(?) . . . empty . . . it races, we race along (?) the downstairs rooms (?) of something's halls (?), which already is changing, howling, clanking. We rush on, bricks are flying, the bombers harry us. A proverbial brick. One. And there are so many here: ping! ping! We raise our collars. What kind of stupid instinct?! We jump. Ping! ping! Just don't yield. To chance. Everything's important. Because he's flying in zigzags. In spurts. Between the walls. Sssshh-booom. Falling plaster. Whitewash. Something. From the rain gutters. Wait? No. Don't stand still. Zoom. That hill is flying, maybe we can sit down . . . I don't know how many times we jump; suddenly ping! ping! Nothing.

Feints. Only. . . . As was necessary, in my opinion.

(From Leszno. 1930. Toy blocks. On cracks. Nanka is peeling potatoes. I marvel that a bullet can hit; after all I'd notice it and jump back. Nanka answers that you can't do that. Now something of the sort has worked.)

After the attack. The other guy goes his way. I go mine. At a run. Dluga. The Square. Dluga. Mostowa. Downhill. The crossing. Below. Rybaki. The cobblestones. Our place. Or rather—he's there! —Swen, with red eyes. He grabs me. Swen's mother says, "What hasn't he imagined—all this time—that you'd never return, that something had happened."

"Eh." I shrug my shoulders.

That's what I'd wanted. And that's also how I overlooked it. It wasn't all that important. Or so it seems. But for me. . . . And for the Radziwill Palace. It was. Important. And for that wall. With the garden. Just as it is now. In the first place, because it's at the rear of the palace (behind the East-West artery, where it descends into the underpass); in the second place, because of its dimensions. Definitely. Its grass. And those statues. It's obvious, of course, that today there is no wall; the whole joke, in fact, is that there is no wall, but instead there are trolleys on either side and the wall is in the center. Those statues, in particular. There was peace, an interlude. Silence. Generally speaking, at least. Anyway, right here. And in the meantime Aunt Limpcia was cooking barley soup (the steam rose from the window, from below; and it smelled so good— after all, she had something to cook). Rysiek and I. Went into the garden. It used to be closed. Nice weather, hot. Of course, it was daytime. That sky. The heat was sky-blue. The grass was green. And they. Those statues. I remember that they weren't there after the war; but that day they were; then they were off their pedestals and just stood there on the grass, stood there, on the grass, in the grass. Then, I think, they were on pedestals once again; I can't remember how they are standing now. But how were they standing then? As if on pedestals. No, not really. Without them. All of them? How should I know? But dust was rising from something. It began to rise (just then). They were shooting. Yes. That's it. Now I know. At the Bank of Poland. The one on the banknotes. Once. Twice. Echo. Ping. A miss. Sometimes it was just the same as that time with the boards. Something toppled too, I think. From among that group of statues. And that's all.

During the occupation Polish children, Jewish children, old ladies, old men, Gypsies, madmen (so-called)—in general, all kinds of people, singly or in groups, would walk into our courtyard on Chlodna Street from morning to night and sing. Most often:

On the first day of September
In that famous year
The enemy struck at Poland
From out of the high sky.

He hammered at our Warsaw
Most viciously of all.
Oh, Warsaw, poor Warsaw,
You are a bloody city.

Once you were so lovely,
Splendid and majestic.
Now all that's left of you
Is a heap of ruins.

That is how it seemed after 1939, after that September. When on one day—the 23rd, I think—18,000 shells fell on Warsaw. September 25—that was the decisive day—from morning to night, for twelve hours, Warsaw was bombarded. On the next day it was set ablaze. There were fires. Raging. Shells. But something was already fated. Prophesied. On September 25 people could no longer hold out. On the 27th those who had survived crawled out from the cellars.

Yes. Afterwards. Afterwards—the deportations. Pawiak Prison. The camps weren't set up yet that first week. They developed. Then the ghetto was organized. And that wall on Krasinski Square, on Holy Tuesday--April 20—the second day of the uprising in the ghetto. A German in an armored car behind Garnizonowa Street, near Miodowa, I think, was shooting into the ghetto, into Bonifraterska Street. People were dropping over there. From the tops of large, blank walls with tiny windows. From those tiny windows, too. And after who knows how many hits he removed his helmet (he was sweating because of the sun, he was tired out, the hero, and he wiped away his sweat).

And afterwards—it was the famous, beautiful, late Easter eve of 1943. The Aryans—we were still called that—were in the churches, dressed up for the holiday; but over there, in that hell, we knew, there was no hope. There were those who helped. There were well-wishers. There were even some who were indifferent. The height of the conflagration was on Easter eve itself. There was fire in the sky.

That began to make an impression on people. But there was an amusement park on Krasinski Square. Carousels. Swings. Well, a few of our people were enjoying themselves on those swings and wheels. In that thick smoke. Which was billowing. And billowing. From Bonifraterska. And from Nowolipki. From Dzielna. Swieto-jerska. Przejazd. The uprising in the ghetto went on and on. The first swallows. I noticed them in May that year, in that smoke, and I heard them chirping. Some time around the tenth, I remember. That was already two days after the collective suicide of the Jew-ish general staff. In a bunker on Mila. The Germans discovered them.

And now we were the ones who were isolated, not sympa-thized with. But at least we had the hope of the front. The Ger-mans were defeated. Formally. In the West, the offensive had been going on since June. And for a longer time in the East. But the par-tisans had badly miscalculated the Germans' strength. Before the outbreak of the uprising they had thought that only a remnant was left. But it turned out that several divisions remained. Yes. And it was of no use at all that they were defeated. Here they were strong.

> *August first, a bloody day,*
> *The people of Warsaw arose*
> *. . . . .*
> *. . . . . for*
> *The Germans were already at every door,*
> *tumtatum tatata tata. . . .*

I don't remember the words. I'm thinking of that song about the uprising, naive, but. . . . And further on it went like this:

> *What despair unfolds in one's heart;*
> *There is nothing with which to fight.*
> *A girl attacks a tank with a bottle*
> *To take revenge*
> *For the destroyed, razed capital*

Again, the question of the front. We still had hope. And yet Zoliborz, Mokotow, Powisle, Srodmiescie, Stare Miasto—all were already isolated.

Bugaj Street runs from the Bridge beneath the Castle, below Stare Miasto to Mostowa. Rybaki Street runs from Mostowa all the way to Mennica (called Wytornia), or rather, to Sanguszko.

The problem was to hold Wytwornia. Teik was there. For whole days and nights there were pitched battles for every room, every corridor. And for the roundhouse on Sierakowska, near the Gdansk Station. In order to break through across the viaduct, on the railroad, to Zoliborz. The attacks were coordinated from two directions (Zoliborz and Starowka).

It didn't help. We lost the no man's land of the ghetto. We lost the roundhouse, the stretch of Muranow outside Muranow. Mennica was still being defended. That was the most famous stronghold in our Stare Miasto redoubt.

Yes. Something else about our holding out. Our defense. Why waste words: it was forced on us. It was well known that the Hitlerites were here, the Russians just barely beyond the Vistula; the partisans here, the Americans, the English, over there in the West. The Allies. But it was all simply a machine that was wound down and shattered into unconsciousness. Those fronts. And this uprising. Here—it is well known—the skull insignia, the helmets, shouts, screams: *rauss! rauss!* The Hitlerites, and terror; we were afraid that they might leap out of a tank, attack, start hurling grenades into the cellars. Because that's how it was. Everywhere. I always imagined those rumblings, the stamping feet, the shouts of *"rauss," "Hände hoch,"* and crash! a grenade, a string of them, into an entranceway. A flash. Sparks. Crash! It might hit something. Or perhaps a pillar would act as a shield. We were especially afraid during our walks through those shelters, from one to the other, that we might suddenly notice on a wall the shadows of big, oversized helmets, worn at an angle.

So there was that dread, that terror. And one wanted neither their sudden appearance, nor an unknown way out of the situation, nor any contact. But the viaduct. Once again, it seems, they announced that people should surrender, and who knows how many women went out with white kerchiefs, but there was something strange about that viaduct. The planes, the shells—these were the typical signs of the machine. When and where in this place, in this uproar, this resounding cauldron, this thunderous crashing, could one decide anything about oneself? to surrender with what? to whom? how? which way? when?

Ludwik, weeping and laughing, tells the story of 1939, the bombardment, the inferno, the crowds; he can't control himself any longer, even here amidst these bombs:

weee-oooo

weee-oooooo

weee-oooooooo

suddenly women are bellowing; one of them, seated on her bundles, comes up with this:

"let's surrender!"

and the others follow:

"let's surrender!"

and the whole shelter repeats:

"that's right! surrender!"

but here there is nothing, only

wee-ooo

wee-ooooo

wee-ooooo

then the women, the crowd, the shelter keep it up:

"let's surrender!"

But nothing came of it.

Let us return to the uprising. An attack. Freta Street. Saint Jacek's. Or, rather, the Dominicans. August 17. It is Saint Jacek's day, exactly. And Saint Miron's too. Only in 1922 the calendar had Miron M.B. (Martyred Bishop)—because Nanka chose my name, Miron, from the calendar. But it was always the day of Jacek and Julianna.

There was no church of the Byzantine Saint Miron the Martyred Bishop (Jacek was Polish, Odrowaz). On this day something moved me to go outside and crawl up the hill. There. As if. . . . And I did crawl up. At the best possible moment. Perhaps it was then that those bullets were flying about Freta Street? Or maybe not then. I was collecting the swirling, loose pages of Titschener's *Psychology* from a demolished bookstore. The bullets were whizzing around my left ear, my right ear, and I bent down seventeen times, because that is how many double pages I collected. To read in the cellar. They came in handy. August 17—that I'm sure of—I entered the church of Saint Jacek. I stood there. I looked around. It was empty. But there were explosions already. From the shells. Churches, especially those large ones, are deadly. The echoes resound in them. Like nowhere else. So there were explosions and more explosions. With echoes. But somehow it was too much. The echoes were already somewhere behind the wall. They were already landing right beside me. Now the church was shaking. Dust was swirling. Suddenly a splash; then it flared up, flew through the wall, into the center of the presbytery. So that a hole was blown right through the upper cornice, with the plaster of the shattered corbel sifting down. A dry taste in my mouth. I ran out. Why not? And then suddenly I could hear the grinding of the "nickelodeon":

krra . . . krra . . . krra . . .

krra . . . krra . . . krra . . .

krra . . . krra . . . krra . . .

In an instant I'm in a doorway with a crowd. A man with a briefcase. The door to the drugstore. Now with the crowd, on the steps. Now it begins to hurl us, to whirl us. And since we had dashed upstairs to the first floor instead of downstairs there was even more dread, more cowering; no one knew what the rocking and our being hurled about really was. The "nickelodeons" had this peculiarity, that not only did they rip and snatch up to the height of four stories, but they also stupefied.

So, that's what my namesday was like. Because I went home right after that. For boiled pasta. I think Swen's mother congratulated me, however. She used to grind out that pasta. Like all the women. Without a break. Also little dumplings, or "rosary beads." The one or the other, in tiny pieces. A similar technique.

I think many people used to take walks. More than I remember. Not that everyone did. Swen walked less. Although he took walks, too. But Mama, Aunt Uff., Zbyszek didn't go for walks at all. Celinka, after that first day when she went to the district clinic on Miodowa, to that job (indeed!) no longer went out. Anywhere.

Well, thanks to our running about, Swen and I discovered a second route leading uphill. The Nowomiejski route. 23 Rybaki Street (the home of Leonard, the guy who wore eyeglasses and a coat, who had fled his shelter and come to ours because ours was made of poured concrete). From the front. To the outbuildings. Up to the second floor. Across the cobblestone courtyard. To the outbuilding directly opposite. Up to the second floor. There were four floors in all. Well, on the second floor you ran through the hall, as in the Gdansk Cellar and then you were on the ground floor on the escarpment. Somewhat like a yard, gardens. Hanging gardens, moreover (as at the rear of the Sisters of the Sacrament, but also somehow different). (Furthermore, the forms of trees and constructed (or demolished) objects, or of things which were covered with dust, were changed and, moreover, kept on changing.) So, there was something suspended (because you ran across a bridge) over the ravines of the Nowe Miasto escarpment. And from the bridge to the baroque erstwhile Church of Saint Benon (now functioning once again), which had been transformed under the tsars into Bienkowski's knife factory. Inside I remember its resemblance to a workshop and its churchliness, and how we ran up to the gallery. Or the choir. That church-factory looked worse each time, more and more pockmarked, the little bricks ever thinner, drier, because of the dryness (everything was dry from the shellings, burnings and hot weather). And nothing could be extinguished because they didn't allow it, because they were bombing repeatedly, setting fires, aimlessly, over and over. Behind Benon-Bienkowski, closer to the hill, towards the Marketplace of Nowe Miasto, I remember a dry, long, splintered and always whiter (?) board, which groaned underfoot. But finally you ran up to those iron bars, that forged iron gate, which is still in existence today and which closes off that same back alley behind the Sisters of the Sacrament and Benon. Along this back alley you at last ran out into the Nowe Miasto Marketplace itself. At the widest point. Or, rather, to the right of it. Behind the Sisters of the Sacrament to the forking of Panska and Koscielna Streets (which at that time went downhill on wooden stairs, intersected Rybaki and continued all the way to Wybrzeze up to the barbed-wire barriers. Up to the tank behind the wall). There one had a view of the whole marketplace. To where it narrows. Into a triangle. A funnel. At Freta and the corner of Kozla.

I know we walked about a lot at that time because once, one day, Swen and I went for a walk, purposely I think, To the Cathedral. To pay it a visit. Once again. To see it. To touch it. That was a necessity. For us. With that Cathedral. I don't remember anything on the way. There and back. No doubt we ran. Crouching. The Staromiejski route. The hole, the cellar, the people lying down, the wounded:

"Oh, Jesus. . . ."

A small balcony. A washtub. That was private. Women. Through the wall. To the Dominicans. I think. A moment: Mostowa—the barricade—lying down—shooting—the view—Praga (another city?). The Gdansk Cellar. The old walls. Red. The Marketplace.

Finally, the entrance to the Cathedral.

Afternoon. Heat. Still, it was more peaceful. And a crowd in the center. The rising dust. We walked forwards. Towards the chancel. And it wasn't a crowd of people. But of sculptures, statues, saints, bishops, all gilded, mitered. . . . A crowd. . . . A crush. . . . Shadow light. Heat. But a dim shadow light. The rest fairly dark. There, in front, all the way in, the dust rising from below (from the door). We went over there. The chancel had pews in it. On both sides. And then the altar. And other cathedral furnishings. Armchairs, thrones, gold leaf, cloth covers, accretions. The pews held sculptures, statues, close together, face to face. But the ones we saw that day were extras, as it turned out. And that's not the half of it. They were gathered together near the door, on their pedestals I think, or simply broken off, saved, sheltered here, gathered together in a crowd from various places which had already been destroyed. There was a kermess-like atmosphere in the air. An assembly. Or an election. Judgment, finality. And it happened in an instant, in two or three days.

The news sheets, always at a run. Someone rushes in. Hands it over. Others grab for it. A woman snatches it away. The others move on. Towards the altar. For the candles. Here is Swen. He has it now. In his hands, in the center. He's already surrounded. They're hanging on him! A bombshell. Literally. News:

"Today, at . . . o'clock the Cathedral was bombed into smithereens."

"No. . . ."

I remember. That "no" passed through all the stalls, pillars, passages, stairs.

"No. . . ."

It was said that our side and theirs had battled there when it was still standing, although heavily scarred. That barricades were made from the confessionals and from sugar (in sacks).

That's what happened in the Mint, too. Ours were here, theirs over there. Or in the Telephone Exchange later on, in Srodmiescie. There, it was in layers. On one floor—ours. On the next floor— theirs. And the struggle was stubborn, prolonged. Days. Nights.

Weeks. Or as in the Church of the Holy Cross, where the partisans were in the church proper. The Germans, near the organ. People said they hurled down the organ pipes. They ripped them out. Or they said that the pipes resounded. By themselves. That they piped and blew. Or take the matter of the sewers. People said that in Zoliborz one could slip into a storm sewer leading to the Vistula. Every so often it would sweep away the people who were walking in it. And to get to Mokotow you had to bend low, hunched over. And from Czerniakow you practically had to walk on your knees at times. In addition, they were throwing gas and grenades in there. And there was barbed wire in the manholes. Stopping them up.

These were not myths but living truths. As at 18 Bracka Street. They attacked. Butchered. Retreated.

Light. Once again. Light and water.

I will be wrong about the light and water a few more times. Light and water were available for a very long time. But of course there were disruptions every now and then. Then the carbide lamps were put to use.

I have already mentioned the outhouses which were near the cellar beside the stairs. The entranceway cellar. Actually, there was one outhouse. A large one. With several toilets that you had to squat over. It is precisely there that I can remember the light bulbs under the ceiling. Or rather, that they were still there. And burning. And that the doors were gone. Well, at least that fat woman from Towarowa was able to sleep on an outhouse door. The stalls for squatting were all missing doors. I remember the hinges. Everywhere. The outhouse was always occupied. So one waited one's turn. And jabbered away. It didn't matter at all that there were only hinges and no doors. No one paid any attention to anyone else. Nor was anyone embarrassed. There was also no impatience, because who had anywhere to rush off to? We chatted. With the people close by. Who were waiting. Who were moving their bowels. Who were finished. Who still had to. Who were there for the company. Who just happened to be there. Who had to urinate. Who had just dropped by.

One time, for example—I remember this—at night under those bulbs I was squatting down in my doorless stall and next door to me was an elderly lady in a white coat. For the whole time we chatted with each other in a neighborly way.

A bad beginning. Not that it was the first time. (Because there

had already been many bad beginnings.) But the feel of it. Of en-
circlement. This time increasing until it was unbearable. Naturally
we became accustomed to it, got hold of ourselves, but each time
by a greater effort.

"Hail, Mary, full of grace, the Lord be with Thee. . . ."

"Hail, Mary, Mother of God, pray for us sinners now and in
the hour of our death, amen."

I remember the glaring identity of "now" and "in the hour of
our death." How many times did I feel it during the prayers, but
people prayed constantly. You could hear them, here beside you or,
during a walk, among those near by, or somewhat distant, as you
walked ahead, and as you just wandered about, whenever something exploded a little more loudly than usual, then it was like a
wave:

"Hail, Mary, full of grace. . . ."

"Now and in the hour of our death, amen."

And the response. The short one. The singing. Only that.

> *To Thy protection*
> *We flee. . . .*

It drifted out from the cellar:

> *Oh Virgin. . . .*

To the second cellar:

> *Our dear protectress,*
> *Our dear intermediary,*
> *Our dear comforter. . . .*

It passed on:

> *Oh Virgin. . . .*

but now other people join in—they have just begun.
Beyond the bend they are already up to

> *Unite us with Thy Son. . . .*

Suddenly it's noisier, the bombs and:

Sacred Heart of Jesus, have mercy on us,
Sacred Heart of Jesus, have mercy on us,
Sacred Heart of Jesus, have mercy on us.

Near the altar people are kneeling:

"For all those who are dying this night, and for all the dead: Our Father . . . in heaven . . . Thy . . . Thy . . . Thy . . . of this earth. . . ."

A hit, the walls seem to buckle.

"Forgive us our trespasses as we forgive those who have trespassed against us. . . ."

That reality—pitiful, smoky—you have to keep your eyes hidden in your collar—or cover them with your hand—the dust, the ruins, gray, red, dry and burning in your nose, in your teeth and on your tongue, breathing it in, the heat, everything stings, sweating. . . .

Oohh Virgin, oohh Virgin. . . .

And suddenly (Most Sacred Heart of Jesus) counting:

One, two, three, four, five (here it comes)

Ooh Virgin.

O o o.

One two three four five six seven . . . (here it comes)

Have mercy on us.

Something explodes:

Our comforter.

one two three four five six seven . . . eight nine ten. . . .

Anxiety would set in so something soothing was necessary. Singing. Beseeching. Standing. Without genuflections. Rosaries. Dumplings. Eating under an archway. Because you took food along. So what if the plaster falls in it. It can't be helped. If it's large, it's removed with a spoon. And you go on eating.

On the other hand anxiety set in on the theme of where to stay. Everywhere. Among everyone. We too. We started feeling a need to change places. For a while it was moderate. Then it grew. The first change was just the tunnel. But in the tunnel—as I have already described—there was a dreadful slamming of doors from people running through, from the "nickelodeons," and that caused drafts, blowing, it was cold. And also because after the initial spaciousness there was a crush once more, because other amateurs like us turned up with bedding, and it was narrow there; besides which it was a passageway, because I can recall that the tunnel connected two blocks. And that it passed under the courtyard. We imagined that a bomb might break through the layer of earth and the concrete ceiling (who knows, perhaps it was very thin). So we quickly returned to our big red shelter, the one with the chapel.

I have already said, I think, that in addition to blocks A and B there were also two smaller blocks. It's time to make this clear. C and D. They were placed sideways, on Koscielna Street, from Rybaki to Wybrzeze Gdanskie. They shared a kind of triangular courtyard. And aside from the courtyards between block B (ours) and those two (C and D) there was no other free space. They were close to each other. So that we didn't distinguish between the cellars, either. There was a maze of passages, cellars, rooms, large cellars or shelters, and in one place a concrete stairway leading down into the cellar of cellars. The boiler room. Little doors. A sub-basement room, iron, iron measuring rods, cauldrons, pipes. And yet another lower level, a hole, and there was also the boiler sump; and somewhere nearby was a manhole leading into the city sewer. Which was carefully inspected by us, considered, measured to determine its possibilities, deliberated over, surrounded by us, by people, especially the men, because we were the most afraid, the young men in particular. Because the first to be wiped out were the young.

Well, somewhere in the neighborhood of this tangle was a concrete passageway, entirely concrete, gray, hard, dry, rough, and there was chaos, frenzy, and bedding in it as in a laundry. The passageway had a door into the tunnel. The one I have mentioned. The tunnel went its way—long, gut-like, gray, with electric lamps. Up to the doors into block A. Near which Mrs. Trocinska had parked herself with her bedding against the wall. And then we. And others.

We went back to our large shelter and immediately started thinking which other shelter to move to. Should we? And when? What were the so-called objective motives, independent of what was called "the law of whirling about" and based on looking at oneself from a distance and knowing the relative value of changing places? Was it for safety? Or just in case? That this cellar juts out a tiny bit and has too few pillars? What? Yes. Something of that sort. Because that next shelter really was deeper or it had more pillars, I don't know which, but it was concrete, completely gray, dark gray, heavily vaulted, and smaller. Yes. Moreover, it was a lower vault, and that was an important consideration. It was under block C or D. Nearer to Koscielna Street. But that old, large, higher one had Wybrzeze behind its wall. It's true. Praga. The Vistula. The gunboats. "There's a tank behind the wall . . . sshhh . . ." Jokes upon jokes. But Wybrzeze was theirs. It had bunkers. Against us. (We had barricades against them.) The Vistula. And searchlights. On the left. On the right. And along the asphalt, on the water, in the sky, and again along the asphalt, on the water, in the sky . . . one, two, three, and a circle, one, two, three, those from the left: one, two, three; those from the right from Kierbedz, and again those on the left from the railroad bridge—around and around. (It is true that the entire panorama was framed by two bridges. Two iron gratings across the Vistula. They were still standing. Oh! They served them, all right. The right one, the Kierbedz bridge, the one which began near the Russian church and the left one, the railroad bridge, the belt railroad, which began near the left end of the Zoo, was intersected by Goledzinow, and beyond Goledzinow by Zeran, to the Citadel here. . . . The railroad ran across its roadway. On two roadways actually. It was a double bridge. On special piles. The cars went past on lattice-work squares, thick beams under the rails clickety-clack; it would jump and throw up dust because it was wooden. . . . But that's not important. How many were still in the red shelter, the original one, the protoshelter, in the protostalls, with a view of the sputtering candles on the altar, then the tunnel, wind and drafts, calculations, returning to the protostalls, but this time nearer to the center or the altar, and to what number (this I no longer remember) relocation. Into the second shelter. Gray. Pillars. It's darker, quieter; there are fewer people, in fact only a few, for the time being. Stalls? It seems they were there from the first, yes; was there a system that it was all ready like that? Something of the sort, I think. Well, right away . . . August 17 . . . Saints Jacek and Miron's day. Freta. The nickelodeon. Whoops! Into the dumplings. Mama was making dumplings.

We were in the tunnel through the 18th, the 19th. That is, we moved on August 20th at the earliest. We moved out on August 26th. And the 23rd (that's when it was, I think!) was a memorable day. But we spent several good days there. Certainly two or three more days before the 23rd. In memory those two good days seem like several days. Almost like a week. And not only in memory. Because they did at that time too. During that period before the worst in Rybaki Street, we began counting time differently, more quickly. It seemed to pass more slowly. But that was just how it appeared. Actually time was condensed.

So, the twentieth day of the uprising. We are in a new shelter, beneath the pillars. In times of war, it seems, there is always a return to matriarchy. And especially during that war. That uprising. Particularly with that descent underground, under Warsaw (into the anthill of the shelters). The outbreak of the uprising was a turning point. For matriarchy. Of the cellars? The caves? What's the difference? Masses of people. The mothers rule. Sitting underground. Hide! Don't crawl out! Mortal danger. All the time. Even if you don't crawl out. And taking things in stride. It's good that candles and big and little carbide lamps were found. Featherbeds, too. Somewhat better weapons than the cavemen's. But not much better. And there weren't many of those weapons. For the chosen. Stocks of food. Although they grew smaller until finally they disappeared. After all, what kind of stocks were there? Animals? There weren't any. The larger ones had been eaten already. And the small ones? Some people kept an animal they loved, took it below and watched over it. But that was unusual. Particularly in Starowka. There were fewer pets there. Or they weren't brought down. Or they were brought along and died. Whatever didn't escape, fly away, burn up, cave in, die, was hunted down. Cats disappeared. Dogs disappeared. There's no use even talking about winged beasts. Only that cricket in the wall when it grew dark. And then, in September—lice.

Well, the shelter near the pillars. At first there was a normal crowd. Or rather, plenty of room. One couple. I remember. Young. How energetically she shook her carbide lamp. From Zakroczymska.

"They bombed the ruins three times. . . ."

I was appalled. Because the conversation had started with me saying precisely that they probably don't bother to bomb ruins. So now I didn't want to believe it. Because we were beginning to count on the ruins as a safer place. That's fate for you.

"Of course they're bombing the ruins. And deliberately, at that."

This is where the question of electricity becomes confusing. It seems it was still on then. But I can remember how frequently she shook the carbide lamp. She had a short haircut. Always in motion. Whenever the carbide lamp died out she would grab it and shake! shake! and "ssss"—the flame would grow bright again.

Aside from that there was nothing new in the shelter beneath the pillars. Dawn. Heat. Burning. The Sisters of the Sacrament. They were still on fire all this time. Almost the whole time. Smoke was drifting over from them. From high up. From above the escarpment. And from below. There was something there too. And over there. And immediately:

"They're here already."

We could hear the planes flying over us. At once, on the first day, I'm sure; I remember a bench beside the wall under the pillars in the gray light from the window. People started coming in from the bombed buildings. In tattered clothing. Hungry. With scarcely anything in their hands or with nothing at all.

"I'm so hungry," a woman says.

"Have some," an old man on the bench interrupts his soup-drinking. And when she'd already begun eating he said, "I haven't eaten anything for two days, but I'm holding out."

At night the shells and the "nickelodeons" had a heyday. And yet, the nights were better. Because they were without bombs. At night there were more activities. The kind for civilians. Volunteer work. Only at night now was it possible to move the barricades. That's what it was all about. Once. I remember. We had obviously lost some ground. Or perhaps it was only a tactical move. It was necessary to move the barricades several meters. In our direction. On Rybaki Street. Not too far from Wytwornia. A gathering. Of volunteers. At one or two o'clock. A lot of us. Twenty-odd, I think. Shovels. Pickaxes. Crowbars. Everything is distributed. We get moving. It's warm. At this moment it's even quiet. It seems to me there are even stars. But how could there be stars! Surely they were veiled by the smoke. A lieutenant leads us. A lieutenant? Could it be? That's what I was told. During the uprising a lieutenant was a somebody. So maybe it was a corporal. Or a civilian warden, a semi-military person. It's worth remembering that there were some 55,000 partisans in Warsaw, all told.

We walked on. Our housing block (B plus C and D), the picket fence across from it, the escarpment with the Sisters of the Sacrament, the wall. The barricade. The intersection of Rybaki and Koscielna Streets. Again a barricade. Various ditches. On the Wybrzeze side, shops and some other residential buildings. Rybaki is all twisted, now wide, now narrow. Cobblestones. On the left, the escarpment; over the low walls, the main walls—the ruins.

93

(That's right—ruins! . . .) On the escarpment, on the hill behind the cupola of the Sisters of the Sacrament, is Our Lady. Gothic. With its peculiar spire. Alongside, the Vistula splashes. Finally, the searchlight's windmills. Different things underfoot constantly. Suddenly, dry grass. Or earth slides. Or piles of something or other. I can remember with some certainty only those cobblestones. And also that on Rybaki Street we could see slightly lower buildings. And the barricade. Which we had to move. And then suddenly a silence. Which went on and on. So that at last we became frightened.

"Ssshhh. . . . The Germans. . . ."

"Shh . . . they'll hear us. . . ."

We go up to our goal. Everything swings into motion. Behind the barricade there was another stretch of Rybaki. And its extension. I think the roadway dipped lower. The moving of the barricade was literal. Slab by slab. Every piece of paving stone. Rail by rail. (Perhaps those tools which I mentioned weren't distributed for this job; I've confused this with another nighttime action.) The night wasn't too long. At any moment just about anything could happen. The silence became more and more suspicious. So we developed a tempo. Tempo. Movement. There were many heavy and jangling objects. Many metal plates, I remember. And metal plates cause echoes. A lot of bustling, people, moving at a trot and rushing to get the next piece, and once more all over again. And all the time, during this hurrying about and moving and passing each other, in this rush, everyone would shush everyone else,

"Ssshhhh. . . ."

But after all, with so many people and things, something had to be sacrificed. Because of all that haste. So putting things down was more like throwing. Only it was also like stacking things up. Just that!

"Ssshhh. . . ."

We ran with the material from the old barricade (which was growing smaller and smaller, disappearing) into the shadows of Rybaki, to the new barricade, which was growing larger and larger. Passing the apartment houses near the Vistula. And the wooden house near the escarpment. Suddenly someone—it couldn't have been me?—dropped a metal plate. Onto the cobblestones. Clang! Crash! A hideous echo. At that moment everything, the background of utter silence and the August warmth, seemed so suspicious to us that we froze. I don't know whether it was really caused

94

by that. But right away a flame sailed over us. Alive. Whining. And crashed somewhere. Nearby. It was a shell.

Then a second. A whine. Like a comet. And crash! From the Kierbedz bridge. And a third: fire—whine—crash! Fire—whine—crash! From the opposite direction, from the Gdansk bridge, without warning. Yet another from the Gdansk bridge. Another from Kierbedz. From Gdansk. From Kierbedz. And crash! crash! Suddenly. They had caught us between two fires. Literally. We had just about finished the barricade. And even if we hadn't we couldn't have managed for long. From a third direction too, I think. From the Vistula. Or the Zoo. I only know there were those flames from various directions. Intersecting. Crosses. Red.

I didn't understand immediately. What should we do? And what about the others? Somehow they began to disappear. We had to disappear. But how? Where could we go? I rush over to a wall. No protection. I slip into the doorway of the stone apartment building near the Vistula. It really did face the Vistula. And all of Praga. I don't know if it had a courtyard. Or how it was demolished. I know there was nothing there. Only the Vistula, Praga, the shells and the echoing explosions. Someone else next to me. How long could I stay there, stand there? One, two, in a minute I jumped out. And up to the wall. And the sidewalk. I see . . . that is, I sense: unexpected salvation—a tiny window leading into a cellar. I flatten myself out like a cat. Jump. Down. Someone behind me. Also like a cat. And someone else. Warmth emanated from inside. And chattering: buzz-buzz-buzz. . . .

I landed in a huddled mass of people, a tight crowd, men just lined up one beside the other. They were ourselves, the men from the barricade. Carrying something, shovels (precisely, I remember the shovels . . .). But how crowded it was here. And there was absolutely no other exit, hole, hidden recess. Only that cat's window above and that little space. Warmth. It was just splendid with all that fear and stench! And pressing together with feline resourcefulness. Barely room for five sacks of potatoes. Every now and then someone else still joined us through the window. One of ours, one of the ones still outside. Jump! And there he is. It got more crowded every time. You couldn't move an arm or leg. So you didn't move. After all, just being here was happiness. So, that cat's leap from the street didn't mean a thing. Something was going on. Splat! Against our barricade. Something spreading. Splat! Against the pavement. Right here. Splat! Into the wooden house. High flames. For a moment. Then lower. The wooden house was burning down.

How long did we stay there? For a long time, and yet not till morning. It began to quiet down while it was still night. Rapidly. It stopped. We rushed out. Our tools clutched in our fists. What we didn't have with us had to be collected. Quickly. What else? I don't remember. Only that it was done quickly. Cobblestones. The sky. August. Something (a shovel?) under my arm. Koscielna. The corner. Near the barricade—the one over here—silence—only a couple—a partisan and his girl—sitting beside the barricade, on duty. And talking away. As if there were no other way, there could be no other way. Only the warmth. Just sitting there. The barricade like a piece of furniture. And talking. I also remember that I was happy to be going home.

Morning. From the start: sun, heat, smoke, planes, bombings, burning. I keep recollecting. If someone should want to picture to himself the three destructions of Warsaw—September 1939, the uprising in the ghetto from April 19 to about May 20, and the 1944 Warsaw uprising—all of them happened precisely under such suns, heat, burning, planes. Heat, that is, sunshine and a blue sky mingled with fires, smoke, explosions, sifting plaster; all this added (and this is hard to believe although it is true) something exotic. Or rather, an extra whirling in one's brain.

Well, that's how it was from early morning. Those were already the days when every hour, every half hour, something collapsed nearby, crumpled, closer, farther off, higher up. Part would be saved, if at all possible. If they could, people would dig each other out. Every so often new people would come into our shelters. Sprinkled with plaster dust, with or without bundles, without anything, with children, with families, or alone. They walked in. They ran in. Everyone was welcome. That was obvious. The plankbed benches became more and more crowded. Gray light from the window. There was still room. Then people came in, all the time more and more new people. Several times a day. Now 23 Rybaki, our passageway, was bombed. Now some house on Mostowa. Now a house on Koscielna. Now Rybaki behind Koscielna. Now Bolesc.

One time, four generations of the bombed walked in. Lusia Romanowska with Mareczek; her mother, Mrs. Ryminska; and Mrs. Ryminska's aunt, Aunt Zosia, in a black cap, a black coat, carrying a dark cane.

"Good afternoon . . . may we. . . ."

"Yes. Please. Of course. Where are you from? There's room here. Please come in."

"From 2 Koscielna. They've bombed us now. We're lucky to be alive."

We made room for them near us. We, all six of us, with our little cook stove of three bricks beside a pillar. I think they sat down on a bench. Mareczek was three or four years old. Aunt Zosia had come to visit Lusia on August 1. Lusia was a writer. We hit it off. Talking, talking. But there were new bombs.

"One, two, three, four. . . ." New people buried. And those who hadn't been injured came in:

"May we?"

"Of course, where are you from?"

They would sit down. They would tell us.

Our entire shelter under the pillars lived in great friendship. There wasn't a single quarrel or argument here. Actually, it wasn't really bad in the other shelters either. The shelters were getting better and better. And the situation was getting worse and worse.

I don't remember the date. August 23 or 24? In the afternoon. That day we stood up many times. There was some sort of instinct which made us stand during a bombing. Not sit. Perhaps you wouldn't sit it out. Or maybe it was because of the pillars, because we would stand around the pillars. Maybe there was one little per cent better chance near the pillars. In fatal situations. About this time, just as my father ran into a cellar somewhere between Marszalkowska and Zielna, something smashed down near by and broke through the cellar and plaster began to rain down at an angle. Everyone stood in place and covered his head with his arms. So that in case a brick should suddenly fall down they might still have a chance. And somehow they survived. Those people. Other people began digging out the people beside them right away.

So that was in the afternoon. We stood near the pillars for a rather long time, as I remember. The planes were flying over one after another. And dropping bombs. Then other planes followed. And bombs. We didn't know what was happening in our blocks. What they had hit already. What was broken. Maybe it was then that people were buried in block A near Rybaki. I know that there weren't any songs; not then. Nor counting "one, two." Swen's mother, her head against a pillar beside me, was praying quietly. The lights were on then; this I remember. Yes, it was definitely then that block A was bombed. Because the planes kept flying over. With that whining. Then the whining of the bomb. Of one, of another. And it would strike. Something would explode. Nearer and nearer. Then, near the last pillar I think, under a light bulb, a woman in a bright, ordinary coat suddenly stood up. No one knew her. And suddenly, in that silence, she began to speak:

"Let us pray that we'll survive. Let us pray to Saint Christopher." She swiftly drew a medal from her purse. Again something pelted us.

And once again, whooooo.

She held up the medal. "Saint Christopher will lead us out of this morass."

New planes.

The woman in the coat began to speak, in a monotone, but so that each word reached me, with its complete sense:

> *He that dwelleth in the secret place of the Most High*
> *Shall abide under the shadow of the Almighty.*
> *I will say of the Lord, He is my refuge and my fortress:*
> *My God; in Him will I trust.*

Swen knelt down. Beside me. Near the pillar. The whining. And then we heard that we'd been hit. The lights went out. Something shuddered. Things began crashing down above us. The ceilings from the second floor broke through onto the first.

> *Surely He shall deliver thee from the snare of the fowler,*
> *And from the noisome pestilence.*
> *He shall cover thee with His feathers,*
> *And under His wings shalt thou trust:*
> *His truth shall be thy shield and buckler.*

Something rumbled. Everything was still crumbling.
But all this time the woman in the coat kept speaking:

> *For He shall give His angels charge over thee,*
> *To keep thee in all thy ways. . . .*

Something was crumbling above us. A moment's interruption.

> *They shall bear thee up in their hands,*
> *Lest thou dash thy foot against a stone.*

I believe it was at this point that she broke off.

Again the vibrations began. A noisy moving about. More and more. Swen squeezed my knee. I winced and hid my head in my collar. Is this it already? Already? Yes, it's hard, only will it strike from the head? To the feet? Will it knock you flat? If only it could be quick.

Two ceilings collapsed from the first floor to the ground floor, so now it was our turn. Swen pressed his head against my knee. Swen's mother stood there without changing her position. It was very quiet. There was absolute silence. Only something rumbled, was crumbling, still crumbling, crumbling. . . .

It was black, except that dust clouds were visible.

Suddenly . . . we understood that we wouldn't be smashed. And only then people began to croup, choke, cough; someone screamed, "The doors! Are the doors still there?"

"The doors! Take a look! Have we been buried? The doors!"

"Matches! Who has matches?"

"The doors! I think we're buried! The window's covered! Matches!"

Zbyszek, coughing, was the first to light a match.

"There's nothing to see. . . ."

Another; he walks closer:

"No, it seems there aren't any doors—they're buried! No! They're here! They're here! They can be opened . . . it's all right, it's all right. . . ."

We inspected the bombed out block A only from the Rybaki Street side, on the next day I think. Swen and I. No one went to inspect what remained above us after the bombing. Not even the next day. No one was curious. I was amazed. It wasn't clear, I think, what had happened with the lights, although probably they were still on. Where the wires hadn't been cut. But I remember people saying on the second day that the showers on the ground floor were working. With cold water. It was difficult to expect any warm water. Swen didn't feel up to a cold shower. I'm also afraid of cold. But it was hot. And besides, I realized that after something like that, those functioning showers might be the last occasion for bathing in such a peaceful time, after the raids, on the second day, at evening, because after all those showers were somewhere above us and who knows what was really below us?

I skirted the corridor, the stairs, the exit, and stood in front of our ground floor on the courtyard side, the second one. I even entered the ground floor. Because it could be done. And those showers really were there. They were in working order. There were even shower stalls. And it was possible, because no one was in a hurry to wash there, to strip naked and bathe in freedom. And what did the rest of the building look like? The rest—those two broken ceilings, that is, fused into one concrete mushroom, which itself was fused with the rest of the ground floor. Our shelter was where the hole with the showers ended and the fusing of the mushroom with the ground floor began.

On that very same day, the second day after that bombing and later ones which went on from morning till night, after my bath, in the evening, after things had quieted down, from the bombs at least, a priest ran into our shelter. Not into ours alone. But to other shelters, as well. And he wasn't the first priest. He came running in order to distribute to each shelter the so-called last sacraments. He just came running in. He had nothing with him. Everything had been used up already or was in crumbs. I am writing about this because it is one of my important memories. It is well known that even in the worst of times, the churches are always well supplied with communion wafers and that they worry a lot about this. *That* is something which is never scarce! Once in religion class I learned about "holy communion of hunger." When there are no wafers and you want to take communion.

I remember that the electric lights were burning then. It happened either in our cellar or the one next door. The shelter was filled with people. I think it was in ours. Because the light bulb and the ceiling vault were near the priest's head. There was a general feeling of great depression. And of concentration. The priest said,

"Now let us all recite aloud the universal confession. 'I confess to the Almighty Lord God, the One in the Holy Trinity ... that I have sinned in thought, word and deed—through my fault, through my fault, through my most grievous fault.' "

Silence.

"And now," said the priest after that recitation, "let us all take holy communion of hunger." A short prayer followed. Silence. Everyone bowed his head. And it was over.

The priest moved on to the next cellar.

Either that night or in the morning we transferred to the large shelter, the old one. Again. It was too terrifying for us in that other cellar, under the pillars. But here too, in this old one, it was also terrifying. We had inspected beforehand the entrances, the descents into our little sewer. But where did it lead to? We thought about the real sewer mains. To Srodmiescie. But there were probably crowds waiting to get in. And to get in you had to have passes. And there were crowds waiting for those passes.

We were afraid that the Germans might enter. We were afraid of the shadows of their helmets. Especially towards evening. Or at night. Swen and I often looked at the ceiling: aren't they coming yet? They could rush out from behind their tanks at any moment. The tanks were really coming out now. From Wybrzeze too. And from Koscielna. The partisans settled down by the windows. And bent over in the window frames, they waited for hours at a time. With a grenade. Or a Molotov cocktail.

I thought about those pillars then. That in case they should come inside (the Germans) and start hurling grenades, then those pillars would always be a kind of protection. At least from the first throw. Later . . . who knows what; they'll order us outside, to disassemble the barricade; they'll drive us in front of the tanks, because they were doing that all the time. After all, Roza Ad. and Basia had gotten here and she had been driven in front of a tank. Probably before this, in this cellar, she had said to Basia, "Don't cry; we won't survive anyway." Although they did survive.

So a person kept on calculating, together with other people, what he should do next. Several times already Aunt Uff. and Swen's mother had been taken with the idea that we should just get out of there. Twice they had even gotten ready to leave. To upper Stare Miasto. But each time I was somewhere else. For some reason. Once, on duty—I remember that. Both times, however, they waited for me, but when I returned there was artillery fire or a raid or some sort of hell, so that our departure was postponed. But August 25 I think we were already very well prepared. We'd had enough of Rybaki Street. Of the Vistula. Of those housing blocks. We. Lusia, Mareczek, and her mother. Aunt Zosia said that even if we went away she'd stay on here. And the Ads. were prepared to go along with us. The question was, where should we go?

"To the Sisters of the Sacrament."

We decided on the change. "To the Sisters of the Sacrament."

"To the Sisters of the Sacrament."

The Sisters of the Sacrament had practically burned down to the ground. But the church itself was still standing. I don't know in what condition. It seems to me it was somewhat battered. But basically it was standing. Was the cupola intact? I don't remember. In those times saying that something was "standing" could be so relative that I simply don't know. But where else could we go, if not there? Throughout the entire expanse of our neighborhood there remained, as everyone said then, only two addresses: 5 Hipoteczna and Krzywa Latarnia (on Podwale), so we considered those two surviving buildings. But if only those two were still standing, what a mob there must be in them.

Lusia said, "It would be best to go to 5 Hipoteczna. I have a friend there."

However (an additional obstacle), 5 Hipoteczna was a long way off.

But to remain here was impossible. The blocks were nearing their end. At any moment the Germans would invade them.

"What about the ruins?"

"That's it! The ruins."

It wasn't the first time that thought had crossed our minds, either.

"But they're also bombing the ruins."

"Perhaps they're not bombing them like they do here, not taking aim."

"Yes, but if they hit the ruins, that's the end, because there's only one ceiling or it's completely. . . ."

And so on in a circle. Always someone didn't agree. But we had the feeling that we must get out of there.

August 25 must have been absolutely dreadful because by evening, I think, we had decided that we would leave at dawn. The passageway to Nowe Miasto and Stare Miasto was already burned down, bombed out. And to reach the Sisters of the Sacrament you had to inch along the escarpment. Or rather along the exposed "frying pan." Under fire.

The partisans came rushing in at night. "Who'll volunteer to dig trenches?"

Several people stood up. I did too.

"Just come back before daybreak," said Swen.

They gave us each a shovel, a pickaxe. And we ran quietly into the street. It was warm. I only know it was Rybaki or one of the so-called streets, because Koscielna and the intersection, too, had already changed radically. They didn't look like themselves or even like streets, for that matter. Or like an intersection.

Various formations jutted out. Hills. Ditches. Barricade-walls. Barricade-ruins. Something more or less slanted. And deep.

I am speaking of changes sensed by smell, by touch, on the run, by extending your hand, with the powdered ruins and smoke in your breath; in general, things sensed in profile, because after all it was night.

How was it that that whole hilly area was still there—that is, whatever was along the hill or on the hill and even the hill itself—Nowe Miasto, the New City of Stare Miasto? Perhaps it would be better to ask how it still hung there? In and on itself? Burnt through with live flame? Scorched? Pulverized? Broken? Resounding? Shattered?

The Sisters of the Sacrament were burning from the top down, from left to right. And collapsing. Farther to the left, the Dominicans were also shattered, resounding, roasting. Also from the top down. What went on below, in our low-lying place, could not be comprehended; what is there to recollect, why revert to the situation as it was—since nothing existed any longer. A fortress —our housing blocks, standing firm, bullet-pocked, dimly outlined. You could still see the Mint, or rather, Wytwornia. There were still fragments, skeletons, between it and Our Lady, the one above Koscielna Street. On the heights.

Nothing. We rushed through the job of digging in the hard city ground, with cables running underneath, and having to be careful where and how long to dig. Having to come close and stop in time! But it took only a little while.

We leaped along those ditches; we walked back crouching. Returned our shovels, pickaxes. Quickly. My labyrinth. My shelter. My people on their feet, with their bundles.

"Are we going?"

"We are."

Each person takes something. We move as a group. The Ads. are there too. Lusia with Mrs. Ryminska and Mareczek. Leavetaking. It's painful. With Aunt Zosia. Dawn was breaking. And that's what was important—to leave before the day began. And yet things got all fouled up. Either it was that someone was packing for too long, or that those others had started up earlier than usual. There was artillery fire already. Even at the exit we deliberated again over whether we shouldn't wait awhile. But the majority, I think, began to shout that there was no reason to wait. Because it would get worse with every passing moment. In any case several people began to run outside and simultaneously the shells started coming in; immediately, there was tumult. Already, on Rybaki Street, you could see clearly. Several figures, bent under bundles, raced past. I had a blanket filled with rusks on my back. We went to the Dominicans' gate (the one with the monstrance) in order to reach the top via the monastery gardens and along the escarpment, because 23 Rybaki was already destroyed.

After a moment's silence they began firing again. Confusion. Mr. Ad., his trousers awry and carrying his briefcase, ran in front. Mrs. Roza Ad., with Basia in her arms, ran after him and called to him to wait, but another shell exploded and Mr. Ad. speeded up. So Mrs. Ad. turned back. Now Lusia, carrying Mareczek, was running behind Mr. Ad., also more and more quickly. Her mother (Mrs. Ryminska) wanted to catch up with them, but couldn't. Aunt Uff. and Zbyszek were already overtaking her. Mrs. Ryminska called out,

"Wait . . . wait a bit. . . ."

The rest of us passed by but she kept on calling, "Wait!"

I felt foolish and went back. The same number of steps. I started to lead her. By the arm. Because the ground underfoot was full of debris. And she was stumbling. Since we were going too slowly and they were going too quickly I pulled her along at first. To make her walk faster. Then I ran up to join them. To tell them to go more slowly. But there was gunfire already. It was thundering all around us. And how! And it didn't help much to call. So I went back to Mrs. Ryminska once again. And again I ran away. In order to maintain some kind of communication. Mr. Ad. was farther and farther away. And higher up. On the escarpment. He was racing over the ruins. His trousers were twisted. Then over the grass. Which was littered with bricks. Plaster. He crouched down. And ran on. I can no longer say for sure when it was that Mrs. Ad., with Basia in her arms, turned back. I turned around. I looked back. I ran up to them. I called. It was obviously the herd instinct (in me). After that, I just ran on. A long time. Through streets. But they didn't. They were afraid. Because they weren't used to it. To shells and bullets. It really was a matter of becoming used to them.

So Mrs. Ad. and Basia dropped behind. And the rest—always more and more stretched out it seems—went on, now past the gate with the monstrance, past the monastery gardens, always higher, at a slant. Along the grass. The earth. A piece of something. At times a tree. That's good. For the eye. Like a shelter. We were going to Nowe Miasto. And the situation was getting worse and worse. The more we went towards the right. And the higher we went. Some other people were going there too. Lots of them. Also, people were descending the hill. They passed us. That fat woman was also with us. From Towarowa. The one who slept on the door from the toilet. She had something tied to her back. Below her neck. I think. Because she was bent over from carrying something.

There began to be explosions from Zeran too. From them. From beyond the Vistula. The front. And the sound of explosions increased. They were German. The bullets too. Around us. Thicker and thicker. Aimed right at us, I think (they had to be). It was getting hot. The sun was already out. It was striking our eyes. Somehow Mrs. Ryminska fell into step. I don't know how long we walked. Uphill. At a slant. We began crawling up to the Sisters of the Sacrament. That is, up to Benon-Bienkowski. Which was also already in ruins there below. But Benon was still higher up. We crawled onto the worst terrain. The hardest for walking. Steep. And the most shot at. We grabbed at branches, I think, at the grass, in order to take one step higher. And higher. At anything at all. Because the bullets went whizz! whizz! At those branches. At the grass. Somehow not at us. But that wasn't absolutely clear. The branches and the grass were gray. And time and again they spurted out bullets. Shells, too. And the front. Thunderbolt after thunderbolt.

During this crawling up over the grass something around my neck loosens, slips from my back and . . . the blanket with the rusks falls off . . . lower . . . the rusks bounce away, scatter. Immediately I begin grabbing at the nearest ones. Back into the blanket. With desperation. One handful. Another. A third. But the rest are lying lower down or in the grass or simply scattered about. My people are already pressing against me, practically pushing me for several seconds already, not letting me be.

"Leave them, leave them!"

"You see what's going on!"

"Miron, Mirek, Miron!"

I do nothing. After all, there's hunger. Each handful of rusks is a day's life.

"Miron! Leave them!"

"Miron!"

"Miron! Get going!"

They were all yelling. Aunt Uff. Zbyszek. Swen. Celina. Swen yelled a lot.

"Miron! Miron!"

I can hear those voices in my ears even today, as if they were calling now. They are waiting. They move a little. They are practically turning back. They stand over me. With their bundles. Hunchbacked. There's no let-up in the buzzing. Shells are landing. But the rusks are lying there. How many of them there are in the grass. The grass is thick. Quick as lightning I gather them up. But. . . .

"Miron! Miron!"

Those who had been below me were already moving above me. Some other people were coming up. Stooping. And still the shells were coming in at us. Not as much any more. Just enough. It is hard to snatch things up from grass. I claw at those rusks.

"All right, all right," I call. "All right, all right!"

"Mirek! Mirek!" I remember Swen's mother calling the longest. A scream. And her bending down all the time. With a blanket just like mine. Filled with rusks.

"I'm coming, I'm coming." I was finished.

"I'm coming!" And I wrap them up, throw them over my shoulder, and run off.

Quickly. Quickly. Because it's bad. We reach the ruins of the factory-church. Boards. Thudding. Tap-tap-tap. The remains of the main hall. I think there were others. The facade of Benon. From above. Boards. A pile of ruins. Pieces of debris. Whitewash. Plaster. Wooden laths. Splinters. Bricks. Eaves. Everything. Whatever there was. Already we're on the escarpment. No longer on that frying pan slope. Perhaps we'll make it. Whatever's behind Benon is there. In any case we make it to those picket fences which are still standing today. A gate. Through the gate. Into a lane. The tiny street from Benon to the Nowe Miasto marketplace. On the right, Przyrynek, Our Lady—brick, old. On the left, the Sisters of the Sacrament. Full of people. With bundles. Humps. With something under their arms. A basket. Anything at all. Or with nothing. Here I remember Mr. Ad., in those twisted trousers, I think, hopping and skipping over the ruins, over the large and small remains of houses. And that's how I lose him in my memory. The marketplace forms a triangle. We are at its base. Somehow we think it over. It's hot. Bright. Smoke. Explosions. The front. People.

A crowd of people is squeezing into the neck of the marketplace funnel; they are all mixed together, milling about, dashing back and forth—because there is something flying past or falling down all the time (after all everything is still *changing*!). Freta. Kozla. The Franciscans. Shattered apartment houses. Superstructures. Several stories high. Stripped down to their foundations. Crosswise. Empty. Into shavings, hanging strips of plaster, laths, boards, bricks. There was an awful lot of that stuff. All Warsaw was made of it. Almost. Those five-story buildings too: laths, plaster, bricks, boards. Or splinters. Powdered substances. Dry. They crackled. When hit, they splattered. House after house. Rain gutters, brackets of sheet metal hung from holes in the balconies, or from nothing at all. They swayed. Clanged. Banged. Thin, empty inside—what one had thought of as a cornice, a wall, marble. Warsaw was betraying all her secrets. Since it was she who betrayed them there is no reason to hide the fact. She was already disintegrating. Sinking. She had been sinking for one hundred years. Two hundred. Three hundred. And more. Everything showed. From top to bottom. From the Mazovian princes.* Up to us. And back again. Stas, Sobieski,* the Saxons,* the Vasas.* The Vasas. The Saxons, Sobieski, Stas, Fukier.* The Sobieskis, Marysienka,* the Sisters of the Sacrament.

We turned. All of us. The woman with the door marks and various others who walked by, walked up, walked away. The front was being lost. Like this land. And all the ruins and the sky. Blue. Smoky. Red. Sun. Dust in your teeth. With lime. The ruins stink. Strongly. And the burned-out buildings—awful! And an explosion with its drifting dust stinks. Through one's ears to one's nose. The nose shares a cold with the eyes. Mechanical crying. Overly salty. Literally. What else? The hands work. Somewhat like blind people's. The feet dig into something. The shoulders get exercise. The whole, pasted together, sweaty, exhausted, says something in the background. Thinks, too. The same thing, only quicker. An entrance. With people. Under something. They look. Into a hole. A chink. Stairs. Into something dark, damp, crowded. And that trap door; was it really a trap door? The entrance (exit) under the Sisters of the Sacrament. Or was it something made of boards? Those masses down below. Their nest. Swen stamps his foot, yells, bangs something.

"I won't go in there. I won't go in there. Let's go away. Let's not go to the Sisters of the Sacrament. I won't go to the Sisters of the Sacrament. I won't go to the Sisters."

We push him. But he insists.

"I won't go into the Sisters of the Sacrament. I will not go into the Sisters of the Sacrament."

Suddenly a Sister of the Sacrament is standing in front of us. From below.

"We're already very crowded, one thousand people under the church." She spreads her hands; her eyes and head are bowed; she continues to speak, grayly, grayly. "Really, as many as we could . . . we accepted." She breaks off confused.

"Maybe, maybe. . . ." we repeat.

"But, as many as we could. . . ."

"But, maybe." We speak again—Aunt, Swen's mother, Zbyszek, Celina, Lusia with Mareczek in her arms (she had carried him along the escarpment, shielded him), Mrs. Ryminska, I. And the woman from Towarowa.

"Perhaps, perhaps anyway. . . ."

"Maybe somehow. . . ."

Except for Swen who keeps saying, "No!"
and again

"No!"

"Not here!" And stamps his foot.

"If you insist . . . take a look, it's crowded . . . the walls are cracked . . . so many bombs . . . have already hit . . . us, the church, you see." (Yes, the church of the Sisters of the Sacrament hardly existed above the ground; yes, yes, by that time already, and they had nothing else, nothing, nothing, only whatever was under the church, under the trap door.) "Well, go in please, if you'll fit; take a look, go in, please." She invited us to come under the trap door.

What was there?

We were upset. Now we were the others. With bundles of rusks. Should we go in? Or not?

"No, I won't go down there, I won't go in there, no, no." Swen had made up his mind; he wouldn't let anyone in.

"Then where should we go now?"

"Yes, where should we go?"

"To Our Lady?"

"Are there people there? It's been covered over. Oh, what it looks like!" Our Lady looked horrible. Yes. Yes. I recall everything now. What it was like then.

"But maybe there are people there?"

"Perhaps."

"Let's go."

We walked to Our Lady. It absolutely terrified us. The church too. And that dark belltower. Like playing store in the countryside, with cocoa made from bricks. Our Lady looked just like that.

"And are there people there now?"

There were. Indeed. Under that "cocoa" made of bricks. Someone gave us information. One of us asked a few questions. In any case, people walked in. Came out. Dragged themselves inside. Looked about. Sun. Heat. The front. Ours: bullets, hisses, whistles, shells. No one could fit in anywhere. Here, too, some people were hiding. Perhaps two thousand of them. How should I know?

To the Franciscans? They've been demolished. No doubt there are people there too. Two thousand. Three. Under the ruins. We go back. The Sisters of the Sacrament, after all.

We stand there once more. We peer inside. Under the trap door. But Swen screams, pulls us away,

"I won't go in. You go! But I won't go. I won't go. Not to the Sisters of the Sacrament. I'll go anywhere. Into the ruins—yes. But to the Sisters of the Sacrament—no. Not to the Sisters of the Sacrament!"

Swen had his way. We walked away. We walked on. Thunder. The front. Shells flying. All the time. Something or other. We squeeze into the neck of the Marketplace. That woman is probably somewhere around here. The one from the door. All striped. She left. Walked away. Separated from us. I don't know. Everything was coming apart. Nothing could stick together. Everything was moving. Disappearing.

Garnizonowa Street? It had had it. The Paulists? The Paulists no longer existed. The Cathedral? We already know about that. The Jesuits? Next door. The same as the Cathedral. The Dominicans. Maybe the Dominicans. We walk along Freta. And anyway, churches aren't really so good.

"Krzywa Latarnia, that's really where we want to be, or 5 Hipoteczna."

"Let's go to 5 Hipoteczna." That was Lusia.

"Or maybe to the ruins? They're full of people; after all, they say there are plenty of people in the ruins."

"Well?"

"Let's go to Krzywa Latarnia."

"Yes, but they won't let us in there."

"But it's also ruins."

"Let's try the Dominicans."

"Look, they're still standing."

The church was still standing. The monastery was in worse condition.

We enter. An imposing wardrobe. Pseudogothic. The portico. On the left is a row of little stoves. More like debris than stoves! But there are large kettles on each stove. And they are all steaming. Indeed! In a row. A woman is standing or squatting in front of each one. Disheveled. Under the gray light. And wielding a lid. A large one. For a cauldron.

We go inside. Straight ahead. Doors. Downstairs. There are still stairs. The church is below us. Inside the church: echoes, reverberations. A crowd. We squeeze in. Into the nave. To the left. It's full. Altars. What a lot of them there are. With gold, silver leaf. Baroque. Dancing figures. Holy madmen, mystics. They are writhing alongside, above, across the altar. There are statues on the stairs beneath the altars, under each one (why was it like that?). Living figures. Half reclining. Themselves baroque. Also. They too were lying crosswise, sideways, but lower down and dressed in crumpled rags.

We go outside. The barricades. Downhill on Mostowa. On the left the Gdansk Cellar no longer exists. Burnt down. On the right is a footbridge. A trough across the moat. And the walls. The old ones. Reconstructions. Brick. Thick. And there are people here. Beneath the walls. Spread out. On the grass. On the bed of the stream. Which is no longer flowing. Which hasn't flowed for four hundred years. The closer to the footbridge, the more crowded it is. And this is how it was under the open sky! Further on it was just the same. People sat around. Lay around. Those walls. They go on, they twist and turn. Parallel with Podwale. And we go on, following the turns of Podwale. The narrow street. It's there. Krzywa Latarnia.

"Here we are," says Mama.

"Here?"

But inside the gate (it was a stone apartment house) an elderly man was standing, bald, perhaps he had a moustache. That's right; everyone had beards, moustaches, long hair then.

"My dear people," he says, "what do you want? You want to come here? There are three thousand people here. You couldn't fit a pin in . . . three thousand. They're suffocating. They'll suffocate to death. There's nothing to be said. You shouldn't even go inside."

We shouldn't even go inside. We didn't speak. We didn't stop. We were walking on already.

"Let's go to 5 Hipoteczna," says Lusia, "and maybe...."

"Where? And they'll let us in?"

"There are five stories there; I have a friend. And if not there, then the ruins...."

"Certainly, the ruins."

"But where? Which ruins?"

"We'll find some."

"Well, let's get going to Hipoteczna. We may as well."

We walk on. From narrow Podwale into broad Podwale. The rear walls of the palaces. People. People. And explosions. Thundering. And the front. Others too. Planes. Somewhere already.... We have to hurry. We gave up any hopes about Dluga Street. There'd already been a disaster there by then. Those hospitals. In the cellars. And the burned pilots. They bombed through. They bombed through. Shattered. Everything. The Dominicans were to experience the same thing in a day or two. Those people. And those saints. Together. Into the cellars. Everything.

"Let's go to Kapitulna. To Miodowa. Kapucynska is almost directly opposite. We just have to get past Miodowa. But it's probably impossible."

I don't remember if we went into Kapitulna and someone there said (because many people were just standing there or turning back) that Miodowa was no good. It was flooded. Fenced off. With barricades. Ruins. Artillery fire. From the corner of Kozia, from the seven-story building. And from Bonifraterska Street. And every so often there were tanks. From Krakowskie Przedmiescie into Miodowa. They could go there and back. They were shooting. Starting fires.

Perhaps it was Kapitulna. To the right, across something which was demolished. Or perhaps we went back to Podwale and through the Chodkiewicz gate with the grillwork. Into the same courtyard, the big one. Or was it that Kapitulna was fenced off with barricades? And we went right through those bars, the fence, into the courtyard, into that pile of ruins, because everything here —the outbuildings, the wings, the front—was demolished, burnt to the ground, with something protruding here and there, bricks, boards. Piles. An entire hill. Through the courtyard. Stumbling.

111

Maybe we should leap over there? To the passageway, the gate. From that gate to the Pac gate. Next, to the Capuchins. Kapucynska Street. And from Kapucynska a passage had been broken through into the rear of Hipoteczna. It's close by now. But how could we cross Miodowa? We could hear what was going on. People were coming back. They warned us.

"No, no, it's full of dead bodies just lying there. Anyone who tries to run across falls down right away. And groans. Or is already a corpse."

We go into a burnt-out, completely burnt-out, caved-in front building; only the foundation piles show. Into the entranceway. Stairs leading down. Black. Into an even darker hole. And into terrible heat. After a fire.

"There's someone below; let's inquire."

"In any case let's go down, take a look around."

We go down.

"This is Miodowa, isn't it?"

"14 Miodowa."

Downstairs, straight ahead, there's a woman wearing something dark, black. She's bending over. Doing something. Around someone. A back. A bare back. And a wound. We can see. From a distance. He's lying on his stomach. On a cot. She's applying cotton, gauze. A cell. Black. And the noise. Water. A waterfall.

"But is there a passageway? Across Miodowa?"

"What? Across Miodowa? Artillery fire. How can you go there?"

We can hear the firing and the noise.

"What's that?"

"The whole street's flooded. It's like a river."

"And coming in here? Falling in?"

"Yes."

A waterfall, literally. She soaks the bandages in the roaring waterfall. What luxury!

"And those cellars to the left?"

"That's the Artisans' Guild."

"Can we go in there?"

"Certainly. It's empty."

We go in to the left. Behind the pillars of this anteroom, practically next door, an oil-painting Christ on the Cross has been preserved. An elderly man with a moustache looks in, comes down, questions us; we mention Miodowa but he says nothing, goes out again.

We go further in. Past the threshold. Or rather past what remained of it, past the doorway which had been burned down to the brick.

"Let's stay here."

"Fine, let's stay here."

We all agree at once. A relief. It's empty. There are ruins. Something is there. Over our heads. The framework. Not intact. Something seems to be missing from it nearer the street. But very little. That's nothing. One or two little windows? One, I think. Yes. One. One or two pillars. Everything black, ashes, heat. Now I know. There were more pillars. And a second window. On the other side. The courtyard. Farther on, to the left, an arch and something else beyond it, identical with the first one.

Lusia spreads out her coat on a pile of ashes and plaster behind the pillars, sits down, the first one to do so.

"Ugh, Robinson Crusoe."

Swen's mother settles into a leather armchair.

"Ooh . . . how nice."

Aunt sits down in another armchair which looks just the same. Nearer the wall.

"Dear God . . . at last."

Zbyszek sits down in a third chair. Celina flops into a baby carriage, in the center of the room.

"Oh, how good. . . ." Her legs and head hang down because she doesn't fit in. But she's happy. Like all of us.

Swen and I grab three bricks. We have a stove already.

"Let's go get some boards," Swen and I say and we go out. Because there's an iron bed with springs there. Bare. But how can we lie on it?

"Oh Jesus!" we can hear from the Miodowa gate. "Jesus, help! . . ."

"That must be him."

He'd crawled out, the man with the moustache, and now he's lying there and how can we get to him? Who will help him if they're killing people out there?

We look for boards in the courtyard. Everything is dry. Bone dry. There are some boards. Long ones. Two of them.

"Good."

"Let's take them."

We carry them inside.

113

The man is groaning. Too bad.

"Oh Jesus . . . help . . . help . . . ."

We put down the boards on brick supports. And we lie down next to each other right away. Swen on his board. I on my own. On the left is a high window. I'm near the window. Which looks out on Miodowa.

"That's good," I say.

Swen says, "That's good."

After an hour, two hours, the wounded man grew quiet. Either someone took him away or he died. We. It's too bad. Our own kind. There are nine of us living together at 14 Miodowa Street, the Chodkiewicz Palace, the Artisans' Guild (the front of the stone building faces Miodowa, the courtyard faces Podwale, the side, Kapitulna).

Across Miodowa was the Pac Palace. The gateway was in Empire style with bas reliefs, grillwork and a little circular courtyard. To its right was the Prymasowski Palace. On our side of the street, to the right, were the Basilians. To the left on our side, the Igelstrom Palace, the Branickis'. Everything with two fronts—Miodowa and Podwale (the driveway). To the left, on the other side, behind the Pac Palace, was a circular driveway, a semicircle, a barely scarred wall, stairs, a terrace, a statue above something or other: the Capuchins. And Kapucynska Street. Also from the Sobieskis. On Krakowskie Przedmiescie, Our Lady of Victory at the fork in the road, adorned with golden hearts, votive, decorated; also connected with Sobieski. The Sisters of the Sacrament were linked to Marysienka. The Senatorska church was the first stop for every king immediately after his election—down on his knees and the first prayers of thanksgiving.

We were lying on our boards. Unsanded. Full of splinters. Swen said, "God grant I should have such a bed for the rest of my life."

"Amen," I answered, meaning that there could be nothing better.

Swen's mother prepared the food. Lately, we'd been eating very little. Twice a day. And only a little bit each time. Mama wanted to please us. She made dumplings with what remained of some vinegar she'd had.

"What's that you've made, Mama?" Swen asked.

"Actually, it's inedible, I think," I said.

Mama and Aunt tried some.

114

"Yes, it can't be eaten."

"I wanted to do something nice for a change. But it didn't turn out right."

Too bad. We poured it out. We got something else. Maybe coffee with rusks. Food was liquid; we got it in jars. Here on Miodowa, at least. I remember. Had we found them on Rybaki already or only here? Colored jars. Green. Bronze. A bit warped perhaps. From the fire. Small jars.

All our happiness on Miodowa Street, in the ashes (we waded in ashes here and they also sifted in through the vent; as soon as something exploded there were piles of soot)—all our happiness was spoiled immediately and forever by the bombs.

At the beginning we didn't move at all. Where could we go? We were in the ruins. A bit of superstructure, that's all. Either they'll hit us directly or they won't. If it's a direct hit, they'll break through. There will be no miracles here. So we sat there. They bombed. All around us. Nearer. Farther. The escarpment, Dluga, Podwale, Miodowa. We didn't even interrupt our meals. Here. We learned not to interrupt our eating at all. Unless the bombs were really very close. Then we'd hunch over for a moment. They the planes would fly away. Mama prayed. She recited out loud. We responded. Then Lusia, Swen and I thought of what we could do. Either Mama or Lusia had cards. Was it Lusia who had the idea of playing bridge? The three of us played. With Zbyszek. I think Zbyszek sat in an armchair. Those armchairs were comfortable. Large. And strangely bowed backwards. Celina didn't want to get out of the baby carriage. She lay there dangling her head, arms, legs. And she was content. I remember that the cards were spread out on those boards of ours. And that we didn't play very much. Because of the planes. The bombing would seem to stop. But not really. They'd fly away. We'd play some more. Again they'd fly over. Bombs. Looking at the ceiling again. And we'd play some more.

Then we had to fetch water. For Mama. For cooking. For Aunt. For Mrs. Ryminska. For washing. For various needs. The water was there; it had to be fetched. I went with a pitcher and a bucket to that dark room where the wounded man, his wife and the waterfall were. It could be collected there in a second. I ran right back to wash. Right away. To wash my shirt. There was no soap. But who even dreamed of soap then? The shirt was black. Celinka had an idea. We could do some laundry. Swen was astounded,

115

for some reason. Because we were doing our laundry. Or perhaps he didn't react until the evening? Because I think we did the laundry more than once. After every thick dusting. Or explosion of soot. It dried in ten minutes. Because it was so hot. Such heat. Unbearable. And I think we walked about in various outfits, as was customary during the uprising; I remember that the wife of that wounded man sat in her slip in that dark room beneath the waterfall. Who cared then about a slip? Masses of people started coming into that room, the next one, the one beyond the room nearest to us. But going out into the courtyard was very risky. Even going out onto the stairs, at least onto the higher steps. But people went out to the stairs anyway. Because it was impossible to endure the heat. Naturally we used the water. To wet ourselves. But we needed air too. When it grew dark we would start sitting around on the stairs. Too low down it was too hot, just like down below. But fragments from the shells would land on the steps more or less halfway up and higher. We noticed that. So we chose the middle steps. Where we could catch a gulp of air but the shrapnel couldn't reach us.

We went to bed. Lying down to sleep was actually a matter of sitting down, each in his armchair or carriage, or stretching out on a pile of ruins, like Lusia and Mareczek. Or, like Swen and me, in whatever we were wearing (and we had only one change of clothing) on our boards. In other words, in the same places we'd chosen immediately (everyone at the same time) upon coming here to stay.

The first night I didn't sleep on the board next to Swen but on the iron bed with the bare springs, just because it was standing there near us and looked as enticing as a hammock. But it was impossible to lie there even in a jacket and I had only my one thin shirt right over the iron springs, which formed small squares. I don't know how many hours later it was or whether it was dawn already or not when I got up and went back to the boards. My whole back was covered with little squares, like a shirt of mail. We also had the idea of removing the springs as a unit and placing them on the boards, on both of them. But no. That was bad too. What could be better than boards? We remained on the boards.

The first night as well as the following ones (the whole time on Miodowa, I think) there was moonlight. And smoke. And more smoke. Fires. And more fires. But somehow, from our boards near the window, we could see the upper portion of the Pac Palace gate.

The frieze, to be precise. In the moonlight, because it was fine weather although the smoke obscured it somewhat—the frieze. Gray-brown, I remember that. At night it had the color of dumplings left to dry (remember, our mouths were always dry). And that frieze. With figures. A procession. The figures were flat, yet they cast shadows. Anyway. In addition, they were in a semicircle. I would look at it for hours. Intrigued. It seemed to me Swen was less interested. I was somewhat offended by this. Dumplings and more dumplings. Everything then was rye, floury, like the dumplings, ready to crumble. And amidst all this there was the waterfall. That too! An accident—a miracle—a luxury. The waterfall hummed. Clattered. The water fell somewhat lower down, I don't remember where any longer. All of Miodowa emitted noises. After all, the river was flowing along it all the time. The Pac Palace. Come what may. Pac. From the palace. That one, not the other. Here (that's how I imagined it) the court of first instance convened in the days of Prus.*

Well, those springs. At night. Dawn. As usual, the weather was exceptional. Hot. It was hot here; in fact, it was like an oven. The building had burned down five days before, according to the wife of the man who'd been wounded in the back, the woman in the slip, in the dark room beneath the waterfall. A building takes a long time to cool off. And in summer? What are five days! And how long a fire can be smelled! I knew that from 1939. You could smell those burnt-out shells almost until the uprising. Yes. Because you could smell the ones from the uprising for another five years. Even after eight years they still gave off an odor. Only there were the rains, and the soaking, and so many masses of people, dried out, new, all the time, that it was hard to know what was stinking. Well, I woke up with squares on my back. We attempted to place the springs on the boards. And lay down on them. Finally we gave up. The bed remained where it was. With the coat of mail. Empty. Rusty, iron. After all, it had been burned. How had the armchairs survived intact? I don't know. There was that Christ too and some plaster which hadn't peeled. In the anteroom. But the chairs? Unexplained. I don't know if it was then or on the third day or maybe it was the second day that there were raids, only not in the morning because we just lay there, lay there. We each had a little colored jarful of kasha or barley soup. I think it was the last of the kasha. Or the next to last kasha. So, with those jars we lay under the doorway between our room and the big anteroom with the

Christ on the pillar. I think He was on the pillar. Or perhaps past the doorway on the wall. We didn't all fit into the single doorway. Eight adults. The child was held on Lusia's lap. So some of us probably went near the pillar. It was right there. And it counted just the same. Like the doorway. It was something which might remain standing in the event of a hit and the collapse of some part of the ruins. The doorway and the walls were still perpendicular. For the most part. They might collapse, too. But they had a chance. The pillars did, too. Somehow. It's true, they weren't concrete, as on Rybaki. Even so. Well, we would take the food in those jars to the doorway and since we were hungry (God! were we hungry!) that was our reasoning. We ate. We looked up. At times soot poured down. On the kasha. The coffee. So we didn't leave any over. That was a second reason. In the so-called hallway a lot of things were sifting down all the time. From above, from the windows. From the ceilings. From who knows where. Of course we brushed it aside. And ate. What of it? Things used to drift down here too. But less.

I think it was that day that I got up from the boards for a moment to do something (after all, when we weren't standing in the doorway we were lying down) and ran out into the yard. Maybe it was to get cups. Into the neighboring stairwell. In the same corner, but next to the stairs. Also a burnt-out cellar. And I found them immediately. Swen's mother had said,

"Mirek, you'll manage to find something, somehow. And I could use some dishes. Cups. Because we don't have enough jars. There'll surely be something there."

And there was. They were right there. Just as I entered. I looked around. Warped. Scorched. But you could see they were porcelain. Flowered. From a set. With saucers. I was happy. I dug them out. Brought them over. Swen's mother was happy, too.

"Oh, how nice, I'll serve in them."

Perhaps it was then that she showed me: "Look, shrapnel, still warm! It fell in. . . ."

"Just now?"

"Yes, right onto your place, where your back was, just after you walked outside."

"You had just gotten up and walked outside and wham! right through the window. You were lucky."

I was. Because nothing else fell in. Not a piece. I looked that one over. It was warm. A fat chunk. It was iron.

And perhaps it was on that second day that Lusia, Swen and I organized a literary contest. We had the idea and then immediately,

"We'll do it?"

"Sure."

"Now?"

"Now."

"But on what?"

"The theme?"

"Well, that. . . ."

"Good. That."

"We'll write. . . ."

"For how long?"

"Two hours."

"Good."

"Attention," said Swen, as soon as we had pencils and paper in hand, "we're beginning."

The contest was interrupted. Several times. We'd run to the doorway. Then we'd read aloud. Taking turns. I don't remember anything. I remember only Lusia's sheet of paper, long, from a legal pad, what a page! And her sloping, tiny pencil writing. And that hers was the shortest.

The vent used to come open. Soot drifted in. Once it covered Zbyszek. So we were always laundering shirts. And we were always wetting ourselves to try and cool off. A common rosary. Evening. Maybe it was a bit cooler. Not in the slightest! It was summer. In Warsaw. And in that cellar. So out onto the stairs. We found the ideal step. The center. We sat there most of the time. Celina, Swen and I. On one step. I remember that once we sat on two. So perhaps two of them were ideal?

At night, a breath of air. The moon. Shrapnel. "Nickelodeons." Exactly. Self-propelled nickelodeons. The frieze was fine but there was really only as much peace then as there was during the day. Though there weren't any planes. And no one thought to stir from his place in response to those nocturnal weapons. We lay there. Listened. Watched. Something drifted down. Farther off there was smoke, smoke and the moon in a semi-circle on the frieze. Tanks would ride up from Krakowskie Przedmiescie. They would stop near us, somewhere near Kapitulna, near the barricade no doubt. And they would fire. And fire. Deliberately. Deeply. Drily.

Thunk!

And after each thunk! something would sift down. Sometimes we counted. Out loud. Once, half asleep, we counted up to 123. Then my stomach ached from the explosions and the dust.

We got up. Sun. Heat. It was like an oven in here. The building wouldn't cool off for anything. Perhaps it had cooled off one or two degrees? But what difference did it make if it was 106 or 108? And it was that high, for sure. The only breezes were from the bombs, the machine guns, shells, grenades and tanks. And these had the negative aspect that they always made something fall down. Something small, powdery, but with a kind of ash-step or, so to speak, an ash-shudder. Or the cornices would break off, the moldings, brackets, walls, low walls, bricks, brick facings, plaster, bits of the foundation; they would topple the heaps of ruins, the ones above us, near the front and by the gate. It seemed to us that something was always being fired from the tanks and the mine-throwers (those "nickelodeons"), hurtling in either from the gate or from the building's front. That front was shrinking all the time, its columns, openwork, pendants. The "nickelodeon" with its one-two-three gouged out everything, gouged and hurled. Its name, mine-*thrower*, wasn't given it for nothing. At the beginning we were afraid of the flamethrowers. That they could reach us. Through the holes, the open grillwork. The same with the tank. That it could hit us. With one of its volleys. Or set us on fire. The same with the grenades. But after two days we got used to them, knew that they wouldn't thread their way over to us. If only the tank crew wouldn't storm us. If only they wouldn't suddenly hold their guns on us. Scream at us. Order us to come out. And at the same time fire at us. And then drive us in front of them as a shield. Everything at once would have been just too much. But the planes. It was impossible to get used to the planes. The cellar no longer amused us as a novelty, as ruins. Perhaps it might have amused us. But it didn't. Every fifteen to twenty minutes, continuously, they flew over. Dropped their bombs. Flew past again. Dropped their bombs again. Every twenty minutes ten people standing in the doorway. Yes. Half in and half out. I don't remember what was happening with the front then. I remember this. The doorway. Swen's mother leaning her head against the edge of the wall, under the oil painting of Christ. They would fire blindly. They didn't care what they hit, as long as they destroyed everything. So the same ruins were hit for the third time, the fourth time. The ruins were disappearing, like the remains of the openwork screening.

We would get up early, but not to eat, because I think that by then we had already begun to eat only once a day. Towards evening Swen's mother prepared ersatz coffee from what remained of the kasha. For everyone. She would give everyone a cup. Without sugar, of course. How long had we been without sugar? From the very beginning, I think. And three rusks each. Thin ones—bent, broken slices of dried black bread. (Later we had only two each.) That was the most solemn moment. And either before or after it we said the rosary. The day was long. Although I think people say that at the end of August the days get shorter, that couldn't be true. Only sun. Heat. And those bombs. And standing in the doorway. Counting.

"One, two, three, four, five, six, seven, eight, nine, ten, eleven, twelve . . . well . . . a dud . . . oh."

And immediately:

"One, two, three, four, five. . . ." Explosion, thundering, chaos, something is collapsing! We? No. . . . And again:

"One, two, three, four, five, six. . . ."

I was still reading from Titschener. Those 36 or 38 pages. From Freta Street. Did I write anything? Perhaps I was still working away at my huge poem. I remember telling Swen the second or third day on Miodowa, in a relatively quiet moment, that I would like to read it to him.

"Good. You know what, let's go to the third room to take a crap and you'll read it to me."

"But, you know. . . ." I wavered.

"What's the matter?"

"No, not while we're crapping."

"Why?"

"Just because; you go and when you come back we'll go behind the pillar and I'll read it to you."

"Fine."

And I read it to him behind the pillar.

At the same time there was trouble with the water. An unpleasant half-surprise. Miodowa was flowing, flowing, roaring; the moon was shining. But the sun shone too. And those pipes which had been hit were clearly emptying out. It stopped roaring. There was still something flowing. But by the third day the waterfall in the dark room was no longer thundering. At first it still fell in a trickle. Then just barely. Then whatever was left. Just drips. We

121

had to stand there patiently with a bucket. To have a supply for the next day at least. Laundering was over. No more luxury. After three days or two and a half we were already without water.

I took the bucket. I ran out into the courtyard. It was cluttered even more than before with various things. The first time I scooped up some water nearby, in our courtyard I think. But that was also the last time. To get water there. In our whole area, in fact.

By then people were already coming to join us. People. Living there already. That Tuesday. They came over. They came downstairs. Just as we had. They walked in. They stayed.

"May we?"

"Of course."

A whole family. Large. I don't remember from where. An old aunt was with them. She groaned. And immediately lay down on the iron bed. On the springs. And didn't move any more. She spoke through her nose. Indistinctly. She was always complaining. That her whole throat burned from the fire. In fact, she was scorched. Those women, several of them, healthy, bovine women, affirmed it, knew about it, had witnessed it. And yet they shushed her. And repeated,

"She's exaggerating."

Then, when she was groaning during the night, they said to her, "You're exaggerating, Aunt."

"You're exaggerating."

There were other people there too. In the corners near the walls. They came over. They also said,

"She's exaggerating."

"She's exaggerating."

They also came into that first anteroom. And the hall behind ours. The women from that family, since we were sitting in our part and eating only once a day already, would go and cook in the anteroom where Christ was. They had a stove there. Once they walked past carrying some fat dumplings. Freshly steamed. White. Flour dumplings. A heaping bowlful. Fragrant. Sheep dumplings, as I used to say when I was a boy. They walked past us behind the pillars, carrying the dumplings. To their nest. I don't remember anymore where it was exactly. In the corner near the courtyard. Not so much in the corner as near the wall. There were three of them. Behind the woman in the slip with the wounded man in that dark room which was now as dry as tinder. And behind us. After all, I've said that the shelters weren't anyone's private property. Underground Warsaw was communal. Swen recalls this:

"Do you remember how that woman carried those dumplings . . . fffull. . . ?"

Perhaps the woman would have given us her dumplings. If we had asked. But it never entered our heads. And it wouldn't have helped the situation. There were still two rusks for each of us with a drink of coffee from the charred porcelain. And what of it that the women had yelled at their aunt? The others did too. After all, they didn't really yell so very much. Although from Wednesday through Thursday was quite long enough. And in chorus. Loud enough. Until she stopped groaning. I have to admit that. The wounded man on Miodowa, the one with the moustache (it was his own fault), was also left alone. In terror for oneself, out of a fear of sticking one's neck out. What about the news? The news sheets? I think they still reached us somehow. They were gotten hold of. One knew things. That the so-called general situation was worsening. I was about to say that it couldn't get any worse in Starowka. But that's not true. The worsening really had no end. It always turned out that things could be worse. And even worse.

We were awaiting the demolition of the bridges. We were astonished that the bridges were still standing. Red Florian was standing in Praga. With its towers. And the orthodox church, too. With its skyblue cupola. Like fair weather. We were waiting for one more symbolic, evil, pre-ordained piece of news. For the end of the Zygmunt Waza statue on its column. It was still standing. It remained standing for a long time. Until we learned through the news sheets that they had demolished it.

Our kings were not protecting us. Nor were we protecting our kings. Nor what had come after them. Nothing. Nothing.

My Piwna Street! Of the Augustinians. Of vespers. Psalms. And the Seven Plagues. I once went to vespers at the Augustinians. There was a crowd. They were burning incense. There were palms. People were singing. Vespers. Jewish matters in a Gothic church, in the twentieth century, in the language of Kochanowski. And when they got to:

> *Thou art a priest forever*
> *After the order of Melchizedek. . . .*

I was very moved. In those words I could hear, I recalled, the original vespers. That is why I am writing about this. Because it is all intermeshed. Everything. My neighborhood too. Leszno, Chlodna, and Muranow. Because the majority of my churches were there. Then the Jews. And Kochanowski.* And that woman near the pillars.

> *Pray for the peace of Jerusalem:*
> *They shall prosper that love thee. . . .*

It went on that something is "within thy palaces."
Jerusalem in Stare Miasto or Muranow. Then in the ghetto. There was yet another Psalm:

> *Except the Lord build the house, they labor*
> *in vain that build it;*
> *Except the Lord keep the city, the watchman*
> *waketh but in vain.*

And further along . . . I remember only this:

> *But they shall speak with the enemies in the gate.*

Only then did I understand that that refers to a defensive gate, like the one on Podwale or in that classic Roman drama by Shakespeare. People are forced out through such a gate. Other people are pushed through it. I used to think then, in the crowd, beneath the palms, on Leszno and Piwna Streets, on Nowolipki, that it was a gate like the one at 99 Leszno or 37 Poznanska, a gate like so many others. A front gate. An entranceway. With a sign: "Peddlers, singers, musicians and beggars prohibited." With alcoves on the sides and iron Saint Nicholases. In any case, of wrought iron. Grillwork and flowers. And farther on, in the center, in front of the entrance to the first courtyard-well: an oil painting of a sphinx on waterlilies, above the stairwell. Or tiles. With garlands. Festoons.

Well, Our Lady on Piwna Street. Who would have thought then when I was listening to those halls, those gates, that now, running out with a pitcher in search of water on Podwale, I would see "Zion," the second one in ruins, gray, red, "Our house, the house of the Lord"—the second one after Muranow, after the elders who "shall judge the people righteously"—that I would see those Augustinians. Their back. From Podwale. Demolished. No more Seven

Plagues. Palms. Crowds. That singing about Jewish problems. It was sunset. Heat without let-up. And bricks, piles of ruins, gray, ashen, stone upon stone. With windows, ruins, the jangling of my empty bucket and the buckets of other passers-by. I associate it with the sunset. Climbing up Podwale. To the other side. Higher and higher. To mounds of something or other. Nothing specific. It seemed to be Rycerska Street. You could recognize it because it was crooked. It was a red path, at second-story level, made of broken bricks. Or rather buildings. There were so many piled up. I ran up to Rycerska Street. Pitchers were jangling. Empty. No water anywhere. Only people searching. No one found any. Suddenly, I can see: several hundred crooked meters ahead, beyond the rise, the red rise, a woman is running; she's carrying something, in a bucket, a pitcher. I run. I chase her. I see: she's carrying something. No jangling. And she's slightly bent over to one side. I run. I catch up with her. I ask: "Where. . . ."

I don't finish. Because she's looking at me and also into the bucket. I look into the bucket too. Soup. I don't know why, when I told this to friends after the war, I said that the soup was made from berries. Only recently, some twenty years later, have I begun to wonder where those berries could have come from. At the end of August? And at the the end of Starowka? There. At that time? And so many of them. So much soup. Yet I can see it and it's black.

But nothing came of it. I missed the cue. I ran. I ran up. I ran down to something lower. I turned. Piekarska Street? How should I know? Again, people. Buckets. And nothing. Planes. Bombs. There was no sense in thinking about taking shelter. Where? When? Already there were explosions. Bursts. The next ones. And again they're flying over. Diving. Whining. Bombs. The only thing to do was to run even faster. With the buckets. Everyone was running as fast as possible. With buckets. Pitchers. But that didn't help the situation at all. Running without bombs falling was different from running with bombs. They were bombing something close by. Bombing intensively. Dust was rising. Smoke was rising. Reddish-brown, gray, brick-colored things passed by, Pompeis, ashes. And suddenly the news spread that water was spurting up on Szeroki Dunaj. From a pipe. From a bomb. At that very moment. We jangled over there. We all ran. There. To that dust. To Waski Dunaj. Over the mounds. At the corner of Szeroki Dunaj. Everyone ran there at once. And suddenly a miracle: we really could see water spurting up, like a fountain, from a large cracked pipe which was pushed up out of the earth. Joy. A mob. Collecting. Jangling. There was a lot of water all of a sudden, just gushing out. Everyone ran off. I came running back to Miodowa. Happy. With living proof of happiness to show. Mama was delighted. And I was proud. Then night. An uproar. Explosions. Rosaries. The moon on Pac Palace. The frieze. We slept.

In the morning there was movement. A raid. The doorway. And then we noticed that the old aunt was very quiet. That the aunt was not alive.

"She hasn't been alive for some time now."

"Since when?"

They carried her out. The women, that is. The family. Out to the courtyard. But since the bombing was intense they only set her down quickly, practically threw her down at the foot of the stairs. Somewhat to the side. So that she was lying bent over. Her legs spread apart. All day, all night. And longer. Because there really was no time or way to bury her. Not even more or less.

I don't know if it was towards evening of that day or of the preceding day that Celinka, Swen and I were sitting on the two middle steps when we started discussing whether we would survive.

"You know," Celinka smiled, "I have a premonition that I'll survive."

"I do, too," said Swen.

Celinka answered with a smile, "Yes, but my friend said the same thing and she died."

My second foray outside for water. Including a search. This time even more hopeless. Where should I go? Count on a bomb hitting a pipe a second time? People wandered about. Searched. And found nothing. Carrying their buckets.

"There is some! 5 Podwale! At 5 Podwale!"

"Number 5 Podwale, the corner of Kapitulna, a well, wooden, it's been uncovered. . . ."

I ran over. Other people too. Thank God it was near us, although down Kapitulna. I ran a long way. The nearer I got the more people were running with buckets, pitchers. They were even passing us already with full ones.

"Yes. There's water!"

I run in through the gate of number 5. There it is. A crowd. The jangling. A line. A small courtyard. A well. In the courtyard.

Wooden. Green. Moss-covered. Square. Such an old one that no one had known about it. Someone discovered it. Who? There are no people here. The house is barely standing. Partly. But it's absolutely unusable. Which means some small part of it is standing. Perhaps not even burned out. Just something left after the bombs. They were falling all the time. And that something, which I think was an office, was serving as a station for the line. Because there was a line. And it kept growing. No one would give up on water. And so people stood there. Patiently. On the ground floor (it was the ground floor). But never above. It was hot. Daytime. Bright. And we stood there for a long time. Because the well was really old. And it was necessary to lower and draw up, with a stick or a rope, bucket after bucket, one by one. That other place was the office. I looked at what was left of the furniture—a wardrobe. Shoved against a wooden harmonium. Which had been pushed aside. Full of papers. Blank sheets. For writing. I took a pile for myself. That was sheer luxury. The very fact. And the quality. I remember the watermark. SIMON, or something like that, I think. I didn't have any paper, so I was very happy. And I waited. For my turn. An hour. Two. I think two. There may have been something else besides the wardrobe. Debris. Nothing else. Ruins, of course, plaster and laths, bricks, openings without door or window. You walked out to the well through such an opening when your turn came. Because it did come, finally. Mine. I lowered the bucket. I drew it up. Someone even helped me. He knew how. And I ran with the water and the paper to my people. To my ruins.

The night was moonlit, no doubt. With the frieze across from us. And something pounding (that tank, all the time). And the hideous heat. The heat from the fire. We were probably eating one and a half rusks each for an entire day.

Those days on Miodowa Street were spent entirely under bombardment. From morning to night. All that time spent standing in the doorway. With a view of two stories of ruins. There were no superstructures in this place. None. Only the doorway. Actually, I've exaggerated about the superstructure. Precisely on August 31, as we learned immediately, the "Chrobry" Battalion, over 200 people, returned from action. To their quarters. To the cellar in the Simons Passage (on Nalewki, near the Krasinski Gardens, called The Heroes of the Ghetto today). They all collapsed onto their field beds and planks. That is, they didn't so much collapse as barely make the motions of pulling back blankets in order to lie down when, already, the explosion had occurred. Only four or five of them survived. Even though they survived, they had no idea when, what, how. Just that suddenly there were bombs and firing. I spoke with them, with those who survived—three or four men and (I think) one woman. In 1946. In September. At that time, from the Saxon Gardens to Zoliborz, Warsaw was a desert. Actually, from Aleje Jerozolimskie to Zoliborz. I was a journalist. I was writing about the exhumations. People testified that here and there there was this and that. And then there was the question of identification. The list of those identified. It was the same in this case. But those few survivors began the exhumation on their own initiative. Several workers did the digging. There was a basin, a large tin basin, for heads, arms, legs. But it wasn't easy to recognize what was whose. I remember this:

"Is this Zdzis's leg? Or maybe it's Rysiek's?"

And it was thrown into a basin which had held carbide.

Don't be surprised. That was common then. A fire was burning. Near the Gardens. The first frosts had set in. But they gave up digging further. Because that Passage was one tangle, a heap of ruins, a strong fused entanglement, with iron rails protruding. The house had been big and strong. And when it (along with the rest of the ruins) collapsed, it caved in. So much for that. Then they took it apart. That was proper. They dug them out. They buried them. But did they identify them? I don't know. That's all.

On the first of September in that famous year it was also splendid summer weather. Also a Friday. Five years earlier (but they included two leap years)—and so history made a complete circle. I remember thinking that to myself at the time.

Now I think that the words about how "the enemy attacked Poland from out of the high sky" are well chosen. Because it was fair weather and in fair weather the sky is high. And the planes are, too. But in 1944 the enemy attacked from a low, roof-level sky.

We didn't know yet in the morning that that first day of September would be historic. At dawn, in fact. I think that day began very early. The planes rose with the sun. At five a.m. bombs were already falling, further destroying what remained above our heads. And people were already dying. Some from cave-ins. They were also dying at night. But from other causes.

Well, on September 1, early in the morning, Swen's mother announced to us that we had nothing to eat. I say "us" because the whole cellar was already on its feet. Each said what he had to say.

After standing in the doorway for a while Swen and I probably decided to go outside. To search. For food. How?

"Maybe something will turn up somewhere. . . ."

"If not, we'll have to steal."

"Yes, we'll have to steal," we told each other out loud.

And we went out on the steps and after estimating the heat and the danger we went into the courtyard. We stood awhile beside the door, above the spread-eagled, half-sitting corpse of the old aunt. What instinct? We stood there and looked at her. She had a ring on her finger. Only after the war did we each confess to the other that we had thought about the ring. But whether or not the ring would have been useful then is an open question. It wasn't money alone that was useless.

I must confess that for a long time I hadn't liked the first day of September. Perhaps school was the real reason but a person convinces himself that he's had presentiments. Or perhaps that date had had something disquieting about it for a long time. It certainly must have.

And then, on that day, besides the need to look for food, something else drove us out. After standing for a long time over the women's aunt we began to crawl through the passageways, the courtyards of Miodowa, in the direction of Krasinski Place. And it became immediately apparent that we weren't the only ones wandering about. That there was unrest. That it was the end. Stare Miasto was defending itself with its last ounce of strength. But there were fewer and fewer people. And nothing to eat. The partisans didn't have anything either. And an attack was in progress. From several directions. Explosions. Shooting. Cave-ins into the last remaining cellars. The sun rose higher in the sky. The heat increased. People were walking in circles. Civilians as well as partisans. Helplessness. I don't know when people began saying that the Germans were already on Freta. And that Starowka had capitulated.

I think we returned to our cellar. Something was being talked about there, discussed. But what? Mainly it was the fact that at some point the Germans would break into the cellar and begin throwing grenades. Again, those pillars. I thought, if only I could be behind a pillar. But would that have any effect? In fact, did our talking, our deliberating have any meaning? Heat, noise, chaos, counsels, smoke (the fires kept on burning and burning), embers and ever greater uneasiness. We went outside once more. The two of us. The rest stayed there. Zbyszek too. I don't remember exactly what happened between the time we walked away from the old aunt to the time we heard the first piece of news. And what happened between the first piece of news (the Germans on Freta) and our meeting our mutual acquaintance, Henio. Henio was wearing the uniform of a partisan—German cast-aways, in other words; a tankist's suit, I think.

"I'm an orderly," he said. And we sat down in Fuchs' courtyard, I think, in the building behind the Basilians. On a step near the wall, maybe only under the wall, perhaps on the ruins of something like an entrance covered by a roof.

"Listen," said Henio, "we're retreating today through the sewers. The severely wounded are being left behind, but the lieutenant has a favorite who's seriously wounded, and we have to transport him. Will you agree to go?"

"Yes!"

"You can both go because I can say you'll have to take turns carrying him since he has to be carried on your backs."

Swen's leg was always painful. His knee.

"That's nothing, I'll be the one to carry him," I said, "and you'll help me a little."

"But listen, there are three of us," Swen answered Henio.

"Three? That's not so good."

"My cousin, we can't leave him."

"It can't be done."

"Well, that's too bad," I replied. (How easy it was to give someone up!)

But Swen was firm.

"No, we won't go without Zbyszek."

Henio began to relent.

"Well, it doesn't depend on me, because if it did . . . but perhaps I'll try to explain . . . or I can simply mention two and the third will join up, or never mind, the three of you come, to Dluga Street" (I think he gave an address), "to the left of Krasinski Place. There's a hospital there. And that wounded man. That's the assembly point. The Germans are taking Stare Miasto but there'll be a defense. The manhole is on Krasinski Place. Don't take anything with you. They won't let you through the manhole with any objects. A bit of bread at the most."

We didn't dare believe in those sewers yet. That was our dream. To get through to Srodmiescie. The legend of the sewers, of entering with passes obtained through friendships and only in

130

the highest circles, had made its impression. But it didn't frighten us at all that it might be dreadful in the sewers, that people drowned down there, that they lost their way, that from Mokotow to Dolny you went on your knees because it was three feet high, that some of the manholes were held by the Germans and kept open, that the Germans tossed grenades inside. . . . We just wanted to get away from here! Only the women would remain, and they always have it easier.

"You'll have to dress the wounded man"(here he gave us his pseudonym), "you'll have to pretend that he's only slightly wounded, because otherwise they won't let him into the sewer. Well, at . . . o'clock" (Henio named the hour, 2 p.m. I think), "be here . . . so long. . . ."

Or perhaps he didn't tell us the hour, since no one had a watch; maybe he just said "in an hour"—yes, that's more likely.

I remember that we ran back to our people. That we rushed in with a great deal of noise. Aunt Uff. was happy that Zbyszek could go too. Zbyszek was also happy. And Swen's mother. For us. Although it was hard for Swen's mother, Aunt Uff., Celinka, Lusia and Mrs. R. to part with us. Especially for Swen's mother. And for Aunt. And even more so because it was for the unknown. Danka, Aunt Uff.'s daughter, lived in Srodmiescie, on Zurawia Street. So Zbyszek and Swen had Danka there, and I had Father and Zocha. And above all, we had Halina.

I think we already knew that we would exit at the corner of Nowy Swiat and Warecka. So Father, Zocha and Halina would be closest. Because they were at 32 Chmielna. Between Bracka and Marszalkowska. So we'd go to them. All three of us. Directly.

After those hopeless hours our excitement about the sewers was so great that the raids, the shelling which must have been even heavier on that last day (although any scale of measurement had long been exceeded) had no effect on us. A so-called final attack had its specific characteristics, which were familiar to me from Wola. But here was an antidote: the sewers.

Anyway, it was a historic day. The fall of Starowka. Starowka was already famous throughout Poland. In the camps too. And in England. And the sewers, the Starowka sewers, were famous. Warsaw already knew that it was a historic day. But the knowledge wasn't so very wonderful.

Our haste was communicated to the others too. Especially to Swen's mother and Aunt Uff. Or rather, to the two mothers.

"Coming, coming; wait a moment!"

"I'm coming, just. . . ."

Did we take anything? No, I think not. But during this time, from what must have been the very last supplies, they had hastily fried up two pancakes for each of us for our journey. On tin plates. The kind that people cooked on then. No, not on tin plates. Excuse me. I forgot. On those three bricks behind the pillar. We found out about it only when we were saying goodbye. They stuffed them into our pockets. We didn't want them. Because we were going to Srodmiescie. And we were taking their last supplies. But they didn't want to listen.

The women all said goodbye to us rather strangely. Swen's mother and Zbyszek's mother made the sign of the cross on each of our foreheads in turn and kissed us. That was probably the most moving farewell of my life. They cried. In fact, Zbyszek's mother never saw him again after that. He's living in England. But. . . . His wife (he got married) sends letters. For him. So he's alive? It seems so. But why should it be like that?

We left the cellar. 14 Miodowa. By the rear. On the right side. To Krasinski Place. You got there by going along Miodowa. Past the barricade. Into Dluga Street. We could make out the assembly point just past a throng of people who were already waiting under the walls.

That house is standing today. Again. The first one down from the corner. I think it had a gate with a niche then. Or does it only seem that way to me? The most amazing thing is that the house was still standing then. Still standing. At least, in part. It was like a beehive inside. It was really swarming. And I think I'm not imagining that it was like that on the upper floors too. On the ground floor and the first, at least. After all, I think we went up the stairs. Yes, right up to the first floor. Henio showed us. Where to go. To wait. What to do. It was amazing that we found each other. Don't think there weren't any civilians there. A crowd of partisans and a crowd of civilians. Running up and down the stairs. No one paid any attention to the bombs. It turned out that the sewers had the same effect on everyone. It was a good thing that a bomb didn't hit us. But none did. We had to hurry. Every hour counted. The offensive was gaining strength. The defense was costly. And since in general the seriously wounded and all civilians were being left behind the rest had to manage to retreat at least, the last ones being those engaged in the defense, who now had to defend only the manhole and themselves. But for the time being there were many, many who were still waiting. In addition, I noticed, there was more than one seriously wounded person. And a crowd of civilians, like us, attached to them. To help out or simply because they knew someone. And all this prolonged the retreat. But the plan was adhered to at all costs. Order. Therefore, there was no room for fear.

We rushed after Henio into a hall which was crowded and noisy with conversations. With movement, above all. With people too. And with plank beds. Stacked up. And with various other things. Stretchers were being made up. Something—was it knapsacks?—was being stacked against the wall. It was forbidden to take knapsacks. So whatever it was must have been something much smaller and more essential.

People were sitting, lying down, dressing themselves and being dressed by others on the plank beds. Partisans, couriers, nurse's aides. And, no doubt, their families. Extras. There was madness in all this method. Chaos with haste. But above all, the main issue was maintaining order during the retreat. Our wounded man was lying on a plank bed on the ground floor. I don't remember if I dressed him or if the partisan women had already done that; I remember that I had to put shoes on his feet. And to tie them. Just getting this done took forever. My wounded man was thin, very young. He had been shot in nine places. I thought it would be hard to pretend that he was all right. He was half conscious. He was groaning. Everything hurt him. And it wasn't surprising. When I began putting on his shoe he groaned, writhed, pulled back his leg. I said something. I cajoled him. I waited a bit. And I tried again. I don't know what was happening outside. In the sky and in the city, that is. Lieutenant Radoslaw* (not the famous one) rushed past a couple of times. Blonde. Over thirty. He introduced himself to us. Also hastily. He was worried about getting shoes on the wounded man. And even more about the sewer. Henio came by a couple of times. And a nurse. A colleague of his. And of the wounded man. From the same division. She looked at my work. I was already beginning to pull on one shoe. I don't know when I finally pulled it all the way on. I think she helped me at one moment. There was some flexibility in our group's schedule. I'm not sure, though. Perhaps it actually depended on packing. And on putting on shoes. Even so, people were entering the sewer nonstop. Finally we got the shoes on him. But then the lacing turned out to be just as

133

difficult. Because his feet had also been shot up. Some people had watches, though. I exaggerated when I said no one did. Putting on his shoes and lacing them apparently took two hours. Maybe a little less. But not much. We were in that hall a very long time. Then we were about to leave. But still we waited. For a signal. I remember a lot of coming and going, bustling about, carrying things out, yells, commands.

Finally it was our turn. I took the wounded man on my back. He was light. But he hurt all over. He tried to help me. And himself. As much as he could. At the beginning, for entering the manhole, he even had the idea of being helped to walk. So I walked next to the wounded man and Zbyszek, Swen, Radoslaw, Henio and the nurse, carrying a haversack, followed. And their men walked behind them. But I only remember those who walked nearest me. Swen walked behind me, Zbyszek behind Swen. Henio behind Zbyszek, I think. The nurse in front of me. Or perhaps Henio was in front of her. And Radoslaw ahead of them.

We walked quickly down the stairs. Straight to the gate. I remember that from the gate we squeezed through into an alcove. And there we waited. Then a bit farther, but still near the gate. I remember that the wall of the house and the gate were yellow. And that there was a dreadful fire across the way. And not just in one place. Flames several stories high. And smoke. It stung our eyes. Blinded us. The sun was shining through the smoke. I think that there were a great many civilians in front of us and behind us. Not only young men. Old men too. And old women. Someone was sitting in line, in a folding chair. The line was very crooked. Because of the alcove. And we had to be right up against the wall. Because as we came closer to the street we suddenly began to be afraid. I don't remember if there were planes. Most likely there were. And we could only flatten ourselves. Against the wall. They were bombing and setting fires. I remember the shells. They were flying in from Krakowskie Przedmiescie and Bonifraterska. From the Vistula too, no doubt. And from Przejazd. We could sense that they were aiming at the line to the manhole and at the manhole itself.

We moved up. From the gate. Right into the street. Next to the wall. Here we moved a bit more quickly. And we could already see people breaking away from the wall at the corner and crawling along the pavement to the manhole. But the manhole had to be approached from the other side of the square. Opposite the left tower of the church on Garnizonowa.

There was time for thinking—the emotional sort. No, don't think. Despite everyting.

"God," I thought to myself, "they're back there on Miodowa —and how they made the sign of the cross when we said good-bye. . . ."

Again we moved up a bit. Along the wall. It was getting more and more dangerous.

"Oh," I thought to myself, "Halina, Father, Zocha are over there. In Srodmiescie."

Srodmiescie! I had arranged to meet Halina at seven. On August 1. I would be there September 1. Also at seven. Since it was afternoon, I figured I would be there in two hours. "And what about Mama? Where is my mother? Is she alive? I still have the keys. Did she get back to the apartment before they drove her out? How is Nanka? Sabina? Aunt Jozia? Stefa?"

Again we move a little way along the wall. Shells were landing. And those fires. Along the other side of Dluga. Here. A fresh one. On Garnizonowa too, I think. 13 or 15 Dluga. Live flame. And yet the sun is shining here. Through the smoke. And flames. It's stinging. Everything.

"And I," I thought, more or less in these words, "who used to read Victor Hugo's Jean Valjean* with Mama long ago in peace-time—Jean Valjean who walked through the sewers of Paris with a wounded man on his shoulders—now I will enter the sewers of Warsaw in a minute or two, with a wounded man on my back. Who could have imagined it?"

But Srodmiescie was far away. Perhaps it's hard to understand this today. Nowy Swiat—Krasinski Place. Both are in Srodmiescie. They're not so far apart. But they were terribly distant. No nearer, I tell you, than, for me, from Warsaw to Paris after the War. In general, the two places weren't thought of as being in any way connected.

It was five in the afternoon when we broke away from the corner of the wall on Dluga and the wall on Krasinski Place and immediately started crawling. Faster and faster. Because the shells were falling without mercy. On us. On the entrance. The Miodowa barricade was fine. But the barricade across Krasinski Place, from Bonifraterska, was low—no higher than our waists. Made of gray paper sacks which were filled with something. Cement, most likely. And that barricade was important. Our defense. We were crawling

135

beneath it. I was dragging the wounded man along the ground. With all my strength. Quickly. Quickly.

In the sunlight, across from the fire, from the flames which were several stories high, was the manhole. Someone was half squatting, half standing over the manhole. One or two people. And directing the traffic. Without pity he tore the bundles and knapsacks from people's backs and flung them aside onto a heap; they piled up. Everything moved like lightning here. The shells were striking noticeably at the manhole itself. From two sides. The fire was raging. And engulfing things. We crawled along. Using all the strength we had. In front of us, behind us too, was an unbroken line. The manhole wasn't big. The cover was thrown to one side. No one explained to anyone else what to do or how. I flung my wounded man over my back. No. He was handed to me somehow, I think. No. I don't remember. With him, perhaps. Into that opening. The last view. The church on Garnizonowa. Burning. Smoke. Sun. Shells. And metal footrests. One foot. The other. Lower all the time. It was deep. It wasn't hard at all. A number of those footrests. It widened out at the bottom. Like a bell. And we were completely underground. Noise. We set off at once. To the right. We'd rolled up our trousers before on Dluga. We waded into something. Water halfway up our calves. We began to walk. In the water. Step after step:

squish . . . squish . . . squishhh. . . .

The first thing that startled me was the peace. Quiet. A humming sound. Those steps. A light. A candle could be seen far ahead of us. Our nurse was also carrying a candle. Peace. After that hell. Relief. Extraordinary relief. The wounded man didn't weigh me down at all. I rested a bit from the effort. He was passive. Joy, almost. After that hell above. The bombs, the shells . . . far away. All that could be heard was:

ooooo . . . ooooo . . . ooooo . . . ooooo . . .

drawn out, terribly drawn out, hollow . . . oooo . . . oooo . . . that was the bombs and the shells; completely distant, indifferent, and their echo carried, carried.

I think we turned into Miodowa Street right away. A whisper. One man to the next:

"We're walking beneath Miodowa."

"We're walking beneath Miodowa."

"We're walking beneath Miodowa."

And the whisper, too, could be heard in echoes, drawn out,

as in a seashell. No. As in a well. That's not quite right either. Because it wasn't just a well without a bottom. But something without beginning or end. And unmeasured. Because it branched. After all, there were as many sewers as there were streets. Another city. A third Warsaw, counting from the top. The first was the one right on the surface. The city of passages through halls and courtyards. The second was the city of the shelters. With a system of underground passageways. And beneath that underground city was this underground city. With traffic. Rules. Signs. At each fork, over the entrance into the sewer proper, or the Stare Miasto-Srodmiescie pedestrian artery, was an arrow and the sign "THIS WAY" in chalk on the bricks.

What do sewers look like? Different in different places. Always shored up with bricks in their entirety. And they always have rounded ceilings and rounded floors. Or, rather, oval. In general, they appear to be cross-sections or, rather, to be seen in perspective, because their cross-section can be seen into infinity. Oval-shaped. More or less oval. I say more or less, because right under Miodowa the sewer was large and had benches (concrete, I think) on both sides. We walked behind a candle. The nurse was carrying it. And ahead of us someone else was also carrying a candle. And someone even further forward, I think. So things could be seen. Naturally, not clearly. The walls glowed. Glimmered. In a slippery way. Because here everything was slippery. We had rolled up our trouser legs. To our knees. But we were wearing shoes. The water was always halfway up our calves. I don't remember if it stank. Or steamed. I don't even know what was in it. Probably various things. It seems we passed two corpses. Exactly twice, I think, something got tangled under my feet. But generally one didn't feel anything but

slosh . . . slosh . . . slosh. . . .

and relief. That we were on our way to Srodmiescie. It must have been an absolute hell in Stare Miasto if our eyes and noses were so deadened.

Just recently someone asked me where the sewage was coming from then. Why was it still flowing?

I don't know.

Those concrete benches may have been for the workers to have something to walk on. After all, normally the sewage flows higher and more rapidly.

No one thought about that then. Benches are benches. Suddenly

I noticed a discarded knapsack on the benches. Then, further on, a jar of lard. Then again a knapsack. Or a blanket. I recall, to myself at any rate, that I was carrying the wounded man. It was wide and high under Miodowa. So I was carrying him normally. We walked on and on under Miodowa. And it was shimmering. From those candles. And the people. And the thundering:

oooo . . . oooo . . . oooo. . . .

So that I grew tired from carrying him.

"Zbyszek," I turned only my head because we were walking, "could you take him now?"

"Sure."

Swen slowed down. Zbyszek passed him. He came up to me. And took him. I was free. I felt comfortable. As I rarely did.

I don't remember if this was first:

"Attention! Put out your lights, a manhole is open."

"Attention! We're slowing down, we're passing under an open manhole."

"Attention . . . put out your lights . . . absolute silence . . . the Germans are overhead. . . ."

Or perhaps the light from opposite us was first. From afar. But moving. In our direction. So that we became uneasy, I think. Perhaps we even asked:

"What's that?"

We, those uniniated people. Someone, a few people ahead of us, whispered immediately:

"A courier."

"It's nothing, nothing," we passed it on, "a courier. . . ."

"Aha—a courier."

"A courier."

"Attention . . . at-ten-tion. . . ."

The light suddenly came closer, moving quickly, the splashing was also rapid.

"Attention, attention. . . ." It was the courier.

She passed us with her candle.

Then again, "Attention, a manhole, we don't know if it's open."

"Attention, a manhole. . . ."

I remember that one of them wasn't open. But we passed by more slowly, more quietly. At each one. During that month we had grown only too accustomed to silences, to the phrase, "the Germans are listening," and to pretending that suddenly we weren't there.

I don't remember any longer those columns of light under the open manhole. Or perhaps I do remember. From far off they were like candles. The same effect. Something shining. Then again, something beginning to shine. It passed. In our direction.

"Attention . . . attention. . . ."

This time it was a boy, I think. That girl courier passed us several times. Once, two people. Once, I think, even more.

We were amazed that it was still Miodowa. There was no fear of getting lost. Because there were lights and arrows. And people who knew the way. And the fact that there was no end to us. Ahead. And to the rear. At the corner of Nowy Swiat and Warecka people had been exiting and exiting for a long time already. But they were still entering continuously on Krasinski Place. And for a long time they would continue to enter. We had hit upon a good time. Teik retreated with the last forces, at night already. They had to walk more quickly and in the dark. And they got lost. The Germans threw grenades in after them. From above. There was a panic. In the end they made it and got out. But not all of them.

I picked up the wounded man once more. He was already tired and feverish. He wanted something to drink. He hurt all over. He was groaning. I comforted him. But what good did that do? He wanted something to drink. And nobody had any water. Not a drop. Nor was there any medicine for the pain. We had to carry him. Which means he had to be touched in many places. And he had to hold me around my neck. I held his legs with my hands.

After a long time the word started filtering back that we were turning into Krakowskie Przedmiescie. And that it wouldn't be as high or wide there. That is, that it wouldn't be possible to walk as freely. That was especially distressing for me and for anyone who was carrying a wounded man. You became about a head taller. But after all, I wasn't so very tall to start with.

We were all curious about this fork. This turn. This news.

"Krakowskie Przedmiescie!"

"Krakowskie Przedmiescie!"

"Krakowskie Przedmiescie!"

Perhaps the first open manhole was really over here. Because Krakowskie Przedmiescie was held by the Germans. But Miodowa too, from Krakowskie Przedmiescie to Kozia, was also theirs, I think, because they used to ride right up to the barricade near the Capuchins. And also because they were occupying that seven-story building on the corner of Kozia.

Finally, we're there. At the fork. The important one. We turn right. The sewer becomes different immediately. Smaller. And oval-shaped. Without any benches. We all had to stoop a little. But it wasn't too bad. That is, we were definitely hunched over. I don't remember any more just how much. Even before that the wounded man was beginning to weigh me down. Once again I took a break and gave him to someone else. To Zbyszek. Or to some other person. From Henio's section. Then I took the wounded man back. I held him by his knees, lower down. And he held his head lower. And he didn't stick up at all. Because his head didn't want to stay up very straight. It kept flopping over. Until it fell. Onto the back of my head.

"Water . . ." he groaned.

"But there isn't any water, there's nothing we can do, just a little longer, we'll get there soon. . . ." That was me, trying to comfort him.

But he kept groaning. "Water . . . water. . . ."

Again I explained it to him. A moment later he called out again, "Water . . . I can't stand it. . . ."

"We'll be there soon, we'll be there soon. . . ."

He began slipping even lower; his head bounded downwards and sideways. There was one stop when I wanted (I don't know if it was a manhole or if we had to slow down, or someone was passing us and it was more crowded so we had to stop)—anyway, I wanted to prop myself up a bit with my hand against the wall. I leaned on it. With my palm. And my palm slid downwards along the thick green ooze. It didn't even give way. I knew, after all, that it was half round and yet I was astonished that it was so thickly covered with . . . whatever it was. Because I think practically my whole fist slid into it. And slid down. With the slime. "So there's no way to lean," I thought, because for some reason I was still protecting my clothing. Oh naivete!

We moved on.

splash—splash—splash

ooooo—we could hear the uprising overhead once more—ooooo . . . ooooo . . . ooo. . . .

"Water. . . ."

"But it won't be long now . . . not long. . . ."

"Water. . . . Give me some water from the sewer. . . ."

"No!"

"Give me . . . give me that water . . . from the sewer. . . ."

"No, no, no. . . ."

The nurse ahead of me heard him; she also cried out, "No, no!"

"Give me. . . ."

He wanted to slip down even lower but he couldn't manage to.

"What should I do with him? What should I do?" I was getting desperate.

"Just a minute." The nurse opened her haversack. "I'll give him a sugar cube. I've got some with me."

"Oh, that's great," I said, "and that's supposed to quench his thirst?"

"Yes, sugar helps, it does," and she gave it to him; "there, that's sugar, take it."

"Good. . . ." He opened his mouth; she put the cube inside.

We walked on. For the time being there was some peace with him.

We walked for a long time. Under Krakowskie Przedmiescie. Forks. . . . The names of the streets in chalk, arrows: "THIS WAY!" People passing. Standing still.

"Attention! Attention! Attention! Manholes!"

"Silence! Put out your lights!" And again we slowed our steps.

Reverberations from the bombs, the shells, from whatever, every so often, without a stop:

ooooo . . . oooo . . . oooo . . . oooooooooo. . . .

Someone (a civilian) took the wounded man from me once more. Suddenly:

"Nowy Swiat!"

"Nowy Swiat!"

"Nowy Swiat!"

"It won't be long now. . . ."

"Nowy Swiat! We'll soon be coming out, onto the corner of Warecka!"

"Nowy Swiat! The last stretch now, exit onto Warecka!"

I don't remember now if there was anything different about Nowy Swiat. Perhaps it was even a little smaller. Or maybe not. Perhaps not. There definitely was a fork. We were definitely exhausted by then. And impatient. Although it was comforting that

141

we had made it. Without grenades. And that we were walking under our own territory. I don't remember in what words that was expressed. Towards the rear, behind me. But it was very much to the point.

I don't think anyone told us the time yet. What time it was. I don't know if that was deliberate. Because they did later. Shortly afterwards. Near the exit. Not that they made an announcement. But the time was mentioned. Perhaps it only seems to me that we didn't talk about it since we'd been walking for so long. Or maybe not. The fact is that on the whole everyone was disoriented and even had we not been disoriented it would have been hard to believe that several hours had passed already. I know for a fact that before we reached the exit there was great excitement. Because it was ten o'clock. Or even past ten. At night. Even perhaps half past ten. Yes. Definitely. No earlier. Because someone said that we'd been walking for five hours. And after all, we'd entered the sewer at five o'clock. There was sunshine. Heat.

I know that I took the wounded man back from Zbyszek or the other person onto my own back. He was at the end of his rope and I don't remember anymore if he was groaning without a stop. Or if he was already quiet. And utterly indifferent. Maybe both. By turns.

At one moment the cry went up:

"Stand still! Stand still! Stand still! We'll be exiting in order. Pass it on!"

"Stand still! Stand still! Stand still! Pass it on!"

"Stand still! We'll be exiting in order. . . ."

We stood still. We chatted with Henio and the nurse. Radoslaw told us, "The entire 'Parasol' group is exiting ahead of us. Two hundred people."

We stood there. Rather far from the manhole. People were exiting, but we couldn't see anything. Or even hear anything. Because we ourselves were chattering. As were the people in back of us. After all, we were still too far from the head of the line. It dragged on and on. The wounded man was groaning. He lost consciousness. By now, it was hard for me too. Difficult. What did my clothing matter now? I leaned against the wall together with him, just as I was. It didn't make any difference to him. Or to me, either. But since the wall was rounded, concave, I bent into a convex shape. I felt as if I were sucked in. There was no talk about cold that summer. The dampness—that was a trifle. And the ooze—

that was also the same by then. It was a good thing that I didn't slide all the way down. The wounded man hung across me. And kept on groaning. I hunched over too. Other people stood about, facing each other, back to back, side by side, in groups; I think several others also leaned. Perhaps once we slid forward several steps. Certainly. Once. And again. Because a commotion, a tumult could already be heard from up ahead, people figuring out (as it turned out) some technical-equipment problems.

Henio or the nurse confided to us in a whisper, "They have a large number of wounded . . . that's why it's taking them so long . . . because they're carrying them on stretchers."

So that's what it was all about. A lot of wounded. Only now did they stop concealing it. So mine was not an exception.

Everyone felt guilty about those left behind. Not so much about the civilians. Obviously, the young men posed a special problem. But the partisans? The seriously wounded? Much worse. Because they wore uniforms. And were there en masse. And were helpless. What would happen to them? We deceived ourselves that . . . yes, somehow, anyway. . . . And then it turned out. What. How. Horrible. Others have described it already. I shan't repeat it. Only to say that what happened in Wola happened again.

We stood there for a long time. Getting closer and closer to the exit and the uproar. We could already see something. Movement upwards. But I was still leaning against the green wall all the time with the wounded man. Now I didn't care at all in how many places my jacket would have to be cleaned. Not at all; if only I didn't slip down the wall.

All told, we spent approximately two hours standing beneath that manhole. Then, once it was the turn of the healthy, those from 'Parasol' and the others who were ahead of us, it went quickly. Expeditiously. We were even driven out. After all, there were those others behind us. And the people behind us were stretched out to Krasinski Place. The entire sewer was jammed with people.

Unexpectedly they started screaming.

"Move out, move out, forward!"

"Get out, it's our turn!"

"Attention! Now it's our turn! Get out, get out!"

"Attention! It's our turn now!"

I remember that at first they pulled up, pushed up a stretcher, I think, with something on it or someone. Then Radoslaw. Then Henio. Then the nurse. Then me. Up the footholds. I ordered the wounded man to hold tight. With his arms and legs. I grabbed onto that spiral. Higher and higher. Maybe someone pushed me. Zbyszek or the other helper. Swen and the others came out behind me. I know that at one point I caught the smell of fresh air. Of night. I noticed the stars. And someone quickly grabbed me by the arms.

"No, no, I'll do it myself!"

"You have no strength left. . . ."

I didn't. I submitted. They pulled me out to the surface. I don't know when. Quickly. Houses. A barricade. Srodmiescie. Consciousness. Odors. Dizziness. The wounded man. Mine. He was already on a stretcher. Two women were walking off with him. Nurses from Srodmiescie. Toward Warecka.

"I'll carry him." I grabbed at the stretcher.

"No. That's our responsibility now." That's literally how they answered me. And they were off. The stretcher creaked. Swayed. I walked after them for a moment. Swen was behind me. And Zbyszek. Many stretchers were being carried. Ahead of us. And no doubt behind us too. I don't know what happened to Henio. I only remember myself. It was quiet. For the most part. The barricades. Narrow Warecka Street. I walked. We walked. Exhausted. Emotionally drained.

Houses? In one piece?! Halina! Father! Srodmiescie! Ohhh!

We entered number 12. By chance. A large courtyard. There was sky here. And stars, I think. Distinct. We sat down on a step. Let water pour from a spout. We straightened ourselves out. I rolled down my trouser legs. All in good faith. And a little for convenience. Srodmiescie. Still standing. Living buildings with living people. Not burning. There is even silence. Maybe some noise. But compared with what I remembered it was completely silent. Halina! Father! Sky. Air. Night.

"Let's go." We jumped up, one-two-three. The gate. Warecka. The square. Szpitalna. Familiar. So familiar. Indeed. We walked quickly and freely.

A corner.

Chmielna. Everything is standing.

We make a turn.

Into Marszalkowska.

The only thing is that it's dark. Barricades. That atmosphere. But otherwise it's normal. Houses. Night. Peace. Midnight. Summer. Warm.

Everything is there.

32 Chmielna.

"It's standing!"

We go inside. The gate. The courtyard. We drop in at the janitor's.

"Is Mrs. Rybinska at home? She is? Yes?"

"They're there; they're there. . . ."

"In which cellar?" we ask.

"Cellar?" the janitor is surprised. "They're upstairs in their apartment. They're sleeping."

That was a shock.

"Upstairs?"

"Yes. . . . In their apartment."

We thank him . . . start upstairs. . . .

"Are you gentlemen from Starowka?"

"Yes, straight from the sewer."

The janitor ran into the center of the courtyard and shouted at the windows:

"Mr. Bialoszewskiiiii! Mr. Bialoszewskiiiiii! You son's come back from Starowka!"

Father shouted something back from the third floor. There was a commotion. Immediately. Thudding on the stairs.

We also ran up the stairs. Quick as we could. I think it was on the second floor that we ran into Father. I noticed an open door one flight up. And Zocha running out onto the stairs.

"Miron! Swen!"

"This is Swen's cousin," I introduced Zbyszek. "He's come here for the time being . . . from Starowka . . . through the sewers. . . ."

"Of course, come in, come in. . . ."

They lead us in, sit down, draw up some stools, chairs.

"I'll make something to eat in a minute; do you want to wash up? You can't imagine what you look like!"

Stacha, Halina's mother, and Halina awaken. In beds. We rush over to them. In the dark I bend over Halina. I am the one from the sewers; she is the one under the quilt, clean. I kiss her.

"We were supposed to see each other August 1," I say. "Well, it's exactly one month later."

Halina is sleepy; she looks around.

"My God, you look awful, your hair is glued down. Zocha, he's got to change his clothing. Swen, you look awful!"

Each of us was given a change of clothing. I think we undressed

145

on the staircase. Then we took turns washing up in the anteroom. There was bustling, fussing, rising, chatting, boiling water, food. Everything hastily.

At that moment we were happy. We talked without interruption. Together. All three of us. They too.

It took us two hours to wash. However, I think we ate something first. Then to the basins. Hot water. Our hair took the longest time. It didn't want to come unstuck. They helped us.

"Throw your clothing into the fire."

"Yes, right into the fire," Zocha and Father decided for me. And flung it towards the kitchen. My shoes too. Everything I had on. Then mainly eating. Then bedding was laid out. After all, it was a big change for such a small apartment. Still more talk. . . . And suddenly we fell asleep.

We awoke in the morning. Hungry. Halina was already preparing three bowls of macaroni with lard for us. She served it. We ate.

"I'll prepare something else for you right away. Zenek is at the Home Army. Downtown. Zocha's at the barracks. She's in charge of the kitchen." (Zenek is my father.)

Again we ate something. Full bowls. With lard. There was a noise. The janitor? Sweeping up? We look out the window. Yes.

Halina cooked and served us something again. Every hour, every hour and a half. Only now was Stare Miasto beginning to show itself.

For the time being neither Starowka, nor the sewers, nor Srodmiescie seemed real. Nothing did. Everything was unreal. All we wanted was to eat. Various surprises. Halina. Ourselves. And that feeling of peace and happiness. If only for an hour. But perhaps it would last till the end of the day. And through the night. Until morning.

I don't remember if anything happened. I think it was then, on the first day, that Halina said at one point, "We'd better go down to the cellar."

But it wasn't anything terrifying. And it didn't last long. It was summer all the time, hot. September 2. Saturday. Like five years before. In 1939. The artillery in the afternoon. Halina explained,

"They begin around this time. We know what streets because they have them under cover. Now it's Zlota and Zgoda. Over there, beyond Marszalkowska, they're worse off."

I think it was that first day already that Halina and I decided to continue our French studies. Halina pulled out Gide's *Symphonie pastorale*. In French. We read through the entire first page with enthusiasm. Which wasn't easy. Because it was dense. And we had to check many words in the dictionary. And even so we couldn't find the right meaning every time.

Father said that here in Srodmiescie you absolutely had to know the slogans and passwords which were changed every day. For protection against the "pigeon fanciers." They checked papers in the evening after dark. There was a curfew. They had so-called detention of pedestrians. For public works. For digging, soldering, barricades. The headquarters of the People's Army was here, on the corner of Swietokrzyzka and Marszalkowska, in the General Savings Association building. For the time being, at least in the central and southern sectors of Srodmiescie, it was touch and go, or rather, the defense was continuing and so was public order. Father said that despite all this he could try to get us work somewhere. Because here you had to work at something. Work was obligatory.

On that foolish day of joy everything both amazed us and didn't. It wasn't that we were afraid of work. We had grown accustomed to it. What hadn't we grown accustomed to? But it seems we had, under our sweetened mood, a great uncertainty about it all. Even a negative certainty. But for the time being, if that's how things were, that's how they'd have to be.

And so we were already talking amongst ourselves about joining the uprising.

"I've thought about it," said Halina.

"But really," I said, "if you want to we can join, it really doesn't make any difference."

Halina said that by now it didn't make any difference to her either.

And that's the way we left it. Provisionally. As it turned out, they weren't accepting volunteers anyway or else they were accepting them but unenthusiastically because there were no weapons.

I think it was still on that same day that after several meals Zocha ordered us to come to her barracks for a meal. Nearby. The corner of Chmielna and Zgoda. The house is standing today. A cake, a piece of cake, five stories high, with a little triangle in the center at the base (a so-called courtyard).

Zocha's barracks, or rather the division for which she cooked, was quartered in the apartment of the Baltarowicz family. Zocha was called Mrs. Zula there. She walked around in a sweatsuit with a turban on her head.

She sat us down at the table. She gave us each a plate of macaroni. In addition, she set out a jar of lard. With cracklings. And some juice. Also in jars, I think.

Somehow, Swen simultaneously greased his own food and mine. With a teaspoon of lard. Then again.

"Have some more." Another spoonful for each of us.

"Have some more." Again another spoonful.

And he grabbed for the juice. Raspberry. No. Cherry, I think. He attacked the lard, the macaroni. I shouted something. But he poured on even more. We started devouring it immediately. And quickly. With great appetite. I confess. With appreciation for everything in that whole mess.

Our first gorging ended with this, I think. It was already dark. I remember that after this Father took us to Uncle Stefan's. The typesetter. On Gorski Street. To the newspaper plant. It was a sweet warm evening. As in 1939. Just the same, September 2. Saturday. A sweetened peace, warm. Dark. The same Szpitalna and Chmielna Streets. Mama and I. We had walked from Napoleon Place to Jedrzejewski's to buy some cake. Because he had good, large cakes. There was a front, too. False happiness. Delusion through physical well-being.

In the printing shop there were many lights, people, the smell of the news sheets, the type, papers, piles, people bending over, tapping sounds. In addition, the radio was on. Tuned in to Lublin. Wanda Wasilewska* was speaking. To Warsaw about Warsaw. It sounded a bit peculiar.

Uncle Stefan was setting type, I think. And it seems he was eating from a piece of paper. He told me (because I asked him) how Aunt Natka, Krysia and Bogusia were; after all, they weren't on Towarowa near the railway where they had lived.

"No, they're at Miedziana, at Marycha's. It's awful there."

I understood that everything was all over there, that on August 26 or 27 there had been air raids, it seems, just as in Stare Miasto. They had survived. They didn't know that they still had Dresden ahead of them; they were deported there after the uprising.

It wasn't only on the other side of Marszalkowska that the situation was dreadful. It was also becoming terrible beyond Nowy Swiat. Beyond the Saxon Gardens there were only ruins and empty lots. The front passed through the Saxon Gardens. So only that chosen belt remained intact, one third of Srodmiescie, at most. A semblance of order. With the headquarters of the Home Army. The five-minute "Srodmiescie Republic." But even here, to be sure, there was more than one peculiar incident.

I have already told how the Hitlerites attacked 18 Bracka Street behind their tanks and slaughtered who knows how many people there. Then the same thing happened on Jasna Street. Also raids, and "berthas" and other things. Once, Father was walking along Zgoda Street; someone was playing the piano. Suddenly — planes. Right afterwards, the bombs. Half of the house disappeared. The person upstairs was cut off. The staircases had collapsed. Luckily a truck came. Firemen. They got him down with a ladder.

It wasn't for nothing that people in Srodmiescie sang to the tune of an old rhumba:

> *The tanks along Marszalkowska*
> *The tanks along Nowy Swiat. . . .*

The huge General Savings Association building itself (headquarters) was already scarred. But it was standing, more or less. Mighty. Concrete. So many stories high. People were living there. Father went to see his acquaintance, Major Brejdygand. To get him out of there. Major Brejdygand replied, "No, it's just fine here. . . ."

The next day, in the morning, Father went to see him again. He found the building in ruins. Major Brejdygand had perished. They had bombed through to the cellars, two stories down I think. The concrete hadn't helped.

I heard from Janck Markiewicz's mother that she and Janek had a wounded friend there. He had to be carried out. They got hold of a stretcher; they rushed about looking for him but he couldn't be found. They called to him. No answer. Plenty of wounded people. In water. And the water was rising. Because something had burst. The wounded were crawling about but they didn't have any strength. They went on looking for their own. Finally, a weak little voice:

"Here I am. . . ."

They look: a mummy wrapped up in bandages. They put him on the stretcher. They carried him out. Others were shouting:

"And when will we get out? When will you get us out?"

149

" 'We'll come back for you,' I shouted," Markiewicz's mother told me, "I had to lie to them. It was horrible. We carried that poor thing. We carried him. It was getting heavy for me. Around Sienkiewicz Street. I stumbled with the stretcher and began to shriek. Janek yelled at me, 'What are you trembling for, you hysterical woman!' But I didn't say anything; I only lay there and screamed, 'Help. . . !' "

"And so?" I asked, laughing. "Did it help?"

"You won't believe it, but it did. Suddenly someone ran up. Wearing a uniform. He and Janek carried the stretcher. Finally he saluted and walked away. And that was the Yugoslav who took part in our uprising."

All that took place right at the beginning of September. Back in August Father had been asked to find a postman. His address: some number on Sliska Street. Father went there; the old man was sitting in his kitchen with his sister. Father told us:

"I say they should leave but they say no, no . . . I come back several days later. They're no longer there. They're sitting in the cellar. But do you know how? Under the courtyard. They dug corridors under the entire house and under the yard in a square. And people were sitting there on benches along both sides, crowded, one next to the other, without any space. Again I try to persuade him but again he say, 'No . . . my sister and I will stay right here!' Just as I was going back to them for the last time I was thrown against the wall in the building housing the Capitol movie theater; I was thrown against the wall, fell through into the basement, and then the main wall began to collapse because they had obviously struck behind the wall and broken through into the basement. . . . And when I reached Sliska Street I learned that everyone in those corridors under the walls had died."

After telling us about the famous battles in the Telephone Exchange and in the Church of the Holy Cross where, it seems, the Germans were on the roof of the church proper and the Poles in the choir with the organ and they even tore out the pipes in order to hurl them, Father and Halina told us about one youth who sat for days in the tram on Marszalkowska somewhere near Zlota and whenever a tank approached he threw bottles at it; it seems he destroyed several tanks like that but finally he was killed too.

What amazed me even more was that Woytowicz* had organized a Chopin concert in a cafe on the ground floor on Nowy Swiat. For the partisans. It was evening. The artillery fire began.

Woytowicz was playing the *Revolutionary Etude* when the shells began to whistle and hit Nowy Swiat. Right there. Woytowicz didn't stop. No one moved. Only the cups and saucers tumbled down and were broken. Irena P. told me about it when everything was all over.

Halina said that there were concerts in the Conservatory. And in the Apollo movie theater nearby a film was being shown. A documentary. Of the battles in the Church of the Holy Cross. She saw it herself. She told me about it then.

But let's return to the situation at 32 Chmielna, on the third floor. I don't remember any more how we slept. After all, there were seven of us and yet it seems we were comfortable. From the beginning Zocha showed a great partiality for Zbyszek, which Swen made fun of.

On September 3 it was already hot in the morning. Sunday. It felt exceptionally holy. Food. Sitting around. Family. On a couch. And peace. As then. In 1939. Also September 3. Also Sunday. Suddenly the bombing had ceased. Heat. People were rushing from embassy to embassy, carrying manifestoes, because England and France had declared war. On Nowy Swiat, near the statue of Copernicus, I had stumbled across a group of people singing the Marseillaise in French. A woman standing on the roof of a limousine was leading them, her black hair combed to look wet and sleek and shaking her large earrings. I asked someone who she was. He said she was Prime Minister Slawoj-Skladkowski's wife.

So today, September 3, 1944, I organized a reading. Of a poem. On a totally unrelated theme. Written on Rybaki Street. And also of a play I'd begun writing about the uprising. With a scene in the shelter on Rybaki Street. The play was written on the paper which I'd taken from the wardrobe at 5 Podwale, where that wooden well was. During my "author's afternoon" all four of us—Halina, Swen, Zbyszek and I—sat on the couch. I was certain that day would be peaceful until nightfall. And it was, more or less.

I don't know what started first, the bombing or the runs. I know that Swen began first. Running up and down. To the exit into the courtyard. From the third floor. He kept dashing downstairs. Diarrhea and vomiting. Huge amounts. The one and the other. I suspect that he came down with them towards the end of that last (holy) Sunday. I got them, I think, on Monday. In the morning. That fair weather. Familiar. Heat. The burning of garbage in the incinerator. Shared by 32 Chmielna and the Palladium theater; we had a common wall with a hole in it. They had hot water. And we didn't. On the other hand, we had corpses lying in our courtyard. Since Saturday. And the rags from those corpses, their bloodied overcoats, hung on the outhouse door handle. So it wasn't pleasant for us when the runs started. And somehow the bombardment started suddenly too. On Monday.

Father says that we lay in our beds then, after our trip through the sewers, for almost three whole days. But it was neither three days nor a complete rest which we had right after Starowka. After all, I have described our first two days. All that walking around. I can recall that we set up camp beds on Monday, September 4—the third day. But because we had to keep running downstairs Swen and I couldn't lie in bed as one normally would have. After all, not only did we have vomiting and diarrhea, but there was the bombing too.

I have already mentioned that there was one crowded room and a sort of anteroom and that so many of us were there. In addition, there were two small cats. One black, the other white. Halina adored cats. I did too. Swen preferred dogs. (People can be divided into dog-lovers and cat-lovers.) But he also liked cats. Take my father. He has raised animals all his life and is patient with them. As few people are. In general, he has a peaceful temperament. He wishes life, the world and people well. He likes to do things. He made rubber stamps during the occupation. He forged signatures. German ones. On glass. Under the glass was a light. He was excellent at it. At night. And by day he'd go with those *Ausweise* (and what large quantities he had!) to the Industrial-Commercial Hall. At the corner of Wiejska and Senacka. There he'd win over the porter. Not really the porter—because the porter was already ours —but through the porter he'd get the "canary," the SA guard, really stewed. It was a question of having easier access to the chief's office at any time. The chief was in charge of stamping the Hitlerite "crows." À la Roman eagles. The chief was a woman. She was sweet on the porter because he was young. And when she went out to dinner she didn't lock her office, leaving it in the porter's care. During this time the porter would leave his drunken "canary," enter the office, open the cabinet containing the stamps with a specially made key, and quickly stamp the "crows" on whatever my father and other people handed him. But it was still necessary to stand in line at the window for signatures. One waited and waited, as for everything else then. There was yet another complication. A person could sign for only one *Ausweis*. So Father would take Zocha, Halina, sometimes me and whomever else turned up. In that manner, four or five *Ausweise* could be obtained. But on the next day the so-called "Cherman" might recognize them. So Zocha would disguise herself. Zocha especially. She'd wear glasses. Put on mourning. Lisp. She became expert at it.

I remember Father in 1940. When the roundups began. Our window on the corner of Leszno and Wronia Streets was on the fourth floor and looked out on the entire length of Leszno. For part of the evening canvas-covered trucks drove along Leszno. In the direction of Pawiak Prison. They flashed by, one after the other, cutting across Leszno. They were the typical round-up vans, packed with people, and soon to be so familiar. Father was standing by the window. In his underwear. Looking out at Leszno. We had gone to sleep long before, the street had already quieted down, but Father still stood there and watched.

Since he had been a postman before the war, on the first day of the uprising he rushed off to liberate the Main Post Office. Then he organized a foray to get sugar for the partisans. The sugar was on Ciepla Street. Near Ceglana. Father drafted twenty civilians. Chance passersby. He announced that it would be shared fifty-fifty. Between the troops. And them. They ran to Ceglana Street. But since there were already Germans in part of that depot they brought an escort. Three 15-year-olds armed with grenades overwhelmed the Germans from the rear. They wiped them out one-two-three. Then they had to start loading. Father urged them to be quick about it. Not to be greedy. Because it turned out that there were many other tempting foods in addition to the sugar. Vodka too. Sliwowitz. They drank some. Took some for later. But there was that sugar. And the other delicacies too. And the trip back. Father also brought back a large amount of sugar. A whole sack. Cubes. I remember the sack. Of synthetic material, so thin it was like net. That sugar was important later on, on the other side of Aleje.

I don't remember the precise date when we fled to the other side of Aleje Jerozolimskie. Around that time, on Monday, September 4, Father, Swen and I were at the intersection of Chmielna, Bracka and Zgoda Streets. Or perhaps even closer to Nowy Swiat. Suddenly we noticed people running in confusion and screaming:

"Powisle's been bombed!"

"Powisle's done for!"

"The Germans are on Powisle!"

They had had time only to flee, no doubt. With nothing. Some of them, with the remains of the ruins in their hair. They were running up from Ordynacka and Foksal Streets. I questioned them. They started running. Just like those people who had fled along Chlodna Street first towards Wola and then away from Wola.

Right afterwards bombings and panic set in near us too. And then that diarrhea and vomiting. And those corpses which later were buried at the rear of the Palladium. And that burning of garbage and refuse. Everywhere.

"Burn! Burn it! It's infectious!"

The air was full of smoke. Panic. Scurrying about.

At the beginning we didn't run down. Because there were those four flights. Three to the ground floor and the fourth to the cellar. But what with the diarrhea and the vomiting we were forced to keep running down anyway. We wanted to lie still all the time. I remember how all day long mobs of people were rushing through our house to the Palladium on Zlota and from the Palladium to Chmielna. Without a stop. In both directions. At the bottom of our stairwell, in the middle of the hall which the route actually intersected, were half-glass swinging doors. Those doors were constantly in motion and squeaked and banged against the wall. I don't remember if the first time it was through the window and the second time through those doors, or vice versa, that I saw two women dragging a man by his arms. His cheek was torn off. Hanging there, that is. They rushed into our hall at a trot. In the direction of Chmielna. The doors were swinging non-stop. And then those same people came back, still at a trot. Only the man had his cheek sewn on already. I don't remember if I saw that it was sewn on or if it was bandaged. But later on, still during the uprising, I was amazed that he had his cheek. It was scarred but he had it. Because I passed him. And I met him after the war too. And his cheek had become normal. But at that time he'd looked terrifying.

Well, we didn't rush downstairs at the beginning. Swen. Zbyszek. And I. Halina too. (Father and Zocha were here but Stacha, Halina's mother, had gone down to the shelter at once.) But they kept on bombing Zlota, Chmielna, Zgoda, Jasna, Moniuszko, Sienkiewicz. The house was shaking. There was no reason to wait. Not a minute. We went down. Because there were shells too. In addition.

And "cows."

"The cow is mooing," people used to say here in Srodmiescie, just as in Starowka people said of the same thing, "They're cranking up the nickelodeon."

The cellar. Or rather, cellars. Square. With passages branching off from them. They were narrow. Some benches for the older people. Temporarily. Right under the walls. The rest stood. Also under the walls. And we did too. Near the entrance. Side by side. In a row. One beside the other. I felt unhappy that it had come so soon. Once more I experienced an acceptance of death. It was only a question of how. Halina said, "I think it would be best to hold hands."

After the second run downstairs that day we stood beneath the wall and held each other's hands. They were bombing fiercely. It had begun suddenly after that idyll, but in the familiar way. There was a lot of dive-bombing and explosions. Shockwaves. Breaking off. Running about. Stamping. Calling. News. So bad. That. . . . That. . . . That right here. . . . On Chmielna too. And on Zlota. And all over. First one place was destroyed. Then another. Digging out the buried. Fires. Right away. Familiar. Familiar. Familiar. But the exhaustion—despite acceptance—the third time. . . . The third time? The same thing? Oh Lord. . . .

At that time we started running farther off for water. Next door, in the Palladium, there was no more water. Something had crashed, most likely. Into something. So we ran down Chmielna Street. Past the tiny square on Zgoda at the corner of Bracka and Szpitalna. Through the gate. To some building. Or perhaps through a gate along that stretch. I don't remember anymore. I do remember that it was crowded with people standing in a line there; already on Chmielna it was four times larger, and it went through the gate, the courtyards and out to Widok, across Widok to a gate, a courtyard and a passageway (complicated, underground) leading beyond Aleje. There was a crush. Beyond Aleje. Wawa was standing there too, I remember. In a hat. With a pocketbook under her arm. With violet false eyelashes pasted on her lids. On those high heels of hers. I don't want to offend her, but she is fat and she knows it, and:

"That's the kind you really like," and here she poured a glass of water on a certain gentleman at Hania's (with a somewhat belated squeal). Then she was sorry, apologized. But that was in 1950.

155

We didn't know Wawa then. Personally. By sight, from what we'd heard of her, from her performances—yes. Who didn't know her? Swen tells how in those days he was rushing somewhere through the cellars into that crowd, all squashed together, rushing about. Wawa was in the crowd, wearing her hat. Swen ran up to her:

"Miss Wawa!"

"Oh?" she replied.

"Hello!"

"Hello, sir."

"You are here?"

"Mm. . . ."

Meanwhile, through that gate. On Chmielna Street. We ran past with jangling containers. Other people were just waiting there. But Father and Zocha had Home Army armbands. Just yesterday evening or, perhaps, two days ago, Father had hidden when they came to look for him. He was needed for something. That was probably the night when we came from Starowka. Or perhaps September 2. After Uncle Stefan, the printing shop and the lard and cherries. Father wasn't such a shirker. I have already described how he rushed about doing things. But at times—nothing doing. He is needed, according to someone. But he thinks that he has his own affairs. For water, however, it was useful. Allowed through immediately. If some of the women, or civilians, made a stink about it, oh well, they always complain anyway. There was water in three quarters of an hour, at most. In the house. Upstairs. On the box.

Perhaps we were already at the Balturowiczes. (After the night of the fourth and fifth, or the last night at Zocha's. 32 Chmielna.) Or rather, in the barracks. Actually, we had our own room. The six of us. There was a first floor here in the shape of a stout triangle and five other floors plus the Klein vaulting. And over there it was unsafe. At 32 Chmielna. So perhaps we had partially moved to the corner of Chmielna and Zgoda. I think so. It was September 6 or 7. Wednesday or Thursday. Because we were living here, sleeping, waiting. At times we looked in at 32 Chmielna, but less frequently with each passing day. Because it was getting worse all the time. They were shelling. Hitting along the trolley lines. Now Zlota, now Jasna, now Sienkiewicz Street. Everyone knows this. What and when. But in the daytime. The sky. It was dreadful. So much. So much. Often. Oooooo. The planes.

Like a toothache. And the weather. The heat. Sky blue. But here it was gray! And

ooo-ooo-ooo-ooo. . . .
whooooooooooo-oo-oo. . . .
whooooooooooooooo-ooo-crash!
whooooo-ooooooooo . . . crash!

Three days later. After massive diarrhea and massive vomiting. We went outside. Why should we sit and sit? In our quarters on the corner of Zgoda. Although it wasn't bad here. Because we were among family. And Halina was there. And that room which was almost ours. Zocha was caught up in her work. A friend of the family. Excited by her own energy. She cooks. She boils. Pours from a huge ladle. Adds something. Wearing her turban and sweatsuit all the time. She talks, tells us stories, tells them to her men from the Home Army. She liked to call out to one of them,

"Hey you, Gloomy," because that was his pseudonym. Like Teik—the Talon. Roman Z. was Atos. Lech—Emphasis. I have forgotten Father's.

Once I was going along at a trot. Down Chmielna Street. There were people there, people. Up to the gate. The one which leads past Aleje. A line was forming. Stretching out. Day and night. Well, I was walking along. Now the bombs were coming at us thicker and thicker. From Powisle too. And from behind Marszalkowska. But now:

wheeeeee . . . the "cows."

I dash into a huge building, a colossus, a safe, seven stories high, arched, bay-shaped, an address on Chmielna Street. To the right of the gate were stairs. Already there are crashes. Somewhere along here. And wheeeeee—crash. The next one, and another. There's no time. Only these stairs. So I run upstairs. A gate was considered one of the worst places to be (in relation to the "cows"). And those gates were the real thing. Typical.

Up the stairs, stopping one and a half flights up, on a landing with a window looking into a tiny courtyard. Very small. I see. Yes. But I also see something which I would never have expected (a supposedly elegant conditional, a polite expression, typical of Warsaw speech). Well, suddenly against the background of the rear of the second building there was a little detached "palace," a small one-story building; and on this building was a hanging garden with tiny paths covered with flowers. Paving stones, little sidewalks, balustrades. And trees. Lilacs, I think. With leaves spattered gray and brick-red. With a fresh sprinkling on top.

That was a shock. Extraordinary. Like the Cathedral with the statues, the rear of the Radziwill gardens (the traffic island, today), the Four Winds on burned-out Dluga Street.

Another time Swen and I were walking on Zgoda and Zlota Streets. Opposite the Bank under the Eagles we saw a sign for a toilet. I think it was at 5 Zlota. We dashed inside. A long courtyard. At the end, somewhere near the wall which had been broken through to the next property, was a toilet. Public. One of many. Perches. Made of poles, sticks. Extremely long. Above long trenches. And on them? Like chickens. In dropped trousers. Hanging freely. Various people. And among them was Wojciech Bak.* Whom we knew from his poems, his slim volumes. A friend had pointed him out to me. Once. That he was here. During the War. In Warsaw. He'd been expelled from Poznan. So he was here. He was waiting. For this moment on a perch. In the danger and the smoke. I saw him wandering about somewhere else too. And, as it turned out, he survived everything.

From the latrines you could slip into 32 Chmielna through holes in the wall. As for those corpses, once their rags had been burned they were buried. In the Palladium. You could see the fresh graves from the third floor. Next to them was a constantly smoking garbage bin. And next to it, one more latrine.

About the Bank under the Eagles. . . . Well, every now and then we would go out of the barracks on Zgoda Street. Halina and I, for example. We go outside. We look at the bank and dream out loud, that if it has to burn (and it definitely has to) then may it happen before our eyes. Because, after all, it will be a sight to see. Five grand stories. The walls with their wrought-iron fittings. The edifice is almost entirely black (or it was at that time). And there were two poised eagles at each corner. Leaning forward. As if they were preparing to soar. They were looking at the roofs at a slight angle. Consequently, everything below them was transformed into cliffs.

Halina and I go outside once more. In front of our triangular fortress, the one in which we are quartered. Suddenly we hear a shell. Boom! And the eagles are already at the edge of a flaming abyss. And how! Instantly. Live flames. Five stories high. Hardly a wisp of smoke. But the flames are rising from the ground floor directly under the eagles. No one does anything, extinguishes anything. What could be done? So the fire raged furiously. But the

158

walls remained standing. Nowadays, who would even imagine something like that?

The panic was worsening. More and more people were crowding behind Aleje. As if salvation were expected over there. Simply, in conformity with a law I already understood at that time, people had to change their locations and decide that one place was better, another worse. And since there was very little territory left to divide, Aleje became the demarcation line.

Naturally, there seemed to be a reason for it. Because in the evening on the 6th I think, when Father, Zocha and I made a foray to the other side (by a speeded-up method, thanks to the Home Army armbands) it appeared that for the time being it wasn't all that bad over there. I can't recall where we ran about or whom we saw on the other side of Aleje. Just a general impression. And the fact that we were succumbing to an ever greater need to flee from here. Then, on the evening of September 6, or perhaps it was on the night of the 5th and 6th, we made serious preparations. On that last evening in the barracks we sat around the table and began to eat. There was still a lot of food of various kinds. And because we were uneasy and on the alert, a ceremonious mood arose, as if out of spite. As at a feast. Because we were eating, even having drinks, and then to top it off Zocha gave each of us candies wrapped in shiny paper. She gave Zbyszek an extra piece. But then she immediately gave me another one. I don't remember if she gave one to Swen. In any case Halina. Suddenly. Got up from the table and walked out. Into the other room. Which was dark and empty. I went to see what was wrong. She was standing in the space behind the door, leaning against it, and crying. I asked her what was the matter. She kept on crying. I comforted her, kissed her head, because I was feeling embarrassed, but she cried even harder. (Recently, when I asked her about it, she didn't remember at all and she certainly didn't know why.)

After supper we decided to remain there after all. But only until the morning, I think. Not long before that we'd had another plan. Father and Swen ran through those blocked gates into Widok and began looking for quarters there. I didn't have the faintest idea why they were looking on Widok Street. Not only did they arrange with a woman there for us to move in immediately but somehow Swen also spoke with her about art and they both agreed that we would organize an artistic evening there that very night. The plan was quickly changed because bombs fell directly on

159

Widok. And perhaps I was there with them after supper. To see whether the place would still do (because the bombs had fallen next door). Or perhaps we didn't cross under Aleje at all and I'm just confused. Maybe so.

The moon was out. It was late, past midnight. It was warm. The streets were crowded. Loaded down with suitcases, sacks (I was carrying on my back a paper sack full of the sugar lumps from Ciepla Street), this time in utter seriousness, we joined the crowd on the route. Naturally not the slow and terribly large crowd but a smaller, quicker one which had passes. Halina and Zocha were dragging suitcases, because they couldn't live without several changes of underwear. Halina was walking along with an uneasy conscience because she had left both cats upstairs. It's true we had prepared a great deal of food and drink for them and had left the window open—as I have already mentioned—but even so we felt uncomfortable about it. We wandered along in the noise of the moving crowd with strange and fragmented feelings. The moon was shining. We passed a courtyard (with busts of Chopin and Mickiewicz) which to this day serves as a passageway, adorned with those same busts. There came a time when we had to yield our privilege (or our arrogance) and join whatever crowds were there. And there already was a crowd, squashed together and winding along in common confusion. The avalanche rolled on and on. Across the entire width of the street. And there were just as many behind us. Although so many had already passed by in the last few days. Wawa crossed over too. During one of our strolls Swen and I noticed a large hat with a rolled brim and violet eyelashes under the brim in the crowd; and a handbag was under her arm.

Why was the line moving slowly? Stopping? Standing? Maybe it was so that those who really had priority could run across? Perhaps there was an obstruction on Aleje from time to time? Or heavy artillery fire? From the Vistula, let us suppose. And from the Central Station. Perhaps it was a tank attack, although the barricades weren't letting tanks through between the National Bank (on the corner of Nowy Swiat) and Marszalkowska—that happened only afterwards. At first it had been difficult to knock together those barricades. And to prepare that passageway. But after great difficulties both were ready. Therefore the major cause of slowdowns and of standing still in the line, or rather, two lines (because people were also coming to our side from the far side of Aleje) was simply the fact that there were two lines. And that permission was first given to move from our side past Aleje, and then to move from beyond Aleje to our side. As usual, people were scurrying about, from over here to there and from over there to here. Despite the fact that the greater press was in that direction. The corridors were too narrow and winding for people to pass by each other. It was impossible to allow a mass collision in that crush. Because—I recall—all the time it was fashionable to rush everywhere. Yet it wasn't a matter of fashion but of artillery fire, haste and air raids. Well, and of impatience too. At the end.

So, when we'd joined the stream of people at the Widok gate or in the courtyard we would stand still for a while, then edge along for a short time in a phalanx. Then again we would stand still. Until when the time came for our side to go over to their side, we really got moving. Or rather, we dashed into the cellar. Into corridors which weren't cellar-like but trench-like, or rather, into artificial tunnels hastily dug out for the circumstances. In the corridors, the turnings, it was very hot. And one could see that they were made of earth, with the roots still in it.

The passageway, or rather the runway, under Aleje Jerozolimskie itself, was even narrower. Flatter. And without a roof. Of course. There were shields from the barricades. I remember that the barricade to the left of Nowy Swiat was directly above us. There was really no way of adding on a roof. Because it would have meant working on it above ground. And the Germans from the National Bånk were taking care of things here. So, to provide a roof, stumps and palings had been thrown over, branches (pines) spaced in rows. Just as they landed. Wherever. The more the better. I get a little confused here with the picket fence supports of the trench.

There was artillery fire. Normal, I think. Nocturnal. Not too threatening, that is. That's what it seemed like to me.

One-two-three—and we're already on the other side of Aleje. We rush into the same sort of tunnels, windings. Corridors. Some of them, however, were made of brick. Perhaps in part. And maybe it was on the other side of Aleje that it was hot. Perhaps because of the fires.

We ran with the crowd into the moonlight on Nowogrodzka Street between Bracka and Krucza. On Nowogrodzka, on the ground floor in an inner courtyard, lived a former colleague of Father's, Mieczyslaw Michalski. Father led the whole "moonlight cavalcade" (as Halina said) with bundles shining in the glow to

161

Miecio's. We crossed the street. We went through a secession-style gate. And right into a three-story courtyard, to a moonlit well with picket fencing at the center. It seemed to be a garden. We all lined up and rested our bundles and backs against the picket fence. And waited. Rather tired. Father immediately went into one of the doorways. To Miecio. Unannounced. As a matter of fact, we didn't even know if he was here or even if he was alive.

That wait with our backs toward the garden must not have lasted long. But it stretched out for us. It seemed like several days. A long, sleepy uncertainty. Somnambulistic. Because the moon was full.

Father came rushing out.

Miecio is alive. He's at home, that is. With his sister. They have a room with a kitchen. They ask us in. We gather up our bundles and our backs from the picket fence. Some of the sacks were completely white. Halina's was, definitely. I remember. In the moonlight.

Greetings, hospitality, we spread our things out, make ourselves at home immediately; it's a place to spend the night. The ground floor represents semi-salvation. You can sleep. On whatever is there. Just to stretch out. On the ground floor you don't take shells into consideration too much. If it's not a vicious attack. And there was nothing vicious. In this direction. The moon was shining. So it was peaceful. A sigh of relief. Food. A table. We sit down. We chat. We wash. Everyone. By turns. In wash basins. In real water. With soap. And so to sleep.

Yes. That was no earlier than the night of the 6th/7th of September. From Wednesday to Thursday. We didn't know what day it was then. I'm figuring it out now. We only knew the dates. Because from the beginning there was that confusion, that chaos. No later. Because as I found out afterwards, Powisle fell on September 6. And after all, those people from below, from Tamka, Okolnik, Oboznia, were running up screaming:

"Powisle's fallen!" (definitively, that time).

That's a proof of the date.

Perhaps I've exaggerated in saying one third of Srodmiescie. That it was ours. Because Powisle and the ghetto, or no man's land, were cut off. And you have to remember that Srodmiescie didn't include as much as it does now.

On the other hand I didn't add (and this is important for people who don't know the history of the uprising) that part of

Mokotow, both Upper and Lower, was always ours. Southern Powisle was ours (the so-called southern part near Czerniakow) and Zoliborz, including Marymont. Only, these were separated.

In the morning, a raid. On our "new" Srodmiescie. A bomb somewhere nearby. An explosion. And something was drifting down on us already. Soot. Father was completely covered. Because he was sitting under the vent. He jumped up. And he stood there black and helpless with his arms slightly extended. We began to laugh. How could we help it? It was impossible not to. And then we cleaned him off right away, washed him, scrubbed him; especially Zocha. We also had to scour ourselves. Once more.

It was hot. After the full moon, a full sun. As there was every day (without exception!). But, how did things work out on the far side of Aleje? Amidst this luxury? It turned out that even this last refuge would be shaky. For the time being it was still peaceful. Relatively speaking, of course. With shellings. Air raids, now and then. But in those days, that was peace.

I already knew that this peace would end at any moment. That for the time being they were bombing over there in Srodmiescie. But that at any moment they could pick themselves up and come over to my new neighborhood.

In other words, that it would be the same thing all over again for the fourth time. And that again it would be necessary to begin coming to terms with death. Or with the tearing off of an arm or leg. It didn't occur to us that just one of us might perish. We always thought that we would die together.

I think Swen and Zbyszek went to Zurawia immediately to inquire about Danka. And Father and I, the two of us I think, went to 21 Wilcza to Zocha's, Father's and Halina's closest friends. To Jadwiga and Stanislaw Woj. To move in with them. Because we had crossed Aleje with that intention. In addition, I think, it seemed better to us to be on Wilcza Street than here on Nowogrodzka. Was it an anti-Aleje motivation? An urge to move southwards? An urge. Indeed! All creatures when terrified rush about, hide, rush about some more.

Before Wilcza, I think, we dropped in on my schoolmate, Zdzislaw Sliwerski. What of his being a schoolmate? I could say a lot about that. 6 Zurawia. The first floor. Zdzislaw's father opened the door. And Mrs. Sliwerska appeared right away. They made a gesture of invitation. But one could sense the uneasiness. In addition, it was on the first floor. So staying there lost its attractiveness.

Because they too must already have been thinking about a shelter. We chatted in the foyer. Standing up. Then for a long time at the door and on the stairs. Everyone was panicky. I asked after Zdzisio.

"Zdzich is on Emilia Plater Street," Mr. Sliwerski told me, "with his unit."

"On Emilia Plater?" I was surprised, because I didn't think we had men there, that far.

"Yes. On Emilia Plater. Would you like to look for him there?"

"Yes. But can I get through?"

"Well, yes." And he gave me the name of the unit. It was supposed to be near Wspolna or Hoza. One of the corners there.

We went first, however, Dad and I, to Wilcza Street. Paralleling Krucza. Because Krucza itself was dangerous. Or perhaps we still used Krucza then. It's easy to forget. Because there were barricades everywhere. High. Cemented. Made of paving stones. Certainly, even if it was possible to use the street, you couldn't take it all the way. There'd be a gate, a courtyard, a hole in a wall, a doorway. Another hole. Into a cellar. A courtyard.

The traffic was unbelievable. That part of Srodmiescie was absolutely jammed by then. People were still arriving. And they were expected to keep on arriving. Every hole and corner was swarming with people.

No doubt a courtyard-hole route had already been prepared by then along the lefthand side of Krucza (as you walk away from Aleje). Then that route descended even further underground. And since like other routes, or rather, "Champs Elysées," which I knew from the uprising, it was entertaining (because there were pipes and holes and little cellars, twists and turns in it) a jingle came into being about this walk down so-called "Krucza." And we read it in the news sheet. Aloud. Laughing. Just as in Stare Miasto. With the wound-up "nickelodeon." Called the "cow" here. Because actually, if you listened to it for awhile (and you didn't have to hear it for too long—it was a noisy creature) then it did sound something like a cow mooing. (I was amazed when I saw the minethrowers, or "nickelodeons," or "cows," after the war in the Army Museum in Warsaw. Especially at the shells. Six or nine together. They looked like milk cans. In fact, somehow having to do with cows.) Here, on the other side of Aleje, I saw apartment houses which had been uprooted by the "cows," narrow ones, but sometimes four stories high. And when I would say that the "cows" weren't anything serious, people would answer:

"Just look out when they hit." And they did hit.

Some people also shrugged off artillery in the same way. Especially those huge mortars, which I associated with something solid, like a metal, brass perhaps, but this name "mortar" was from the mortars used for grinding pepper and cinnamon.

People would also say to me about them, "You'll see. . . ."

I answered, "But they can't break through into the cellars."

And they replied to that: "Ha ha! They can't break through? You'll see how they'll break through!"

And that was the truth, too.

I have already spoken about how acute our hearing had become. To distinguish what was the front. What was another sector. What was beyond Aleje. What was two streets over. And what caliber. By ear. Halina and I had our own terms. For flying missiles. Some shells miaowed strangely. We would say: "Aha, the cats!"

The "berthas" were the worst. They were, as far as I can remember, three-quarter ton bombs. Three quarters of a ton isn't too bad. Only it was three quarters of a ton of bomb, and straight from the sky, at a slant. I think that was the decisive factor. Well, the ones from the sky fell slantwise, at an angle. And those from the side also came in at an angle. The difference wasn't so great. But yet there was a difference. I insist on my interpretation. I'm talking only about the toll among the cellars.

Mrs. Woj. was in the shelter. They had all gone down to the ground floors already. Or rather, to the shelter. Mrs. Woj. said they had gone down and told us:

"Come over, you're most welcome, really, come over; only it's a cellar. Anyway, Stasio will be coming right away."

Mr. Woj. was on duty. He was guarding the roof. With others. He came down right away. At any rate, not too long afterwards.

"We lie on the roof in case anything should happen and keep watch with wet rags."

"In case of fire."

Mr. Woj. got the bright idea that we should try to stay on the ground floor. They had a neighbor, an elderly woman who lived alone, Mrs. Rybkowska. She had two rooms and a kitchen on the ground floor. She herself was staying in the shelter. She'd been there for a long time already. She was very frightened.

"We'll arrange it right away!" And he rushed off.

"Good, it's taken care of, she agrees, come over. Come on over!"

The building at 21 Wilcza was five stories high. And it had a sunken courtyard. So being on the ground floor in such a house wasn't the worst alternative. Especially since there was an apartment. For us. And a shelter is a shelter.

Another thing about the height of buildings. The best part of being here, in southern Srodmiescie, was precisely this: it was the tallest district in Warsaw. The buildings were five, six, seven stories high. And even higher. Often solidly built. The streets were narrow. Or rather, crowded together. In general, southern Srodmiescie was the largest district in the uprising. In length and width. No, I'm exaggerating. And I'm not justified in dividing Srodmiescie into two centers. Throughout Srodmiescie there was one more characteristic feature. There were drafts of civilian labor. Not exactly round-ups, but, in case of need, passersby were stopped and half commanded half requested to do such and such. And since it was for two or three hours, everyone went gladly. Generally, people didn't refuse such tasks. Although it's not safe to speak of everyone. At that time practically everything was done. But since there were an awful lot of people, probably more than 200,000, no one asked me to do anything. And so I went about on my own.

One more thing. In Srodmiescie there was an extraordinary mixture of civilians and partisans. There were many who sported armbands. Various semi-partisans. Intermediate positions. A tendency to "free enterprise." In short—variety.

Mrs. Woj. told us right away that at the beginning she had sewn huge quantities of underwear, forage caps and other uniform parts.

We returned to Nowogrodzka with our encouraging news. Swen also came back with encouraging news. They had found Danka on Zurawia. With the Szu. family. She'd been renting a room from them. Except that by now they were really all in the cellar. Not in their apartment on the second floor (I think). Danka would drop by there but she was a radio operator in the Home Army. So she lived in the cellar, and broadcast and received messages. After all, it was close by. Also on Zurawia I think. Zbyszek remained with her. He was going to enlist. Or rather, they were going to accept him. If they had weapons. I think they did. Because they had captured weapons. Also, from the parachute drops. Not as many as were needed. But it was really beginning to amount to something. It seems there were a lot of people there too. New volunteers to replace those who had died. I remember—Mokotow, Zoliborz were ours. After the fall of Praga and then of Ochota, Powazki and Wola were in a geographically favorable position for a long while. But I don't want to exaggerate. There was something wrong there within a week.

Let's return to our story. Swen had practically settled in already with the Szu. family. That is, in the cellar. He stayed with us a while longer on Nowogrodzka. We were still able to eat something here, perhaps get something to drink too. But probably that's wrong. We had drunk wine on Chmielna Street. Because we had it. Another "bertha" or a bomb must have landed somewhere. Because Father was covered with dust once more. This time it was blue. There was a pharmacy near by. Or a soap factory. It was hit. Right in the bluing. And again it fell on him. Again there was laughter, cleaning, washing. I can still recall our daily eating of soup. And I think I was the one who found a hair. Hers. In the soup. But I could be confusing her with someone else's sister who looked like Miecio's sister, at some other, also dangerous time. Also in the soup.

So, on to Wilcza! Swen to Zurawia. And thus we entered a new topographic-residential phase.

The first thing we did on Wilcza, at Mrs. Rybkowska's, was to build a stove. A more solid one this time. Made of several bricks. Held together with clay. With a grate in the center. And a pan to catch the ashes. Zocha started cooking something right away. I think our stove may have fallen apart right away before it dried and we had to put it together again from scratch. Mrs. Rybkowska was more afraid than curious. We met her only on the second or third day.

We got plenty of sleep. Because there was a lot of room. In front of the windows there was a bin for something or other. Near the bin was a water barrel. In case of fire. On the left, a gate. On the right, a wall with a hole in it. Into 7 Krucza Street. Because there was a latrine and water there. The wall was gray—the color of a cat. The whole building was the same color. One more detail: opposite us, a little to the left, squeezed into a corner, stood Mrs. Trafna's little house. Mrs. Trafna was a Jew, according to what Zocha told me afterwards. I don't know if they knew each other before or not. We became friends with Mrs. Trafna. Quickly. As people did in those days.

On the first or second night I was on duty. In our courtyard. 21 Wilcza. There was one other person with me. Mr. Woj. was also there for a long time. He was smoking. And Father was there. They stood around. Talked. So did I. We stood on the mounds, in the little valleys, on the boards of the excavations. At night you can sense the terrain without visual preconceptions. The moon was shining. It was waxing. For the second time already. Clear nights. At least without any fires very near by. It was very warm throughout the night, so that I wore only soft shoes without socks (where could one get socks?—a luxury), trousers and a shirt. A light one. Perhaps because of the moonlight.

Swen arrived on the second day. We sat there with Halina. The three of us. In the first room with the sofa. The one with the window right there opposite the water barrel. Perhaps we played some sort of game. Perhaps I read something. Maybe Swen did too. I'm almost positive that I wrote something. But I can't remember so well anymore. Or so it seems. But no. It was precisely here that I wrote that play about the shelter. Still on the paper from the corner of Kapitulna and Podwale.

Perhaps it was then that the "cow" started mooing. Started hitting. It was certainly close by. Because when the second one began to moo we ran downstairs just as we were, not completely dressed, without shoes on and (somehow) in socks. They were right nearby. We flew down; that's an understatement. One turn of the banister in a flying squat! And we were already in the cellar. Just as on Rybaki Street.

Swen took me over to his place. To show me where it was. Then, I think, to Zbyszek's. Zbyszek had enlisted already. Nearby. On one of the streets between Zurawia and Hoza. Or was it Wilcza? From Krucza to the Square of the Three Crosses. We entered on the ground floor. From the gate. Into a room jammed with partisans. On a couch in the crowd sat Zbyszek already in uniform, I think, with his legs stretched out in front of him.

"For the time being, we're sitting and waiting, because we don't have any weapons," he said.

Somewhere near Swen's place on Zurawia we entered a cellar. In one of the bins for coal or potatoes, Danka was sitting on a chair between two walls, manning an apparatus like the back of an exposed radio. She had earphones on. And she was connecting and disconnecting various plugs and jacks with both hands simultaneously, at a very quick pace. She was talking at the same time too.

Numbers. For example:

"Bee-vee! Bee-vee! Six! Em-tee-aitch! Em-tee-aitch here! Hello, hello, we're transmitting. En-kay—eighteen! Hello!" There were even more such outpourings but they were cut off right away, because something had happened.

And so on. Continuously. Rapidly. Once, after a long wait (ours), she leaned a little in our direction. Something like, "Hello, what's new?" And then again the same thing. She couldn't break away. How could she? But we weren't bored. Absolutely not! It was the first time I was in such a transmission center.

Once on Zurawia, either upstairs while we were still at the Szu. family's place (they were all in the cellar) or in the courtyard, I remember that I could hear many voices and the jangling of forks and knives as at a party from the corner windows on the ground floor. I am certain to this day that it was a name day celebration. Which means I'm not at all certain. That's what it seemed like to me. And still does. But it was strange. And it seems even stranger now. It was afternoon. Sun. Heat. Dust. A lot of that in the courtyard. Of what? Various things. Chaos. People running around. That name day party both amazed and depressed me. Even made me nervous. Not just its carefree quality. But as a definite sign that something ominous was approaching.

Because something was approaching—closer and closer.

The apartment on Wilcza was splendid but we already had a place in the shelter. And we began to spend the nights in the shelter. Once we only sat through the night, or rather we slept through the night sitting up, Halina and I, on a green plush couch. It stood near the door to the stairs. And that's where we remained. Because I was yearning for the luxury of space. To have it just once. And Halina wanted companionship. And because she hadn't yet gotten accustomed to spending the nights in cellars. She was wearing a dark cloak (a winter one; she wore it in order to keep it with her). With ash-gray fur trim. On the sleeves. And on the collar. She snuggled against that fur as she had against her cats.

We had some bedding in the shelter. Something made of down. It was puffed up in the center and red on top. How many featherbeds did we have? Two? We had something to cover ourselves with. What we slept on I don't know anymore. Stools? Benches? I think a little of everything. We also snuggled up. Into the bedding. There were a lot of feathers and down scattered about our cellars and basement compartments. They glowed. Some were crimson. Others vermilion. Could it have been under electric light? I don't think so. The carbide lamps! Candles! There were people all over. In every nook and cranny. We were the only ones who had settled in on the ground floor. Though only at certain hours. And in daylight. Mrs. Trafna was in her own home. But I think then she moved into the cellar for good. Which was all for the best. Because soon they began firing into our courtyard. Sometimes large caliber guns. Persistently. Grenades. "Cats" (so-called), "cows." "Berthas." Intermediate range mortars. Something from overhead it seems. Because the house began disintegrating from above. Little by little, in installments. First it was cracked open. Then it began to get smaller. Perhaps it caught fire. Yes, definitely. But they always managed to extinguish it. Mr. Woj. ran about a lot. (He was tall.) He took care. Of the roof tiles with wet rags. Until he'd fall flat on his back, a bit bent over, head down, over the rain gutter. Have I pictured him correctly? Imagined him? Mrs. Woj. would scream at him in the cellar:

"Don't go! Stasiu! Don't go!" And when he did go she would brood. And since he would go at the drop of a hat she was only a little accustomed to it and so she was upset. She was a seamstress. So she was Stacha's and Zocha's fellow artisan. She and her husband, Stas, had lived together at first for fifteen years without getting married because they were afraid of legalities, of deromanticizing. Once, in great trepidation, they got married for real. A wedding. And fifteen more years passed by. In marriage. Nothing was spoiled. And so they lived together later on in Jelenia Gora until the end.

Jadwiga Woj. preferred to have a pallet near us. In our bin. Because we were like one family. They (the two of them), Stacha, Zocha, Halina, Father and I. Mrs. Trafna was next to us. Other women, men, children. A whole herd. Beyond the right entrance, farther on. On the left side, in the first cellar, were the earlier occupants.

And Mrs. Rybkowska was there, wearing glasses. Sometimes she looked in on the ground floor, her home, or rather us. Very infrequently. But she had a need to check up. Once she checked to see if we'd broken the glasses in the breakfront by accident. Another time, she was sorry that we moved the breakfront. That was in her presence. I don't know why it was standing at an angle. Another time she was worried about an ikon, a wonderworking ikon of the Mother of God of Czestochowa, which hung behind the breakfront. Just an ordinary little ikon. Behind dusty glass. Colorless. Now she herself pushed the breakfront away and slipped in behind it. Often Mr. Woj. would sit awhile with us on the ground floor while supper was being prepared and the stove put together, because a "cow" or mortars were always knocking it over. (Zocha just barely cringed at Mrs. Woj.'s constant, "Stasiu, Stasiu, don't go." Finally they quarreled over it. Both of them. A short, mild misunderstanding. Because the times weren't propitious. Then they became good friends once more. And addressed each other politely as "Mrs." Only after the war did they stop. But after the war they were angry at each other for good: from Gdansk to Jelenia Gora. Until they forgave each other at last. That was when Stasio died.)

And when Mrs. Rybkowska would go on too long about the breakfront, the ikon and the glasses and begin to check up on us, Stanislaw Woj. would join in saying:

"Oh no! Planes!"

"Really?" Mrs. Rybkowska would ask.

"Yes," we would say.

And she would flee to the shelter. She believed us. Why not? Once while we were sitting on the couch (Zocha was cooking) they hit the water barrel. A fountain burst from the side of the barrel. Then they hit here and there. Then they struck Mrs. Trafna's little house. Once. Twice. The dry whitewash, walls, laths disintegrated. Dust was sifting down from the stone building too. And plaster was falling. Window frames too. And sheets of metal. The roofs were still made of zinc then. Predominantly. Mrs. Trafna's little house was growing smaller and smaller.

Also in the shelter with us, or rather somewhere near the door . . . there's something connected with that doorway . . . was it drafts, quarreling? I think so. . . . Anyway, there was also a Mme. de la something. A Frenchwoman. Or only the wife of a Frenchman. But a widow. She lived on the fourth floor. I think. Once, there was a fracas. Throughout the courtyard. A huge gathering of men—block leaders, semiblock leaders, quarter Home Army men—surrounded and were screaming at the terrified Mme. de la something, who was dressed in her thin coat. They had just caught her relieving herself on the fourth floor, in front of her own door, which let out onto the stairwell which we shared.

But that was nothing. That too passed. The latrine was in the next building: 7 Krucza. I no longer remember if we first went

171

through a back courtyard (naturally, initially through a hole in the wall). And further on there was the front courtyard. From Krucza. From the street. Or if right after the hole we entered a huge courtyard with a huge depression in the center. With a whole valley dug out with shovels. From bare earth. And there in the center of the depression in an even deeper depression within it was a pump. There was always a line of people. Sometimes a long one. Which wound around three times. So that it filled the narrow valley. Which is what it was intended for. The crowd was at its largest in the afternoon. Also towards evening. When there was hope that it would begin to grow dark. Because it seemed as if the planes went to sleep then.

And the latrine? The latrine was more or less to the right of the hole. At the end of the courtyard. It doesn't really matter which one. Off to the side. Somewhere in a corner. So that because of its narrowness it had room for only a kind of perch. With a hole. And a path. To reach it. When you sat down on the perch above the hole you had—practically in front of your nose—a shed with something inside it. And something above it which rose higher and higher. The side of the outbuilding, I think. Windowless. And behind your back or, rather, behind your a–, was a huge wall several stories high. Also windowless. Above you there was a tiny strip of sky (narrow and long). Shells were flying across it. I wanted to say: creatures were flying. But they were only artificial ones. The live ones were in the cellars. One of the women in our cellar had a dog. What breed? Small and fat. Mr. Woj. used to say that you could set a glass of water on that dog (a bitch perhaps?). And he would say to the woman who owned the dog or bitch:

"I'd advise you to watch out for him!" Because it seems, in fact I'm sure, that dogs were eaten then. And cats.

In the shelter, not this one but the one next door, under No. 23 (a huge six-story building of the old sort, secession style, we envied them their Klein vaulting)—well, next door we had a radio station. It was in one of the potato bins. Behind thick boards. But with chinks in them. I say "we had" because we used to rush there. Because of the radio.

"Beep-beep-beep-beep!—BBC. . . ." Several times a day—the news. We would stand in front of those boards. We would place our ears against the chinks. We would run there straight from our place. From our pallets. From our own shelter. Through other shelters. Corridors. Holes. Gaps in the wall. Until we got to somewhere

172

in the depths of those shelters. Under No. 23. Or rather, we would race through the cellars. As we did everywhere. Without need of surface paths.

I remember a Sunday morning and mass during the early, perhaps the very first, days on Wilcza. One of the women had lent her apartment for it. On the ground floor. At right angles with ours. With windows onto the courtyard, naturally. She even prepared a carpet and palms. Perhaps a palm. Just one. And the other one, was that a dragon tree? Something of the sort. Ecclesiastical. Or so it seemed. After mass there was confession. Communal. Because there were a lot of people. With the condition—stated aloud—that we would go to individual confessions in case we survived all this.

Sunday fell on September 10. That was the second Sunday in Srodmiescie and the first one we were aware of on the other side of Aleje. Or rather, which we realized was a Sunday. Later, until the very end, until the middle of October, no one anywhere distinguished the days. Because the date is significant, not long ago I figured out what day October 1 fell on. And to my amazement I discovered for the first time that it was a Sunday.

You remember. August 6 on Chlodna. ("Perhaps the Good Lord will change something.") The consciousness of it being Sunday. August 15—Rybaki—a holiday—the miracle on the Vistula—but they are not coming closer. September 3—a Sunday like that day of gun salutes in 1939. On the same confluence of date and day. Kanapa. Chmielna. And this fourth one. Famous. Holy. Now. And that . . . is all.

In those first days the route along Krucza Street had already descended underground. On Krucza itself between Wspolna and Hoza lay a woman's bloody shoe (with a chunk of heel). From then on people began to be a little more careful. Only one stretch —from our Wilcza to Hoza—became famous for its safety. People began to swarm over it. They swarmed between Wilcza and Piekna too, or rather, from our corner to the end of Krucza. Up to the square at the intersection of Piekna, Krucza and Mokotowska. Across the square, facing the intersection of Krucza, along the whole southern side of Piekna, was a barricade. Long. Solid. Made from sacks and bags filled with something. And from paving stones. But the barricade wasn't high. You had to run. And crouch down. And watch out for Krucza as you approached the square. Because at that point the firing from Marszalkowska and the Square of the Redeemer would start.

173

But people rushed about. Many of them. A great number. On Krucza and Mokotowska there were many billets for partisans and civilians. So both partisans and civilians were running up and down Krucza. And hybrids. Krucza was undoubtedly the main street of southern Srodmiescie. Probably because it resembled a street. And had traffic. Despite the various ruins and barricades. And despite the fact that it was only this one stretch. But that was enough. For it to dominate. It suddenly became the Aleje for all of Srodmiescie. On Krucza you could take care of many things. On Krucza people would meet their families, friends. Arrivals from various neighborhoods. People who had acquired this area as the third or fourth property of the uprising. Here you could meet someone you hadn't seen for ten years. Suddenly. As I did. Also. I met Count Franio Z. From school. After so many years. Then someone else.

On Krucza we met Roman Z. In Home Army uniform. "Atos." The fellow who came to Chlodna that time on July 31, when there was that storm and the raid simultaneously. To say goodbye. To Mama. And me. And who knew Halina. I think he knew Father and Zocha too. That's not important. He called on us right away. Once and then another time. Zocha treated him. To freshly made soup. A whole bowlful. Roman was getting ready to eat. But suddenly there was a "cow":

moo-oo! ooo-oo! ooo—oo!

—and plaster started showering down from the ceiling. Right into the soup. Roman spooned up whatever could be eaten. He ate the smallest pieces of ceiling. The second time it was the same, I think. With the difference that the stove collapsed too. Which didn't bother us. Because we put it back together immediately from scratch. The ceiling was falling every day, it seems. In large chunks of plaster. In strips. Into the soup. And onto our heads. And there was plenty to fall down because although it didn't look so good from the outside, on the inside it was also a secession building. Or rather, that fifth or sixth Warsaw classicism. Covered with stucco. Rosettes. Garlands. Cornices. To say the least.

A row over the laths. In our last lifeboat in southern Srodmiescie. After renting the place on Wilcza (for nothing, because there was no money in circulation. At that time!) and after a couple of nights spent thinking, however, about No. 23, next door. Our place had those five stories above it. But it was already somewhat shrunken. Eaten away. In addition, it turned out that it was in fairly poor shape. From the beginning it didn't look too sturdy.

Or too firm. But then the gray plaster started falling off in bits. Whitish-yellow boards, so dried out that they crackled. Laths. And that turned out to be the framework. So we left. The whole group. From under No. 21 (literally from under, because we moved underground). To look over No. 23. Under the guise of moving. The tenants in No. 23 knew us. We knew they agreed. And even had they not known us it would have been the same. There was still a little bit of space. So we looked it over. I remember how each of us in turn praised the Klein vaulting and the rest looked it over, patted it. Various people, old ladies. Everyone valued, was knowledgeable about, patted that "Klein." It seems that Klein, simply a certain Mr. Klein, a Jew, a German, had made a good discovery. And just in the nick of time. So that people had managed to build a good many buildings like that in old Srodmiescie in the days of Prus and Proust.

Clearly, the bombs must have been falling because our decision-making didn't last too long. We began to gather our belongings, our bundles, and quick as a wink, under Klein we went! If it hadn't been for that Klein, or rather, that barrel vault made of bricks and gleaming iron, that cellar wouldn't have differed so very much from this one. We lived in a communal set-up there. With an exit leading farther on. With an entrance into our place from the preceding cellars. And again featherbeds. Benches. Bags. Families. Sitting around.

Just about everyone from Wilcza made the transfer.

Bombs. And shells. Were raining down. Large ones. We would sit in the central corridor, the farthest from the openings to the outdoors. To the left the corridor had one little cellar after another. Each one with tiny doors. Only they were open. In the nearest one lived the Wi. family. Mr. Wi., an engineer, and Mrs. Wi., his wife. They sat on sacks. Which had something in them. All day long. That's how they managed. She looked like Gioconda. But her neck, voice and speech were like a turtledove's. Because that's what Halina called her. They had two small children. The children ran around with the other little children. They walked up and down the corridor. They would play like this:

"You go over there with a shopping bag and then we'll meet."
So they would separate. With their bags. They meet:
"Hello."
"Huhwo."
"Has your house burned down, dear?"

175

"Yes, it's burned," and a shrug of the shoulders, "and is your house b-burned?"

"Yes, it is. . . ."

There was also a game with tanks. Jozia Woj. used to take care of the Wis.' two little ones. She was a teacher. As soon as there was an explosion she would stick her fingers in her ears. And since there were so many explosions she would sit or stand with her fingers in her ears. But since she took care of the children and talked with them or with the Wis. or with other people she was always unplugging her ears. Then again she would quickly plug them. She'd ask:

"What?" Yes, she'd adopted the gestures of a deaf person. Or a mute. Once, little Ewa (she was Ewa, I suddenly remember that) wants to go potty. The potty is there. Mrs. Woj. sits Ewa on the potty. In the corridor. Mrs. Wi., in the little cellar-drawing room, is sitting on her sack. And she cries out:

"In the middle! Right in the middle!"

So Mrs. Woj. transfers Ewa to the very middle. She plugs her ears. Because they're shelling. But Ewa is becoming frightened:

"Auntie, give me your hand!" Mrs. Woj. holds Ewa's hand while she's on the potty. And with her other hand she plugs one ear. Well, even that was better.

So. Their mother from Bracka was also there. And young Jadzia was of some help to them there. But, more likely they were just sitting there. Because each family was large then, but their little cellar was tiny. Explosions echoed along the corridors. Shock waves. And songs.

> *Into Thy care. . . .*
> *Holy One. . . .*

Right beside this, other lines were being sung:

> *Oh Virgin,*
> *Oh Virgin,*
> *Oh, Our Virgin—*
> *Our Comforter. . . .*

We had Klein above us. Good walls. A few iron plates. And those six stories. With a mansard roof. Bay windows. Bow windows. Pendants. Six stories. Plus a whole domed roof. Plus the ground floor. Eight levels. But only seven which could be penetrated. Because the eighth was—us. They ought not to be able to break through all seven. There were exceptions. At times. But one relied on the norm. And what if a bomb should land at more of an angle and not hit the roof but strike one floor lower? Then only six. Well, it shouldn't penetrate six. And if it should strike the fourth floor? Such a thing had happened in those large stone buildings. Not to mention the example of the General Savings Association. Then only five would remain. Only this solid structure . . . Klein. And if a "cow" should suddenly rip downwards from the third floor? And strike the ground floor and rip out something? From the cellar? A dumb "cow"? Or a "bertha"? Or rather, something which is seemingly not considered as serious. Or it would be enough if it hit one of the compartments. And it wiped out one of us. A family or an individual. Or next door. Because we worried about our own. And about those who were still nearby but already somewhat farther away we worried somewhat less. About those even farther off but still at this address, we worried a little bit. But about the neighboring building? Or the one across the way? We didn't even think about it. But who will dig us out if we should be buried? —They will. —Then who will dig them out? —We will. —And what about those really far away? Those were strange calculations. Which everyone made. Everywhere. On the basis of probability. And how many of those who calculated that way perished? Well, how many? No one knew. But it was a horrifying percentage. I am not counting the wounded, the rescued, the extricated. The more of us there were—the better. Seemingly. Because the possibility of so-called accidents (for war is like a collection of unfortunate accidents and an uprising is like the explosion of that collection) is spread among a larger number. Or rather, fewer of us would have to die. At the same time, what's the difference if there will be 300 or 500 of us in this cellar if it will bury us to a man? And crush us? There was an incredibly large number of people in the ghetto. Not 500. Not 5,000. But 500,000. And practically all of those who didn't flee died. Death was the basic premise. The greatest probability. Almost the only one. Almost 100%. Because it was that way for many without any "almost." That too was an error of statistics! Besides: if the bombs are falling now it means that someone is dying. For every explosion you hear, something is struck. Let's say, not every one. Because there were duds. Or misses. Or they hit a roadway. Or a lawn. Or the center of a yard. In addition, if something is struck it may collapse and yet not collapse into the cellars. Then people may be buried, but not wounded. But then it's a matter of digging them out. Which is also risky. Because who could clear away the ruins of such a building as ours at No. 23 Wilcza? Who would attempt it? And how many? And with what? And for how long? And meanwhile we could suffocate. Or something. And the lack of water? And during that time there'd be more air raids, chaos. And so on. Now, if only a part is buried and it can be quickly dug out, and if only some people have died and the rest are basically uninjured—this time round—then that's probably not such a bad average. As an average. For these times. But is it right that anyone should die? Even if it's only ten people? And won't the next time, then, be the end for all the rest? It could happen several times in the same place. Moreover, everything depends on the number of bombs. But it's known that they're dropping them only in great numbers. And not on such a vast area. A large one, to be sure. Because they still have Mokotow. The other end of Srodmiescie. Zoliborz. Czerniakow. But there are houses there too. Under the houses—people. Not to mention the partisans in action. With even worse protection. Or without. The more of us who die the worse it is. Because it weakens us. From the statistical point of view, it's also worse. Because now the same number of bombs can fall on a smaller number of people. Or more bombs. And what about the other weapons? Accidents? Cave-ins? It's happened, it seems. And transports to a camp?

And on top of that there's the destruction of protective structures. If the building should collapse, if it disappears, then our chances become worse. Or it could shrink even more. And more. Go somewhere else? Where? Houses are dwindling everywhere. And the crowding. People are dying. That's true. But buildings are dying too.

Or fires. Because they happen. Fire itself is nothing. In comparison with bombs. One can flee a fire. People sit in the cellar until the fire is on the ground floor. Until the neighbors call out:

"Come out! The ground floor's burning already!"

And then they come out.

But then one's shelter is lost. And the shelter? The better it is the greater possibility that it will remain. Or so it would seem. But on the other hand, should a so-called fatal accident occur, then everything good becomes bad.

And you can keep on in a circle, calculating, pondering,

observing, fleeing.

Swen doesn't come. One day. Nothing surprising. Neither does Roman Z. He told us he would but he too doesn't come. Maybe something has happened? An action? But on the other hand, those air raids. . . . But the next day, too, they don't show up. We wait. Well, they'll come. . . . Although it surprised us.

We sit around with our beards growing. We don't wash. Only once in a while. Mainly from a bottle. A bit. Here and there. Washing is thoroughly out of the question. There's only a little water. It's over there more or less. In that valley near Krucza. But that's a large area. And they're firing. But to get along without water? Everyone has to wait until twilight. But at twilight the grenades, mortars, "berthas," "cows" go wild. In the courtyard the weapons have a different meaning. Not only bombs but everything else is important. And very much so. Despite that, people go to fetch water. That day, Father goes too. He takes a bucket. His armband on his sleeve. It's afternoon. The rest of us—Zocha, Stacha, Halina, Stanislaw Woj., Mrs. Trafna—stay behind. The Wi. family is staying put. Father is away a long time. Bombs are falling. Nearby. Far off, too. Somewhere, all the time. But that's nothing. We know that there's a huge line there. It seems they're coming back. Some people. With buckets. Of water. And they tell us how many people there are. An hour. Two. Suddenly there are explosions. Right beside us. Did we get hit ourselves? Did someone rush out to check? Or rush back? Yes. I think people ran back. Without water. Terrified. Because something had exploded. Once. Or more often. Apparently it was a bomb. Nearby. And shells. One hit the well itself. It seems some people died. Hm, yes. The well destroyed, the source of water cut. Tough luck. But the people. . . . What happened to Father? Zocha-Zula and I jump up. We run. Through the hole. To that huge depression in the great courtyard. It's about ready to grow dark. Or it is growing dark. It's like a battlefield. The wounded. The dead. They've moved them away. Already. Father's not there. He's disappeared. We go back. He's not there. We sit down. It's evening. He's not here. Where is he? Why isn't he here? Where can we look? For his traces? In case. We don't sleep. Zocha and I. No one does. In our family. We wait. Maybe he'll still come. And if he doesn't? We'll have to go from hospital to hospital in the morning. Begin with that. But he will come. . . . Yes. And it's nighttime. . . . And late at that. But he's not back.

Finally, towards morning, I think, or in the morning, when we were already certain that something dreadful had happened, he returned. With the bucket, I think. Healthy. Sound. Wearing his armband. So it was nothing. A bomb fell. It hit. It destroyed the well. And people? Some of them, too. Something. But mostly they managed to scatter. Father also fled. He ran to Chopin Street. For water, I think. Right behind that little square with the barricade across it. A colleague of his lived nearby. Whom we knew. All of us. An eternal soldier. Jolly. Mr. Kowalski. He tempted Father. To drop in. With the bucket. He goes in there. Upstairs. Because his billet is upstairs. Because one side of Chopin Street is Polish and the other German, the're not bombing over there. So as not to hit their own. The billet is in an engineer's house. With a daughter. A grown girl. The windows are open. It's fair weather. The devil take it! They'll play cards. Probably bridge. Because the four of them sat down this way: Father against the wall, with his back to it, between the windows; Kowalski facing Father; in one window, the daughter; in the other, the engineer. They play. A shell. Soviet. They hadn't remembered about the front. Fragments fly in. Through one window. And the other. Nothing happens to Father or Kowalski. The engineer is wounded but that's only half the trouble. The daughter's side is torn open. So they run down for a stretcher. They bring it. Set it up. Bandage her. I think they carried her somewhere.

"The daughter was in a bad way," Father remembers to this day, "that side, ech . . . completely torn open . . . her liver was damaged . . . something . . . else . . . I don't know. . . . It was bad, you know."

The next day Swen came running in.

"A bomb hit. Our low building. It broke through to the cellars. Half the house is gone."

"Four stories and it broke through?"

"That's just it. I was standing right in the part which collapsed. With other people. At the last moment I managed not only to rush over to the part that's still there but I also shoved a whole family over."

That was Swen's reflexes. And his experience from Starowka. That you can manage to do a lot between the time a bomb hits and a building collapses.

"The corpses are lying in the yard right now; come and see."

We ran over. Half the building was gone. Sheets were strewn

about the courtyard. That is—something in sheets. I think they'd buried some already. The yard. The house. Everything here looked hideous. Wrecked. You couldn't tell by what. Windows without frames. Heat in the air. Like after a volcano. Something gray. All the time. Hanging there.

On the third day Roman showed up. With his head in bandages.

"A 'bertha' got me in my billet on the sixth floor of Mokotowska. The others ran down to the shelter. Two of us stayed there. Suddenly we heard a 'bertha.' We were already lying under the bricks. The door had collapsed over me. And the bricks were over the door. A piece of wall. I couldn't be seen. I had a chink to breathe through. I could hear people. Walking around. I yelled. They heard me. They ran in. They started digging. And they got me out."

A bomb hit the well. Next door. And we began to look for water elsewhere. I think that's why we were rushing across Hoza, from Krucza towards Skorupka Street (called Sadowa today), until we were practically at Marszalkowska. Suddenly there were ruins. Fresh ones. They had bombed. Through to the cellars. The movie theater "Urania," the pre-war "Seagull." (There was a revue here in '42/'43, Polish, with the best singers. Warsaw was buzzing with revues in '42/'43.) As we walked out, people were leading a lot of Germans out of that "Seagull"–"Revue"–"Urania." Covered with bits of plaster, walls, in those thin green uniforms. Unbuttoned. Somewhat tattered. Prisoners of war. For an exchange. They'd been sitting under the stone building which was the post-"Seagull" "Urania." A bomb. Hit. Or bombs. And broke through. Those who weren't killed were dug out. Now people were escorting those who hadn't been wounded. Simply to another place. We passed by them. In fact, crowds of people passed them. Rushing by. Some from the bombed-out houses, others to help; some to search, others looking for water, still others on official business. Amazed. And the Germans looked at us and at the buildings, and at everything—with fear. That was because of what they wanted to happen to us before this. They had wished it. Perhaps not all of them had. And now their own bombs. A paradox. But not a joke.

I'm confused by two moons. One, from August 26 on Miodowa, on that frieze. The other, around September 6 on Nowogrodzka. So, a span of thirteen days. That might be possible if you

181

counted it as the interval from one phase to another. However, on Nowogrodzka it seemed to be a full moon. In fact, it most definitely was the moon. But there shouldn't have been a moon on Miodowa. It could only have seemed that way at times. Memory has already transformed it into the moon. But no doubt it was the reflection of fires. What would the moon be doing there?

And what about the front? The Soviet front, as people said then. ("Soviets," or simply "Russians," sometimes "Bolsheviks." But during the uprising they used the term "Bolsheviks" less frequently because it had a traditional connotation among us which was inappropriate. And in this situation words which smacked of something like that weren't used. After all, "beggars can't be choosers.")

Well, it seems that on the night of September 9-10 the first air raid on the German sector took place. They dropped flares; the kind that sway and illuminate everything for such a very long time, that you could find a needle on the ground; but most of all it was the shadows of the grass that swayed for longer or shorter times. I remember the explosions. And the flashes. Everything was near us. Onto Koszykowa, Aleje Szucha, Aleje Roz, Chopin Street and Bagatela. Until we ran out into the street from joy. Then, on other nights, more raids took place. On the night of September 13-14 a small reconnaissance plane appeared for the first time. Soviet. Twin-engined. Renowned for its versatility. It stuttered. Trr-trr-trr, trr-trr-trr. . . . We called it the stutterer from the first time we heard it. It flew quietly. Stealthily. Low. It was hard for the Germans to shoot it down. They never shot one down. And it made drops. Of arms. Of food. Without parachutes. So they plunked right down, because they weren't dropped from very high: plunk!—a sack of rusks; or, plunk!—a sack of arms.

People said the weapons were broken. I don't know. People also said that the majority of the other allies' parachute drops fell on the German sector.

The next night there was another stutterer. It flew on and on for a long time. Like a glowworm. Trr-trr-trr-trr-trr-trr-trr-trr. . . . More or less in a circle. It came back. It grew quiet. Then again it stuttered, trr-trr. . . . As if it was confused. It hadn't found its target. So it seemed. Like insects. What they know, they do. However, the partisans lit flares each time. And waited. The stutterer's circling was made easier.

So the front was truly on the move? So it seemed. The radio announced it. And the news sheets. It was moving. That meant it was already on its way here. Opposite us.

Until at last it arrived.

September 15.

In the heat.

In the afternoon. At four o'clock. Maybe. Or five.

It started.

Suddenly.

Everything at once.

And so it went.

You could hear the "katiushas" in all of this, or rather the so-called "Stalin's calliopes." That is, a series of explosions; and did they go at it! And the rest of them too. But I think I'm describing it poorly. Because a single roar exploded instantaneously. As if the sky had collapsed upon the earth. Or, I think that's how I felt then, that it was completely torn into pieces (so that it was remarkable that it was still hanging there). And so it went. The same. Without change.

I had not known that there could be such a roar.

We knew so much. And yet. . . .

That was one of the major strikes. On the eastern front. In that war. Simply because so many were fighting at the same time. Bombs. Other artillery. Guns. And "Stalin's calliopes" (the counterparts of the "cows"-"nickelodeons"). So that, by and large, there wasn't even time for echoes to be heard. We all ran outside. From wherever we were. Immediately. Whole crowds. We crawled out of the cellars. People were standing higher and higher. On boards. On hillocks. On the ruins. As if that might help us to see. And yet we saw only the sky. But it seemed that by standing on some ruins or excavations, and using boards, paving stones, we would be nearer. At least we would hear better. As if that were the problem. Precisely. We were shocked, incredibly shocked. Despite certain previous signs in the sky and from the sky to the earth. It must have shocked the Germans even more than it did us. Despite everything. Because we wanted it. At least for that reason.

What was happening over there—in Praga—was hard to imagine. The familiar places, streets, gardens, in which Dantean scenes might be taking place now. After all, the front must be passing through all the houses, ditches, squares. (Unless it suddenly stumbled across an empty space. As happened to someone in Slask in February

1945, but that was because an entire group got drunk and fell asleep.) And such scenes did take place. One of the greatest cauldrons it seems was right in the middle of Skaryszewski Park. After the war, no matter how many times I walked through that familiar park, particularly near the walled outhouse which was badly scarred by bullets, grenades, shell fragments, I would picture to myself how important this stupid spot was then, that history had touched it in those days, that for more than one person this outhouse was the last refuge or the last view of his life. The second cauldron, it seems, was near the Praga approach to the railroad bridge, the one from the Citadel. A lot of Germans were massed there to defend the bridgehead. The Russians attacked them. By air. The Germans, pushed back to the Vistula because the attack was driving them from the land, threw themselves onto pontoons. Afloat. Into the water. But nothing helped. They were massacred. We, who observed with our ears, looked at each other. Then we shouted warnings at each other. Afterwards, I remember, I shuddered violently from my ears to my stomach and back. I would not have assumed before then that such explosions could be the cause of so much joy.

The assault must have been awfully intense. One could feel that. By the ongoing tension of the battle. For two, perhaps three hours. Not longer. Because we were standing there all the time under extreme tension. And suddenly everything grew quiet. It was all over already. The sun was still shining. But Praga had been taken. Yes. That was truly the first happy day. Without a shadow of gloom. Hope emerged. And, to tell the truth, certainty. That it was the end of our misery. Of the bombs. Of the Germans.

That certainty weakened somewhat after several days. I don't remember if it was then or during the time of the Czerniakow bridgehead that there was certainty even among the leadership. In the news sheets too they were reporting how we should behave when the Soviet army entered. Well, why waste a lot of words on this. An order was issued. Not to give them an ovation. Also not to display hostility. But something on the order of indifference. I remember two words, but I no longer know in which of the news sheets, perhaps a right-wing paper: ". . . maintain silence." Simply "maintain silence." That astonished us. We shrugged our shoulders. After all, some contact had been made. Soviet observers had been dropped among us. In our sector. In order to give instructions to their forces on how to direct their artillery fire. There were attempts at conversation. And requests for help. We heard about Mikolajczyk on the radio. That he was going to Moscow. By plane. I was impatient because he didn't board a plane immediately. Because he was making preparations first. Because he would certainly take a long time to get ready. Oh God! What naivete! And what was it all for since nothing came of it anyway?

Efforts at reaching an agreement here, on the spot, across the Vistula, also were only attempts. One could sense that. And somehow it was known. I have no intention of entering further into matters which have already been clarified. I insist on this. It's essential. The English radio also upset us more than once. Although we were constantly running along the twisting corridors to those chinks to listen. So, first of all, it upset us because they wove too many extras into their broadcasts to us. "Best wishes for the Jewish New Year." "With the smoke from the fires."* And a new, although ver old, hymn from the time of the Confederation of the Bar:*

> *To arms,*
> *Jesus and Mary, to arms. . . .*

At that time Halina and I thought it was brand new and we liked it very much. Furthermore, we were irritable out of jealousy. Because the front was moving. Because there was an uprising in Paris. Four days. And already Paris was free. Or rather, it was the way we had imagined ours before it began. Or again in Holland—all the time, new names of liberated cities. Arnhem cut me. To the quick.

September 18, in broad daylight, suddenly a squadron of American planes flew over. And the whole sky started to flutter with colored parachutes. They really were colored. Assorted colors. They took a long time falling. For our short patience. They had something tied to them. We waited to see what. It turned out there were weapons there, bandages, and books. It didn't become known right away. Because not a single parachute landed near us. I think there was a little wind that day. It seems to me that, atypically, the weather was not so very hot. So the parachutes were carried away somewhere. Finally it seemed as if they were landing on us. And then, no. But it didn't do anything for us at all. Because most of it fell on the German sector.

After that diversion our mood was spoiled. Because the front was really in action. Or shooting. The stutterer flew over by night. But we simply wanted to be liberated. And somehow that didn't occur.

One thing important began to happen. Very frequently, as soon as they started to bomb us, the others simply drove them off. With their own planes. But the Germans were stronger over here. Because those who had been driven from Praga to this shore were included in the anti-uprising actions. The artillery began to rage. The armored train fired continuously. From the belt railroad. From the west. And also there were attacks on the partisan divisions. It wasn't known if the front would hold near the Saxon Gardens. And in western Srodmiescie. What really struck me, after the hell on Chlodna and Wronia, was that the front from Ceglana-Lucka was holding right on Wronia.

Immediately after their loss of Praga the Germans attacked whatever wasn't theirs over here. From the Vistula. Sielce fell. On the night of the 15th/16th. Marymont fell on the 16th too. We definitely read about that then. But I had forgotten. And not only I. How had Marymont held out for a month and a half? A little heap of houses on sloping sand. Only, it was propped up on one side towards Zoliborz. Bielany was separate then, much further off and smaller. Zoliborz was several times smaller. It didn't have as many streets. Rather, construction was in housing blocks. So it was difficult to run through there. Very few hidden niches. The blocks weren't too high. The only housing blocks which were somewhat higher were near the Square of Wilson and the Veterans (called the Square of the Paris Commune today). There were a few narrow streets. Built up near Winnie-the-Pooh Street. So how could Zolyborz hold out? And yet it did. I know very little about that. On the other hand, I remember what burnt-out Mickiewicz Street looked like. And the center, which was bombed to bits. Wilson Street. Krasinski Street. And the rear. Where the terrain slopes downhill. The Germans were attacking southern Powisle at that time. Or the former upper Czerniakow. What went on there I know from Teik who, after all, had already survived Wola. Then Starowka. Then this. He survived. That's a bit too understated. After all, it was they who were falling from the roofs. Men like Teik. They defended Wytwornia (in August). And attempted to join Zoliborz. Via Muranow. Zoliborz was late. The Germans expected something. And began to attack. Teik and his colleagues defended themselves in the depot. At the Gdansk Station. I don't know how many of them came out of that alive. At one moment Teik found himself in the toilet. It was not for nothing that I recalled the Ska- ryszewski outhouse. I know several other tragic outhouse stories. Zygmus M. told me (in a sanatorium already) how as a soldier dur- ing the German attack in 1939 he had leaped inside a wooden out- house. How the outhouse took a carbine round. And Zygmus thought that that was the end of him. I myself, in '43, during a So- viet air raid, rushed into my so-called courtyard lavatory on Chlodna Street. Some other guy rushed in after me. The Soviet planes were aiming at the tracks of the old "Siberia." Not too far from us. The bombs were falling with a thud. As if someone were hammering on metal. And they went somewhat astray. Because they were dropping from a great height. At one point the latrine shook. And we thought it was our time to be buried. The bomb hit the corner of Zelazna and Chlodna Streets. But let's return to Teik. Well, he's there in the depot toilet in Muranow. With a friend. Both of them are lying there for the time being. Unconscious. Then they realize that they can't move. Because the floor and a piece of the wall are pinning them down. Then they want to talk things over. But they can't hear anything. So they dig out. They pick themselves up. And in the meantime they wink at each other. And now it's time to clear out. They rush into the hall. The Ger- mans are astounded. They throw two grenades and run for it. Teik calculates while running. They have the grenades and then what? He took off. He chose well. Because he's still alive.

Teik was on Solec too. The farther end of Solec was peculiar. Cobblestones. I hadn't known that Solec stretched so far. Once, when I was young, I took a long walk there. There were stone buildings, people, women. And since it was fine weather, spring, there was lots and lots of blue sky and water. But where was it, where was it? I don't remember. But those people. Exactly. They caught it there; woe is me, they caught it. And they had the land- ing there too.

"Tonight the Soviet (I think that's the word they used) troops landed on the Czerniakow beachhead."

That morning I was at the radio chinks myself. As soon as the news came over I started running back to my people. Along the corridors. The turnings. In leaps and bounds. What joy! Until sud- denly there was an explosion in my head. Pain. Blood. Well, it was nothing important. I'd forgotten. How low the passageways were. With those Klein beams. And I'd banged my forehead against

187

something iron. Everything went dark before my eyes. For many years afterwards I had a small scar in that spot.

Well, that landing. And the Zoliborz landing too (on Krasinski Street) which I think we didn't know much about at that time. They didn't succeed. People died and died. For the rest—retreat. Some went with them. Some of ours, I think. Some of our men from down below and of theirs, too, I think, broke through uphill. To Upper Mokotow. And after several dozen hours of renewed hope or even certainty, together with the rumor (or perhaps the truth):

"The Russians seem to be on Ksiazeca Street!"

Which meant only the Place of the Three Crosses and Zurawia Street (how far was that?—a kilometer) and then—us. But no. Later, after that hope, the radio. I hear:

"Today at . . . o'clock . . . the Kosciuszko Division . . . from the Czerniakow beachhead . . . driven back. . . ."

In Starowka people had said with a sigh:

"The fifteenth day. . . ."

"The sixteenth. . . ."

"The twentieth day of the uprising."

Now, here, after so many reverses, there was no longer anything to count.

"The fortieth—the fortieth."

"The fifty-second—the fifty-second. . . ."

We began to treat it as the only reality (because we felt it that way). What was. Is. And will be. People joked:

"Well? And when winter comes?"

"Indeed. And Christmas?"

"So? We'll be sitting here then too. . . ."

"Perhaps there'll be Christmas trees . . . from somewhere."

Problems of cold weather were foreign to us. Distant. That year. Particularly.

We went to Chopin Street for water. At first, I think. During the period of the Soviet night raids. Past the barricade. Because of those gray sacks. And bending down. They were gray at night too. A stretch straight ahead. Then a sharp left. It was safer at night.

Then to Wilcza. I don't know if we went to the house just beyond the corner of Mokotowska, on the right side, right away. Because once we walked on Krucza and Wilcza. Then again on Mokotowska. In any case, somewhere around there. I remember many trips in daylight. But there were trips in the evening too. And at twilight. Because we learned the passwords. And the responses (the response was more important). And sometimes we replied. Lots of people went with us. And lots passed us by. Civilians. And partisans. And those who were half and half. With buckets and without. The evenings were warm. I remember dry earth under my feet. And sand. Near the barricades. Anti-tank trenches. Near holes. Ruins. And those silhouettes in the darkness. Hurrying.

I remember Wilcza Street once in the daytime. On that stretch between Krucza and Mokotowska. The sun was out. Large buildings. Tall barricades. The smell of paving stones. From the barricades. Narrow passageways. One of the partisans on duty. And, as usual, a crowd. It remained in my memory because I was surprised at the outset. That there were people there. Walking around. Even the remains of streets. Buildings. It was still summer. A blue sky. A peaceful hour. Such sights. And the truth. Sad. I suddenly felt sorry. Because it could have been normal. I don't know if I thought about all of Warsaw. Probably not. It was enough that on this stretch of Wilcza something still remained, something was alive. It was warm. If only one could begin to live normally on this stretch.

Another time Halina and I were out walking. With Zocha or Father. Towards Wilcza. Already near that address which afterwards we came to know much better. It was late afternoon, almost evening. After the heat of the day. It was dry. Dusty. You could feel the soot in your teeth. Jagged fragments, earth, obstacles underfoot. It was right after a bombing. Right there. From a distance you could already note the absence of the three- or four-story stone house at the corner. No. Not from afar. It was as we were going back. But somehow we already knew it. Because we were walking on Wilcza. And the corner of Wilcza and Mokotowska was bombed. Completely shattered. Precisely—shattered. Drily. Crackingly. Into boards, laths, walls, bricks. The rest, badly scarred, stood there, hung there. The stone house was pouring out into the streets. Onto both of them. Into the intersection. And falling apart. Sifting down. It just kept on without any let-up. But the farther away you walked, the less frequent it became. Now boards, now bricks. And everything was so dry!

On our way back, since we were carrying water, we picked up several boards for fuel. Everyone was doing it. Why not? It was the same in Stare Miasto. Throughout the whole uprising. Everywhere. Because it was something to burn. We didn't have any idea if people

189

had been killed. We didn't see anything wrapped up. In sheets. At that time, by the way, there must already have been a great number of graves. In the squares, the grassy areas. After the potatoes were dug up. In the courtyards. And the sidewalks. In our shelters on Wilcza, not far from the radio station, a certain old lady died a so-called natural death. And a funeral was held. In the yard.

Janek Markiewicz's grandmother also died then of natural causes. In the same sector, only a bit further south. On Mokotowska. Or Sluzewska. I remember that the two of them had to look for boards for a coffin. They ran about. Janek and his mother told me about it. Until they found some. They nailed together a coffin. They buried her at the edge of Mokotow Field. On Polna Street. Later, it was hard to find it. People had already been brought there for the exhumation. They asked:

"Where should we dig?"

Then Janek's mother knelt down in the mud, for it was muddy, and placed her ear against the ground. And she seemed to hear her mother's voice. From underground. With her burring "rh":

"Don't worrhy, daughterh, I won't cause you any trhouble...."

It wasn't enough that her husband had been taken to the Gestapo on Szucha Street. That he was probably shot there on August 4. After all this the Germans sat Janek's mother and other women on a tank and moved with them down Aleje Ujazdowskie to the Square of the Three Crosses. They used them as a living shield for their attack. Janek's mother sat on the tank. And thought:

"This is all very well, but what's going to happen now?"

They were getting nearer and nearer.

"Another moment . . . now what will happen. . . ."

For some reason the partisans didn't shoot. . . . Because in such cases they never shot. Then the situation took an unexpected turn. It seems something hit the tank. They jumped off. The Germans disappeared (either they lit off or were taken prisoner). But the hostages were with their own people. Ours. It was here, I think, that Janek's mother first saw him. And they stayed together until the end. He was quite young then. Still almost of boy scout age.

Let's get back to the question of water. To those outings. Later Halina and I went most often. We learned the passwords. We carried buckets. Mostly at twilight. And we'd be off. With the crowds. To Wilcza. Or a bit further. Where. . . . I'll describe it right away. I know that on Wilcza, beyond Mokotowska, you turned left into a gate. But was there a second gate somewhere around here? Because you waited in a nocturnal line inside a gate (a second one, I think). A long line. The buckets were placed upside down. People sat on them. And chatted. Two hours. Three. It didn't matter. Anyway, we treated it as an excursion with discussions and other pleasures. No impatience. Did the line move up a bit? Did the buckets creak? So we'd drag them along a bit. Then, we'd flop down on them again and go on talking.

Once Halina said we should go a little farther. She may even have said that we should go past Aleje Ujazdowskie. It was already good and dark. So there we were. Walking through the courtyards. One. Two. I look out. Where is Ujazdowskie? We're in a medium-sized courtyard. With low walls or something. Black walls.

"That's Aleje," says Halina.

"That? That?" I ask.

"Why yes."

"You mean it's not a courtyard?"

"It's Aleje Ujazdowskie."

"How can that be?" We look more closely.

"Yes. Aleje Ujazdowskie."

Our inspection didn't help at all. Those were definitely barricades. Those low walls. The space was enclosed. But was it pitiful! Those black walls were the facades of buildings. Other main streets looked just the same. Marszalkowska too. We went on. To the other side of Ujazdowskie. Past Ujazdowskie . . . I'm not sure if we were there only then. That time. But that shock, realizing what it was, will remain with me till the end of my life. To have mistaken Aleje Ujazdowskie for a lousy back alley!

Our stove kept on collapsing. Also the building at No. 21. And Mrs. Trafna's little house. And the low walls. And the courtyard with the grenades. There was a time when I think we didn't cook on the ground floor. We stayed in the shelter. Then, I think, the food situation was already becoming serious. For everyone. By that time we were down to the last sugar cubes. Once, when Zocha went out of the cellar, I grabbed at her bottles. And tipped one into my throat. It was sweet, like juice. Sweet. But suddenly a shock! Something (unusual!) different. Revolting! I swallowed. Because there was nothing else I could do. And I began to think what it could be.

"Oil!"—a sudden illumination. After all, I like oil. Well, yes. If only I'd known it was oil it wouldn't have been revolting.

Once we had a lot of water in the cellar. Even in the kettle.

Stacha was pouring something. Swen came in. With a small bottle.

"May I have some?" he asked, as if the answer were obvious.

"No . . . no. . . !" Something had gotten into Stacha all of a sudden.

"Oh, excuse me," Swen retreated.

"No. Why don't you go for water yourself, just like everyone else does?"

Swen hasn't forgotten that to this day. Perhaps he's right. Because in those evil days Roman brought me a small but real loaf of bread. Rye.

"Here." He put it down. I took some. How amazed I was. And touched. After all, I've remembered that about him for so many years. And that's why he lived with me after the war. Because of that loaf of bread, I think. So one shouldn't be surprised at Swen. Although Stacha wasn't at all mean. She just had a fit. . . .

Exactly. It was a matter of fits. I return to the stove. The clay one. When we were there in a group. Cooking time. Zocha was taking care of things. Setting things out. She was angry at something. At Father. Or at me. Usually she was kind to me (after the war too). Even splendid. But suddenly she was furious. And said something. About my mother. Who, after all, as I found out afterwards, had had to dismantle a barricade and was driven with Stefa and Aunt Jozia between piles of corpses. Beyond Pruszkow. Stefa disappeared at one point. She bought her way out (like so many people). Then came a transport. To Glogow. In Glogow they met Michal. Who had stayed in Leszno with Nanka. And didn't know her address. Only through the family from Skarzysko. But after her return Nanka lived with Sabina. Michal came. She didn't want to go with him. The end! No! At last she agreed. But what? What was going on? At one moment (the bombs were falling, the Germans were creeping up, they were slaughtering people over there) he (I don't know why) said to her, out loud, in the cellar:

"Damn it, I hope the first bomb kills you!"

And Nanka went right out to the Germans.

Well, let's get back to Zocha. At the stove. Something stupid in connection with Father. Against Mother. Just to hurt him.

"After all, she was living with your Father." That she said to Dad.

"What?" I suddenly responded.

"Well? Didn't she sit on her father-in-law's lap? . . ."

Now I. Unnecessarily. Spat. And kicked the stove. It collapsed.

There was a short silence. Then Zocha rebuilt the stove. Like new. It didn't make any impression on anyone. That the stove was smashed. For how many times had it happened already? At once there was an effort to ignore what had just occurred. Then conversation. Already something like conversation. Probably I felt embarrassed the longest. Mama is Mama. But I know why Zocha said that. It didn't mean anything. We talked with each other once, twice. Normally. And the next day I don't think there was any trace left. Except that I felt ridiculous.

I will add another fit. Before the uprising. Back in '41. When Father sometimes still spent the night at 99 Leszno. (Because we were living there at the time. With Nanka and Michal.) Returning to the place of my birth. Snow was falling. It was morning. Zocha came. My mother wasn't home. Zocha had checked that out. Father was lying in bed. Zocha didn't know that. In the room. I was sitting by myself in the kitchen.

"Knock knock!" Nanka opens the door.

"Excuse me, is Zenek here?" Zocha asks.

I quickly close the door to the room. Before Zocha can see. And I remain in the room. I see. Father is terrified. He's sweating. Nanka says something. "No!" Father covers himself. "He's not here." Zocha asks something else. In a normal voice. Nanka says something else. In a normal voice. I think she still wasn't thinking about what she was doing. But already her voice was changing.

"And after all. What are you doing here? By what right?" And she grabs a brush. On a stick. Zocha runs out the door. Nanka after her. "Get the hell out of here!"

And you could hear—bang! Then they were surprised. The neighbors. Because they overheard from the hall. Mrs. Bachmanowa. With her thick lips. With a mane of hair. Whom I called King Sigismund the Old. She said,

"Nanka? Look here . . . Nanka. . . !"

Nanka used to be considered, and still is, a paragon of gentleness. Because that's what she's like. Nanka is an angel. But even in angels something interferes sometimes.

And fate is also fickle.

It is 1945. Zocha has returned from Austria. Through Czechoslovakia. On foot. With a cart. Writing a diary. For the time being she is living with us. On Poznanska Street. I brought her wood every day. Boards from apartment houses. She would cook. As during the uprising. And it was good.

193

It was the first Corpus Christi. I was sleeping. Morning. I heard through my sleep. Something. Someone. I awakened.

"Nanka?" I jumped up. To greet her.

Zocha, meanwhile, was preparing breakfast.

"Please . . . please eat. . . ." She offers some to Nanka.

Yet, after all, they hadn't seen each other. Since that brush.

Well, Glogow. The one from history. From Krzywousty. Mama is there. Michal. At work on the earthworks. Nanka walked thirty kilometers on foot each day—fifteen there and fifteen back. To work. And from work. In wooden clogs. Through the snow. Through the hills. And she would return full of energy. Although she used to go to the "Comet" on Chlodna Street and would walk until she'd say:

"Ech, my shoes are pinching me!" And she wouldn't go on.

Is that what we had to have a war for? And an uprising? To shake up the people? For those vice-versa-brushes, for magnanimous gestures? I don't know. They don't know either. Finally, Mama (also before all that, a long long time ago) used to go every so often to find out about Father. Once he was coming out of Zocha's hallway. And he said it wasn't from her place. Then there was another scene which Zocha made. Because Mama was there. After the war, when Mama was already Mrs. Piekutowa, even earlier in fact, Zocha told me. Once, twice, a third time:

"Your mother is a wonderful woman. . . ."

And Sabina told me:

"So what? Mama ought to buy her a drink now."

And both of them, Sabina and Mama, would say,

"He ought to marry her now. After seventeen years!"

He came back to Warsaw, because in 1945 he and Zocha had gone to Gdansk. He had married Wala. Nanka and Sabina came for the wedding. But they didn't visit afterwards. And they were his sisters. They visited Mama. Mama visited them. Not so long ago Zocha got married. How pleased she was! Father saw her. They wished each other well.

Let us return now to the thread of our story. After September 20. When it was becoming more difficult to wash. Because it was a long way to go for water. Our beards were growing. Growing. Tangles of hair. So that when I heard unexpectedly about a barber on Wilcza, on our side of the street, three or four houses down, I dreamt of a haircut, a shave.

"How much does he charge?"

194

"One hundred zlotys."

I was surprised that he even cared about those hundred zlotys. Even before, one hundred zlotys were worth so little. In fact, I was surprised that he was charging. Or taking customers.

Swen was sitting there with his beard. Reddish.

"Well, you know. At such a moment. . . ."

The moment had already lasted fifty days. Why shouldn't I go? I took 100 zlotys. From Father. They had a lot of money. Father, Zocha, Halina. And I crawled there. Through the courtyards. Or perhaps in the street. In the direction of Marszalkowska. Under those great secession-style buildings on Marszalkowska. They were shooting. Of course. Rhythmically. Artillery. I entered the yard. And either from the yard or the gate, from the rear, I reached the barber. He took me. He had sloping doors. I think he had just finished working on someone. Because someone left. He asked me in. To take a chair. There was an armchair. I sat down. In front of the mirror. There was a mirror, too. The water was cold. And only a little of it. But he had some. A comb. And clippers. And a razor. I think he put an apron on me. There was soap too. But everything seemed artificial. The whole place was dark. The front, which faced the street, was carefully boarded up. But the boards had chinks in them. And so it was half-dark. The whole place was dusty. Powdered. Everything, of course, was covered with powder. The chair. The barber. Not to mention my head. I remember sitting there. Patience. Traditional. The patience of a haircut, a shave. That half-darkness. My likeness in the mirror. Or a half-view of the whole scene. The parquet floors. Yes. My hair flew off. A lot of it. Every now and then something exploded somewhere and the boards rumbled. From the artillery. The barbershop was large. It echoed. The street was a tunnel. It added its own echo. The barber said nothing. I said nothing. As if there were nothing wrong. I paid.

"Thank you."

"Thank you."

I ran back to my relatives in the shelter. Renewed. Without a beard. Without clumps on my neck. My ears. Never before or after has a barber had such charm and style. Except. September 10, 1939, on the tenth day of the war, on the fifth day of our "wandering," in Rowno, I went to a barbershop for the first haircut of my adult life. That barber, however, was still part of our pre-war life. That was barbering!

Lice. It had to be. It was already too long. For there not to be any. Yes. Without water. Those clumps of hair. The cellar. It's an old story. But who gave them to whom? First, half timidly, some people passed them to others. Cellar to cellar. Street to street. I exaggerate. Perhaps in families. It amounts to the same thing. In one day, two, it was clear. Obvious. No one was ashamed before anyone else. But we gave advice. How to find them. Everyone was searching for lice.

I don't know who was first in our family. Maybe all of us. Zurawia Street had already announced the appearance of lice. Swen came. He said he had them too. Everyone did. They were around. Lice. Had appeared. It was hard. Your sleeve too sometimes—one crawls out. A person delouses himself a little. Washes up. Looks for them. Flicks them off. And keeps sitting there. It's no secret. Others will crawl over.

We felt them on ourselves. Right away. Like something burning. Everyone at 21 Wilcza. Quickly! Look for them! Halina and I rush into the kitchen. It seems the Woj. family had already found them. They killed them. In Mrs. Rybkowska's kitchen. The kitchen was private. Where was the entrance? I don't know. From the anteroom? Maybe. We run from door to door, to the kitchen. Halina and I quickly tear off our things. Halina grabs her clothes. She searches for lice.

"Nothing."

She grabs mine. I wait, half naked.

"Nothing."

But perhaps I searched my own first. And she took them after me. Mine. And found nothing. We had made a fire for the occasion.

"That's impossible!" Halina says.

Zocha is already preparing to look. And Father. Zocha also says it's impossible. Halina grabs her clothing. Then mine. At random.

"Give me!"

She looks them over.

"I think I'd better look at the seams. Oh, there's one! Got you!" Flick. Onto the stove.

"Oh, another!" Flick.

"Four! And you?"

"Four."

Or perhaps it was eight each? Anyway, later there were more. And for a long time afterwards. Searching for lice became fashionable.

We became experienced at it. The right time. The right place. I've described only the beginning.

In the meantime, as I've indicated, there began to be signs of hunger. Someone traded matches for tomatoes on the corner of Wilcza and Krucza. Then someone brought bread to that corner. Maybe rusks. Someone else traded cigarettes. Gold, too, I think. And so the bazaar got started.

We heard that a mill on Prosta Street was in our hands. Still well stocked with lots of rye, wheat, barley. That expeditions were being organized. Caravans. Whoever wanted to go. Fifteen kilos for the troops. The rest, as much as you can carry, for yourself. It seems people did go there. At once we saw people with sacks under their arms. Going to that mill. It was far. It's true. I was surprised. That it was beyond Zelazna. That far away. And that it was ours. But it was far. There would be trouble on the road. Unsafe. Artillery. From the railway. From "Siberia." From behind Towarowa. From the armored car. That didn't terrify us. We thought that perhaps we should go there. And quickly. Tomorrow. An expedition was actually being organized for tomorrow. The assembly point was on Hoza.

I don't remember how many of us there were. In our group. Groups left every so often. Of twenty people. Or was it thirty? Forty? We went: Father, Swen and I. The rest were strangers or half-acquaintances. I think there were probably some women too. I remember one for sure. With a sack under her arm. Each person had a sack. His own. It wasn't hard to find sacks. We had a guide. The collection had to be completed in a hurry. And the tempo of the whole expedition was quick too. I don't remember any waiting. The partisans, or the organizers of the expeditions, were counting on a large return from the grain groups. Each person meant 15 kilos for the troops. It wasn't so certain that we could hold the mill.

I think our group got under way immediately, walking more or less in single file. That was the style then. Anyway, you couldn't walk any other way. Through those cellars, holes and vaults of Krucza. Then under Aleje.

So, we were "in front of Aleje" for the first time by moonlight. Having to walk along Marszalkowska made a great impression. The first time. Swen and I. And several others, I think. I don't remember by what route, exactly, we reached Marszalkowska. A general debate began while we were running. Which way to go. After cutting across Marszalkowska. First we were supposed to go along Zlota. But the news was like a bombshell: Zlota was impassable. So we went along Sienna.

I think we turned somewhere behind Sienkiewicz Street. And then we ran across Marszalkowska. That means first there were cellars. And people were singing in them:

> *Under Thy protection . . .*
> *Holy Mother of God. . . .*

Then lingering awhile. And splash! Through that black ravine. What else could you call it? Stealthily past the barricade. I didn't see much. We could tell that Marszalkowska was under fire from the tower of the Church of the Savior. Black walls. The undersides of the trolley cars. And I heard, while running by, how someone on our side (our Chmielna) was banging out the "Warszawianka" on a piano. And immediately we dived into the cellars on the other side. Here they were singing:

> *From all evil. . . .*

We rushed into the next cellar.

> *Our Lady,*
> *Our Lady,*
> *O, Our Lady. . . .*

I remember that definitely, that in three cellars in a row, in three different places, there was that same antiphone. Clearly, we didn't feel very secure, since we were singing. Or rather, because those others were firing. Firing from that armored train. Father has sworn (on three separate occasions) that there was a shell every seven minutes.

"Every seven?"

"Well, I remember that we looked at our watches and hurried on, to make time before the next one. . . ."

But it seemed to me that others were striking too. In addition. Or perhaps that was all. In any case it was dangerous. For us who were running.

An explosion came, I think, right after we ran past Marszalkowska. Perhaps in those cellars. Then we ran out. Onto the surface.

The beginning of Sienna. But what that street and that whole area looked like! The street itself, those sides of buildings, and those rear yards! Just why were we running along it? Well, simply because everything was covered over. Even the passageways. Bombed out. The ruins were some two stories high! As far as the eye could see. To left and right. Here and there something stuck out. But nothing seemed real. We assumed that people couldn't be living under something like that. But they were. Those who survived. I thought of dropping in on Staszek. At least to find out. He lived in those left-hand "Tatras." But, in the first place, our group was running. And secondly, I was certain he wasn't there. How could he be? Practically certain. My experience in Stare Miasto down below suggested the possibility that they were there. But common sense prevailed. And we ran on. We ran along the spine of a mountain chain of ruins. There was even a trail. Red. Of bricks. With a sprinkling of gray. Father remembers that I stumbled over something while running and tore open my boot.

"And?"

"Nothing, somehow you kept running."

I don't remember this.

Only that running. To catch up. Shouting to them. And the ever mounting fear. At one point something exploded. Struck us. Only not the three of us. At the rear of our group. Panic. In one jump we dove under the wall. To the right. There was a wall there. And we turned. Into a street—Komitetowa, I think. I don't know if that made sense. We waited a minute behind the wall. Perhaps because of the people in the rear. We had to help. Actually, those who were nearer helped. We ran on at once. Still along Sienna. Or perhaps on Sliska already? But Sliska was just as horrible. And also covered with mountains. So, we walked out one at a time. Just be quick about it!

At Twarda there was an excavation. Under the street. Very narrow. One person wide. With pipes in the center. So that you had to wriggle past. Farther on—I don't remember what there was. Also mountains. Running. And a second identical excavation under Zelazna. I think we were running along Panska. Because there were those excavation mounds there. I no longer remember what there was beyond Zelazna. The mill was nearby. On the right. But first we ran into a courtyard. And from that courtyard up a huge ladder. Across the wall. Really high. And from there we descended on a second ladder.

"Hurry! Hurry!" They rushed us.

We went right down into the mill, or rather into a swarm of people in the yard. And onto a ramp. That ramp was the goal. Because the sacks of flour were there. Two-hundred-pound sacks. Perhaps there was something like a line. And perhaps not. I think we leaped onto the ramp right away.Tore open the sacks. And loaded up. Or rather poured into our own sacks. Mutual help. The ramp was high and long, and it seemed to me that I was on Towarowa at the foot of the line. I knew that I wasn't. But at moments I think I almost forgot. And I was amazed that it wasn't Towarowa. I held the sacks. Or supported them from the bottom. I think I was under the ramp. And Father and Swen went up. And poured. There were huge scoops. Swen and Father quarreled a bit. Hastily. Only for a moment. I don't know about what. Everyone here was quarreling. I don't know about what. And pouring. Probably about doing it more quickly. Because they were hurrying us.

"Come on! Come on!"

But everyone wanted as much as possible. And they were already firing. German bombers had appeared too. They began aiming at us. There was confusion. Suddenly Soviet fighters. They drove the others off. We were saved.

With the sacks on our backs. We walked to the wall with the ladder. I took only 60 or 70 pounds. Swen took more. And Father took the most. They outwitted themselves with their good intentions. Swen was afraid of hunger. After all, he didn't have too much to eat. And Father thought it was for others too. Both of them, after all, were eager to share. For Swen that was obvious. Father, on his side, had a family instinct. And in general an instinct for hoarding. On the other hand they had heavy, horrible loads. They could barely make it up the ladder. Those ladders were awful for such loads. They swayed. And how could you keep your balance with such a load? And here others are rushing you. Why weren't there holes in the wall here? I don't know. There must have been some reason. I remember: Swen had 70 pounds. Father had more. I had 60. I turned out to be the greatest egotist here. I was simply afraid of wheezing beneath a sack which was beyond my strength. But I wasn't afraid that I wouldn't have something later. I think for the time being no one touched the barley (there was barley here too). It remained in the sacks. As something inferior.

Only now were we really hindered by the excavations under

Zelazna and Twarda. We squeezed between the pipes with those sacks. And we had to help each other prop up the sacks, push them along, flatten them out and drag them through.

Beyond Twarda we passed through courtyards and holes from Panska up to Sienna. To the courtyards of those two or three houses in the modern pre-war style. Those which remained intact and were standing. We knew one of them well, because the literary evenings at Teik's had been held here. In the courtyard, the one belonging to Teik's building, near a hole in the wall leading to Zlota Street, we sat down, out of breath. The sun was still shining. It was hot. Some women brought out a bucket with coffee, or several buckets, and distributed it to everyone. They were good, kindly women. It was they, I think, who told us that we could return along Zlota Street. That it was just a rumor that Zlota was impassable. In the courtyard, this one and the one bordering on Zlota, there was a lot of dug-up earth, ditches, gardens, plants, plaster. Everything mixed together. In the sunlight. And also in the coffee from the buckets. My God! How much kindness there was in Warsaw then! Simple kindness. So much!

Farther on it must have been uneventful. Along Zlota. Because I don't remember anything. There's nothing to say about Marszalkowska. Also, it was different now: a return from the known. After all, that was important to me: to become familiar with that last western section of Srodmiescie. Because it happened that in addition to central and southern Powisle (you know what the northern part was like!) I got to know all of Srodmiescie during the uprising. And what was called district IV. After crossing Marszalkowska somewhere at the top of Zlota we turned and walked along Zlota carrying those sacks. And either on the corner of Zlota and Zgoda in a small courtyard, or in a yard on the corner of Zgoda and Szpitalna, was the place where the grain was weighed. It was a small triangular courtyard. Built up on its three sides to a height of four or five stories. So it was safe. We waited in line. A long one. For a long time. For the scale. At which two or three people were working. Shells were coming in. It grew dark. The shells were still coming in. The line became longer. Perhaps not ours alone. Perhaps there was another expedition, or several others. From that sector. People had gone out from all the areas nearby.

It was already completely dark (and warm) with shells coming in while the scale was still in operation. The line had grown smaller. Our turn came. They weighed off 30 pounds each. And with our diminished, that means lightened, loads we ran under burning Aleje. Perhaps it was only now that it was burning? After the fires here? I know that the passage under it had changed in some way. Krucza was still all right. Familiar. Swen turned in to his building. We floundered on to Wilcza with our treasure.

I assume that it was in those days when we had grain that hopelessness returned. Not as in August. Because they were already transporting us to Germany for labor. And even (those who were unable to work and people with children) to the Government General.* Hopelessness about the front. And the fate of the uprising. The Kosciuszko division had retreated. The front was standing still. And there was uncertainty on our small front, the front of the uprising. It was said that they could drive us back from the Krolewska line. Even so, I was surprised to learn that that line was being held. That, in general, so much was still held. Once I was walking on Marszalkowska. To Zdzislaw S. At the corner of Emilia Plater Street. (And here I come up against the fact that the expedition to the mill was not the first time that I crossed Marszalkowska or, if I was at Zdzisio's after the mill, it was only then that I became acquainted with the last quarter of upper Srodmiescie. Quarter is also an inexact definition. Let us say, part.) So, I ran past Marszalkowska along one of those streets. Hoza. Maybe Wspolna. I was amazed that it was possible to run past. And then I was surprised that it was possible to continue walking there. But perhaps that was only on the corner of Poznanska? No, I think not! In any case, the territory we held stretched as far as Emilia Plater. Or a bit farther. Because it was a corner house. That billet. Many partisans. I found it easily. I also sought out Zdzisio easily. He was there. We sat down on the stairs on the ground floor. In a crowd of uniformed men. Who were either sitting or running about. And the mood was pleasant because of the fine weather. In addition, they were not firing at that moment. But in general the mood was melancholic. Or perhaps I was there twice? That time, one of two or perhaps the only time, was when we already sensed the impending failure of the uprising. We sat there. Zdzisio a step above me. In order not to block the passageway. We spoke very little to each other. Although we were relaxed. Zdzisio gave me a lump of sugar.

"Here."

I began sucking it immediately. At that time treating someone to a lump of sugar was significant. That was our last meeting. Perhaps we will yet see each other sometime. Because we are both alive. We simply have lived in different countries since then.

Our trip back along Zlota with the grain had inspired Father and me to look in on Sabina. Sabina and Czeslaw lived on Zlota. Beyond Sosnowa. I think we ran there the day after the expedition. Zlota looked better than those Siennas, Sliskas, Panskas. Buildings were still standing. There were gates. We found Sabina without any difficulty. In the shelter. Or, rather, in the cellar. An ordinary one. With a little corridor. Or, rather, in a bin (for potatoes). Somehow, it was strangely roomy there. And peaceful. Sabina and Czeslaw had a door. They lived by themselves. They had a couch. And we sat with them just like guests. The carbide lamp was lit. It was evening.

We had to return. Out onto Zlota. With its iron gates. For a moment we were reminded of good times, until our heads whirled, until it smelled like a normal street. It was warm. And completely dark. And suddenly:

oooo-ooo!

We jump into a gate. A shell. It lands not far away. We rush out. Because we have to go farther. The next one. Again we take shelter. As best we can in an alcove. As if that could protect us. Once they begin to shell, they really let loose. It is obvious that they won't stop. There is no way to return. There is no way to wait. We go on. Straight ahead. Right to Marszalkowska. But I don't remember what came after that.

What else happened? In those days? Bartering sprang up on Krucza Street between Hoza and Wilcza. From day to day. On the third day it was already a small bazaar. On the fourth a full-scale bazaar. On the fifth a huge crowd. Standing. Milling about. (That stretch was "chosen," or safe, until the end.) Practically everyone held something in his hand. Anything. Anything could be exchanged, as long as it wasn't for money. Money was worth as much as garbage. It seems someone began to trade in gold. In addition to the sellers a lot of "window shoppers" or others, like Swen and me (visiting), milled about there.

Another diversion was grinding grain. Every day we did more and more grinding. Just like the bazaar. And also quickly. Because more and more people were dragging grain home for themselves. So that two or three days after we were there only barley was left. People were pleased with that too. And the grinding went on. In all the shelters. From morning to night. Using all sorts of mills. Small ones, big ones. For the most part people began with small ones. Like ours. In coffee grinders. shch-shch-shch-shch . . . around and around.

But it was too slow for us. Too small. We had a lot of wheat. (We were already eating it. At every meal. Platesful. With juice. And with the husks. Mmm, good!) We shared it with people who didn't have any. We gave some to the Wi. family, because they didn't have very much to eat. So we changed from a coffee grinder to a mill for something or other, a bigger one. We borrowed it. It seems to me that the bigger one demanded more effort, since it had a larger crank and larger grinding wheels. Then Zocha went and tried to borrow a large mill from some acquaintances. But it was such a large one that it couldn't be lent out. Or moved. We had to run over there with the wheat. To grind it. Practically all of us ran over. The mill was like a mangle. It had a huge crank which moved in a vertical circle. We poured in the wheat. And kept grinding. By turns. Zocha once. Then me. Halina once. Father. We looked into the drawer. And it was just barely there in a corner. The flour. Of course, perhaps it was ground more finely. But so what if it was so slow? Again we ground. By turns. Each of us had our fill of cranking. Till we were sweaty. We looked inside. And again there wasn't very much. We gave up on any more milling. We said thank you. We took our leave of that family. Pretending we had to, since it was almost evening. And in the morning we returned to those despised little coffee mills. They were irreplaceable.

And so until the very end all of Srodmiescie was grinding grain, cooking and eating with the husks, with great appetite and with pleasure.

During those days when we were turning the mills and going to the bazaar, the Germans threw themselves against Mokotow and Zoliborz across Czerniakow. I recall: September 23—Czerniakow—southern Powisle; September 27—Mokotow fell; September 30—Zoliborz capitulated. And now the whole force of the offensive was to be directed against the remainder of Srodmiescie.

Once more I must strike down false legends about how Zoliborz survived. And Mokotow. Nothing of the sort happened there. I remember how they both looked in 1945: not only burnt-out houses but piles of ruins. In 1949 I was on Dworkowa when a mound of corpses (around two hundred, I think) was discovered in a filled-in sewer. Where the stairs were. The gloomy history of the Mokotow sewers is well known. It was precisely there and then that the worst sewer incidents occurred.

After the war, Warsaw sang the "Mokotow March" with enthusiasm:

> *. . . after all, those August nights*
> *and strained arms suffice for us . . .*
>
> . . . .
> *This first march*
> *has a strange power . . .*
>
> . . . .
> *Something quivers in your breast*
> *and sobs in your heart . . .*
> *And the trumpet plays, tra ta ta*
> *Tra-tatata-ta-ta . . . .*

But to return to our subject:

I was not in Mokotow or Zoliborz. Others were. They survived or they didn't survive. Those who experienced the emotions, torments and reality there know what it was like. And have described it already. And will yet describe it.

Zoliborz, I think, awaits its history. But Mokotow has its own great tradition about the uprising. As does practically every section. Of left-bank Warsaw. Let us move from the Vistula to the Vistula, from north to south, like a fan:

Zoliborz.

Powazki. Here I know little. Lost on August 4, I think.

Wola. Well known.

Ochota. The famous vegetable gardens where hunted people sat day and night. Once a volley of rifle fire was emptied into a line at a pump. And those rapes—I know about them from a number of people including Ludwik (he was driven there—he, Ludmila, the whole family); every so often one of the women would return to her family "plot," to her husband, wailing.

Mokotow. As described above.

Czerniakow. Well known.

After the capitulation of Zoliborz on September 30 there was clear weather, heat. (Don't be surprised that I suddenly remember something. That's how it is. And I make no corrections because I want the difficulty of remembering and of separating events to be apparent.) Only Srodmiescie remained. And what was there in Srodmiescie? Krucza? With intersecting side streets? Or Zlota?

205

Even that's not so sure.

And the rest?

In ruins.

So?

A couple of streets which were one-half or one-quarter intact, which vaguely resembled streets. That's how it seemed then. Now they wouldn't even seem like streets. How could they?

The granary was emptied. The grain we had brought out for the troops, which had seemed like so much, had already been exhausted. There weren't very many weapons either. And after all, what kind of weapons were they anyway? (Laughter in the hall.) It was known that in a moment the bombers would arrive, the "cows," the armored train, all sorts of artillery, tanks—against Srodmiescie. Against Krucza. What then?

A heap of ruins? Broken-through cellars? And a mound of corpses?

I'm playing the wise man unnecessarily. Long ago others created history out of this, made deductions from it, and proclaimed them. And it is known. I am speaking like this for myself—a layman. And for others. Also laymen. To the extent that we can speak because we were there. Laymen and non-laymen. All condemned together to a single history. After various rumors in September we felt more and more hope. For survival. Perhaps we were not condemned? If only there weren't a catastrophe in this area. Perhaps it was worthwhile to defend, to rescue what and whomever could be rescued. Perhaps someone will smile pityingly at this point. Now? After so long? Well, yes.

We were alive. Still. That man with the torn-off cheek was walking along Krucza with his cheek already sewed back on, without a bandage. Capitulation hung in the air. Sunshine too. Also dust. Or rather, heat with explosions and rubble. Because they were firing! firing!

And I ran right to Zurawia that day, I think. To Swen. Upstairs this time. Because for some reason I imagined that Swen might be upstairs. No. I think that was the second day. I couldn't have thought that. That on September 30 they would be on the first floor. And yet it seems I did. I think it was September 30. Because there was still a sense of danger from the sky. And there was already a sense of the end, of collapse, of cessation. Like a thunderbolt, if you'll excuse the metaphor. Because people weren't only talking about capitulation. There was, it seems to me, an official announcement about forthcoming negotiations.

September 30. I am on my way to Zurawia. It's clear in the yard. Sunlight at the exit from the stairs, the apartments. Perhaps the other doors weren't open; only that one, on the first floor, the Szu. family's, was wide open, with doors and doors open behind it. Something exploded. Something was lying everywhere. One could sense a lot of people. Where? Below? Here the air was shimmering with emptiness. In the sunlight. Here, in the stairwell. It was still early, before sunset. And I was pulled, drawn to that azure by a song. One person, alone. Hoarsely and staunchly. And piously. In a masculine, peasant style. Solemnly-beerily. It came from the first floor. As it turned out. From that row of doors. So that I wanted to listen to all of it. Someone at the Szus'. But, however . . . I slip through the first door. I want to find out about Swen. The song is more moving with every moment. A second door. It gets louder. Here it is! But I see, because I walk further, that someone is sitting in a chair, in the center. Now I see that it's Mr. Szu., the elder. His back is to me, to the stairs; his face to the window, the court and the opposite lot. What is in the room? Space. Everything has been carried out. Only that song. A howl. Properly, with pauses: "You are absolutely beautiful, my friend"—Half-spoken, as it should be. Again howling. Exertion, then silence. Professionally. And again: "As the hands of the clock are moved back."

What would you want from the text of "The Hours," from his intention, from his concentration under stress? I was stunned. It was truly "The Hours." I walked up to Mr. Szu. Who was sitting motionless in his chair. With his hands in his lap. He didn't see. He didn't hear. He sang. I stood behind him. Should I ask? No?

"Excuse me, did. . . ." No response.

"Excuse me, sir, did. . . ." No response.

"Is Swen here?" Nothing; he kept on howling, motionless.

"Is anyone here at all? Here? Are they here??? No?! Downstairs???"—loudly, and still no response. Stupid Miron. Mr. Szu. howled. Miron ran. Ran around to face him. Mr. Szu. Who had his eyes fixed on the window, the sky; his hands as above (lowered); he sang (howled) and nothing else. I walked around him and, flustered (yes, flustered, that's it exactly—flustered)—I walked out rapidly. I don't think I found Swen that day; the song roared after me all the way down the stairs, through the yard and even farther, I think.

Nonetheless, the house on Zurawia was peculiar. And Mr. Szu., under the tension, performed "The Hours" for the end of the uprising.

That was Saturday. They were still banging away with mortars, "cows" (not bombs); at night too—I don't remember with what; I got used to it. People were sleeping in crumpled bedding in cellars beneath the protection of secession architecture, under that "credenza" (No. 23 Wilcza Street) which survived, which remains standing to this day. The morning was irritating. Sunshine. The same. Without change. A dry summer. And it was Sunday. Which no one knew. Today too. Instead it was known that it was already October. October . . . October. . . . Unbelievable. The third month? The third. Then which day? The sixty-second. But then suddenly in the morning everything grew still. The main front was quiet. The Germans were quiet. And we were quiet. Silence. Such as had not occurred since August 1. Did we know before this already, or did we figure it out immediately, or was an announcement made right away, that there was to be a truce and negotiations until nighttime? I think it was an announcement. So it was the end? Really? It was known that if they were negotiating they would agree. It was believed that nothing dreadful awaited us; people wanted to believe in that, because they'd had enough of the uprising and of the war in general and of hatred and killing and dying. Suddenly—everyone—wanted—to—live! To live! To walk! To go outside! To look around! At the sunlight. Normally.

And at once everyone started coming out from all the cellars, vaults, holes.

Onto the streets!

It wasn't a day of mourning. Nor was it a holiday. Who knows what it was. Everything at once. It was simply the population crawling out onto the surface.

And we went out too. Our whole cellar. Onto Krucza. There was such congestion already on Krucza that you could scarcely walk past. But who was in a hurry? Our whole clan walked out: Halina, Zocha, Stacha, Father, Swen (he'd come by), Mrs. Trafna with her bag under her arm, and I. It really was a holiday. Why deny it? We walked with the crowd. And we passed a crowd of people going in the opposite direction.

The crowd poured out of all the gates, courtyards, ruins, exits and side streets. There was no lack of ruins. All of Krucza was barricaded, dug up. Covered with ruins and crowds. But sunlit. And that silence, disturbed by the bustling about of people crawling out "into the city." On the corner, acquaintances, both close and casual, met. Passed each other. Talked. Stood awhile. Looked at the sky. Everyone—men and women. On the corner of Nowogrod-zka we ran into Irena P. with her mother and her aunts, too, I think. There were excavations here too. Barricades. We stood there. We said something and looked up. And suddenly way, way up in the blue sky Swen and I saw two storks flying. October 1? I pointed them out; the others looked and said nothing; they kept on talking. Then we said goodbye right away and walked on. With the crowd past Aleje, or rather in front of Aleje by the underground passageway.

We were drawn to Chmielna, to our old haunts. In general we were drawn to walk—walk—look—check. There was such a commotion; and such a confusion of impressions; those crowds, and the sun; and the fact that there was silence and so many things along the way, the crowding, people passing by, that afterwards I didn't remember what was what. We made our way to 32 Chmielna. That I know. Through the gate. The outbuilding was standing. I remember that we could see from the gate that our outbuilding was standing. We noticed the first floor. The second. And the third. Ours. And our windows. Undamaged. Open. Hooked back. As we had left them. We ran upstairs. Everything was bathed in sunlight, in the dry heat, in transparent light. The cats weren't there. Otherwise, everything was there. Unchanged. The cats' food too. Where were the cats? We ran downstairs to the janitor. The janitor told us that one day someone noticed that the cats went out through the window onto the roof and never returned. All the other people stayed at Chmielna. Only Swen and I went on, to the square, to Szpitalna and, via some other street, to Jasna. Across Napoleon Square (the Square of the Partisans). Right past the square things became horrible.

And got worse. Ruins upon ruins. Piles of rubble one after the other. I don't know what we expected. After all, I think it was known that those stumps of Krucza or Wilcza were only stumps and nothing else. Still, here and there something was still standing —half a house, one and a half houses. But they no longer had any meaning.

Anyway. It certainly was like what Adam said when I told him about that day:

"Well, unexpectedly there's a return to normality and suddenly there is no city, there are no houses . . . despair. . . . "

Yes, that's it exactly, there was peace already. The end. Everything was over. Two hundred thousand people were lying under the ruins. Together with Warsaw.

It was worst, I think, on Jasna. We walked over gigantic mounds of ruins. Now high. Now low. It was deserted here. And suddenly Swen began to cry. Out loud. So the whole street could hear. That tore me apart completely. I howled too. Maybe a little more quietly. We reached Dabrowski Square. Ruins on all four sides and in the center. And emptiness. That sky. With a lurking echo. Because it was sundown. And something was firing somewhere. In the Saxon Gardens. Farther on—silence. We turned back. The firing began again. During the night there was some action.

On the morning of October 2, 1944, everything grew quiet. This time for good. Capitulation. The end of the uprising. Announced. Starting today everyone is to leave. It has to be empty by October 9. The whole city. The partisans are laying down their arms. People capable of working will be transported to the Reich. Invalids and sole guardians of children will be distributed throughout the Government General. It seems the sun wasn't exceptionally clear that day; we ran outside quickly; Zocha, Father, Halina, Swen and I, this time to Piekna, just to be nearer to Marszalkowska, to get there more quickly, to check the first people who were leaving. It was rather subdued. It is hard to speak here of the first people who left. Marszalkowska, if you looked to the right, was swarming. People . . . people . . . already in line. . . . By the exit, with bundles, in family groups. Marszalkowska was dug up, blocked off. With barricades, ditches. So the crowd assembled on the other side from us. My eye caught the sign "Imperial" (cinema) above the crown and in the crowd I noticed Wawa. We looked to the left: the crowd here had already spread out across the entire width of the street. We walked along our sidewalk, from our side, to the corner of Marzsalkowska, Koszykowska and Sniadeckich. One departure point was right here, from here across Sniadeckich to Politechnic Square. And the other was by Aleje or Towarowa to Zawisza Square. Crowds were coming down Marszalkowska from the direction of the Church of the Savior. From Koszykowa, on the left, even greater crowds were coming. They all either packed in to Sniadeckich and moved about there slowly or stood in place, teeming, swarming about, or looked around, ran about, dashed back and forth as we did, or kept returning from Mokotow Field, from the gardens, with beets, carrots, parsnips, pumpkins, armfuls of produce.

And there were those leaves, odors, colors and a greedy haste to carry them to one's own kettle in order to cook them as quickly as possible and eat them up! At once! To have such things at long last. These processions to and from Mokotow Field grew larger and larger; people were rushing there, ripping up the vegetables, carrying them, cooking them, eating them, and rushing back, tearing and eating, in order to remain here at least a couple of days more, to rest up a bit, eat something, and only then to leave.

A lot of people, already loaded down for the journey, milled about at the main departure point. People were sitting on bundles. They were searching for their relatives. The remaining ones. Those who were lost. Who had promised to appear. Suitcases. Children. Some people spread out in entire camps. As if for a night's stay. At the intersection of Koszykowa and Sniadeckich. In the very center of the confluence of the five streets there was a large bomb crater surrounded by people who were sitting all around it. That's right. The truth. About those bomb craters. Every so often I recall an important sight or sound.

The whole departure proceeded slowly. It resembled an assembly for the Last Judgment. I think it was right then and there that we decided to leave on the second day, October 3. There was no reason to delay. What will be will be. Perhaps it won't be so bad. It's clear that they'll take us all to work in the Reich. If only not to the west. And not to a Bauer (infamous for sweat and starvation):

> *A dog is howling on a Bauer.*
> *He ate slops for breakfast.*
> *And for dinner a piece of tripe,*
> *So he'd bark at Poles.*
> *Oj . . . lala-lala-la-la*
> *Tra-lala-lala-la-la.*

We were supposed to leave together. Jadwiga and Stanislaw Woj. The entire Wi. family, with their children, Jozia, the mother, Jadzia. All of us. Mrs. Trafna. Both Zocha and the Woj. family knew that Mrs. Trafna was Jewish. Many Jews were supposed to leave with the Poles as non-Jews. Others, if they wanted to, remained behind in the ruins. But generally the Jews trusted the Warsawites at that time. The situation, after all, made it easy to trust, to not recognize people and to ignore the question entirely.

211

My meeting with Jews, with Kuba's whole family:

Kuba was a charming, handsome, simply beautiful young Jew.
He wore a cap and high boots. And he was tall, had splendid black
hair and splendid white teeth. I knew him. I and others. He was
extremely well-liked. He walked around, smiled. He was very se-
ductive. But not excessively. He knew how to make an impression.
I had met him for the last time in Dabrowski Square, where I live
today. It was summer, June, a thunderstorm; there was lightning;
we were standing under a roof and Kuba laughed at the thunder,
showing those teeth of his. And then once again, when he was carrying a sack or something for his family. Then he disappeared.
Which was normal. We remembered him, and thought that perhaps
things had gone badly with him. And suddenly now, October 2,
we were standing around, walking through our Wilcza-Krucza
courtyards. We passed some hillocks. There were a great many of
them. And depressions too. We were discussing. What. How. Who
will leave with whom. I look to the side. Those white teeth smiling.
That same splendid profile. I look and don't believe it. But he
smiles. Runs up to us.

"Kuba!"

"How are you?!"

"Is it really you?"

He smiles. Broadly.

"How did you hide?"

"Well. . . ."

"Where are you? How are things? What are you doing? Are
you alone? Are you leaving? No? Kuba! Imagine that. . . ."

Kuba with complete trust in me and Father, for he is standing next to me and Mr. Woj., says:

"We've been here in the ruins. On Wilcza. The whole family.
All the time. Twenty-six people. We are set up here. And you?
Are you leaving?"

"Well, it seems so."

"You're really leaving? For Germany? Why?"

"Well, really, we don't know exactly why." Because actually
Halina felt like remaining in the ruins. I did too. Father and Zocha
also half felt like that. But it was somehow decided to leave. And
here is Kuba persuading us:

"Stay with us. We're well off. You won't be badly off. We
have what to eat. We have supplies. They won't find us."

"Father," I say, "perhaps we should?"

212

"How should I know?" Father began to think it over.

"Stay with us."

I began to yield to Kuba. It pleased me. To stay. They had experience. Kuba was clever, worldly. I really wanted to. Very much. Halina did too. I ran up to her right away. I told Kuba:

"Well, we'll see."

"Stay with us."

Halina and I made up our minds. We absolutely didn't want to leave for Germany for the unknown, for labor. People were counting on its not being for long. But the devil knows how long it will be. Maybe another half a year? Wouldn't it be better to stay here in the ruins?

"Who'll find us?"

Zocha reconsidered the situation too. And Father. For a moment it almost seemed as if we would. But then we began to be afraid. Perhaps it was dangerous. If they find us they'll kill us. But if they transport us (if we leave), then it will be to labor and only that; to life, and not to death.

We didn't want to break up again. Although in the end it turned out otherwise. We foolishly began to separate, not to stay together. It happened by degrees. More and more. Beginning with Swen. Instead of leaving with us, he and Zbyszek (who wanted to leave as a civilian) decided not to. Somehow we didn't make plans. We didn't agree to anything. It was my fault. Halina's, too, a little. But how could Halina be at fault? I was! Slovenliness. Practically relying on a chance meeting at the right time. And then we didn't meet. Swen was with us that very day. Or I was at his place. Was it that Swen was estranged because of what Stacha had said about the water and other such trifles? So what? I didn't act. And I'm the one who lost. Swen wasn't well off in September. With living. With washing. With heating. Everything went badly. He even had a drafty place. Despite the heat. In 1939 Ludwik had stood in a gateway on Kercelak between two fires and had shivered from cold in the draft from the flames.

Mr. Szu., the man of "The Hours," hadn't gone mad at all then. For now he and his family were preparing whole jars of lard. Their son had a suitcase full of money. Just in case. What I know now I learned many months afterwards. After meeting Swen and his mother. Because we had somehow lost each other here, drifted apart. Swen left with the Szus. For Ursus. They were driven out. The old people were separated. The Szus.' son, the one with the

213

money, and Swen were placed in a freight car for a labor transport. But it was an open car. They rode. And rode. It was nighttime. Somewhere. Far away. Still the Government General. The
train prepared to round a bend. Slowed down. They jumped out.
Someone else jumped first. A shot. What happened? Who knows?
Then Szu. threw his suitcase of money out; Swen threw his bundle.
And then they jumped! They were successful. They ran to a village.
Schwanzdorf was right nearby. The Government General. Kielec-
kie. In Polish: Ogonowice. . . . They went up to a cottage. A
night's lodging. Questions. Lights on behind covered windows.
Mama, Aunt Uff. and Celina. And Lusia with Mrs. Rym. They
were all there. It's unbelievable. But that's what happened.

Our Starowka family: Swen's mother, Aunt, Celina, Lusia
and Mareczek and Lusia's mother had left when the Germans attacked, several hours after our departure for the sewers. Grenades
were being tossed somewhere nearby. But it wasn't so very dangerous. They were taken to Pruszkow or Ursus. Swen's mother and
Aunt were in no danger. Celina faced forced labor. (In 1942 she
had been in Majdanek for four months.) They disguised her. That
is, they put on her whatever came to hand and covered her up.
With kerchiefs. To make her ugly and old. And that's how they
got by. Through the selection procedure. All of them passed as
unfit for work. To the Government General with them.

Let us return to the main scene of departure. The final one.
To the so-called exodus. The day of capitulation dragged on and
on. Some people left. Others made preparations. Others thought
things over. Some passed by. Consulted. And everyone walked
about. Meetings multiplied. Gatherings. Indecision multiplied too.
Stupid separations. Sheer idiocy. Neither here nor there. And in
addition: carrying water, as much as possible, for a grand washing
before the grand exodus. All Warsaw started bathing. In families.
In shelter groups. In every possible vessel. I don't remember what
happened about shaving. No doubt whoever had what to do it
with shaved. After yesterday's holiday of crawling out into the
street today was a day of preparation. We put off our washing until evening. Meanwhile a discussion began about what to take with
us. Whatever could be moved. And what to leave behind as useless.
Everyone held such counsels. The Wi. family suddenly had more
kasha than they all could carry. We had a lot of wheat which it
was also necessary to leave behind. At least part of it. There were
those who had nothing. But a great many people had to leave

something which would have come in handy, either food or clothing. It didn't make sense to drag it along. After deciding what to take we began to discuss what to take it in. The best thing would be if each person would take something on his back and carry in his hand whatever else he wanted. Father and Zocha came up with the idea of sewing backpack-sacks for the five of us. On straps, à la knapsacks. The bags from cloth. And the straps from cloth. Because there was no leather. There was cloth, though. And a sewing machine was found. Zocha, Halina and Stacha began to sew those bags. I began to rush around looking for a supply of notebooks and pencils. In a corner of Mrs. Rybkowska's apartment I found a bulging closet. Completely stuffed with stacks of notebooks. Perhaps it hadn't bulged originally. But only began bulging from those notebooks. It was musty. The notebooks were old. So I quickly tore out the pages which hadn't been written on. Just at that moment Mrs. Rybkowska walked in.

"What are you doing? Those are my deceased daughter's school notebooks."

"Yes, but. . . ."

"Excuse me. . . ."

My buts didn't help at all. Since it wasn't at all obvious why I should be tearing out pages from old notebooks, there was no way to convince her. Even if I should treat them as souvenirs. I decided to keep ripping them out after Mrs. R. left. After all, I had to have something to write on. For the road. And for the transport. She left soon and I went on ripping.

I think we separated for awhile after the bags were sewn. Did we go back to Chmielna again? I know that Father and I went to Zlota. We wanted to see Sabina once more, to say goodbye. It was afternoon, overcast, but without rain. The haziness came not so much from above as from below, it was so crowded with people in motion. After all, people were also leaving in that direction—via Zawisza Square. And they were passing each other just the same, returning, discussing. The houses were black and gray. At the same time. Like the crowd. Balconies ripped off. And suddenly in those balconies—because it's hard to say on them—there were people. Heads in the windows. It was astonishing that people were looking down into the street. They hadn't been upstairs for a long time. Every so often someone walked by carrying a wounded person on a stretcher. Or a sick man.

Sabina and Czeslaw were bustling about in their little cellar.

Calm. They were eating something. They had something to eat. They had no intention of leaving tomorrow or the day after. The later the better. When it would be completely empty. Why rush? They left on October 9 or 10. After all, Sabina, Czeslaw and Czeslaw's sister had an apartment on one of the upper floors. So I went upstairs and stood on the twisted balcony. The crowd was passing. Crookedly. Massed together. Avoiding obstacles. On the left. Now on the right. Now in the middle. The street was noisy. An insane drunken voice could be heard in all of this. Loudly. Nearer and nearer. An oration? Well yes, an oration. I noticed a drunkard—if not a madman—in the crowd. He was raised somewhat above them, and seemed to be walking along but also seemed to be stopping on the mounds. He was haranguing the crowd:

"Pee-ople. . . . Where are you going to? Pee-ople! Napoleon has already declared. . . ."

No one listened. The oration was a bit peculiar, to say the least.

We left Sabina and joined the swarm. To Krucza. While it was still light. To bathe.

This was a major process. Long. By turns. In a basin, in water warmed on all four burners. Everyone bathed. Halina, Zocha, Stacha, I, Stanislaw, Jadwiga, Dad.

The Third Day of Holidays arrived. That seems like a metaphor. But it only seems that way. I sensed it then already. And I wasn't the only one. The day of capitulation came to an end. Which in the morning had been the last, the sixty-third, day of the Warsaw Uprising of 1944.

> *Tanks down Marszalkowska,*
> *Tanks down Nowy Swiat . . .*
> . . . .
> *Do you remember the July night . . .*
> . . . .
> *Jump to the left, jump to the right . . .*
> . . . .
> *All Warsaw will call out hello to us . . .*
> . . . .
> *Hand in hand across Mokotow . . .*
> . . . .
> *To arms, Jesus and Mary, to . . .*
> . . . .

Under Thy protection . . .
....
Without hesitation, confront the fierce lion. . . .

Our brains were reeling.

October 3, Tuesday, we went to Chmielna once more. People were walking about all the time, preparing for the exodus, going out, meeting, bringing back beets and carrots from Mokotow Field. We, too, were really still wandering about. The Balturkiewiczes, the landlords of the billet on the corner of Zgoda, took us down to their storeroom so we could get enough clothing. I don't know if that's when I got a coat or even whether I got it from Zocha and Father or from them. I did get winter shoes from them. For the exodus. I wasn't the only one. The whole family rooted around in the cellar. Among the shoes. I was deeply moved by the fact that these people worried about others all the time. I left the manuscript of one of my plays in the coalbin in this cellar. It was never found. The door to Chmielna was locked with a key. Unnecessarily. For the house was burned down by the Germans. Later. But who knew that it would become ruins, that some months later only Father and I would be here? That we would come here with a brush and a pot of dye and write in large letters:

ZOCHA, HALINA, STACHA
WE ARE AT 37 POZNANSKA APT. 5

Dressed in those shoes, with something on our heads (ski caps, no doubt, because that's what was worn then) we made our last trip across Krucza. Crowded. I think Swen dropped in on us once more. Anyway, we saw each other. Settled for a stupid parting. Neither saying goodbye nor not saying goodbye.

At the last moment Father and I gathered some things to bury: our documents, Halina's diploma, a camera and my notes (a play about the uprising, not the same as the one on Zgoda Street), written on Kapitulna Street paper. We took them to the cellar, or rather, the shelter on 21 Wilcza. People hadn't been in the shelters for two days now. We went down. It was black. Empty. We wrapped the camera in rags. We put the paper together in a tin box. We dug a small hole. Covered it over. And tamped it down. After our return in February we dug it up. They were there. Other things, on Miodowa, on Zgoda, which we had covered carefully with bricks, were sodden. Swen also went there, by himself. And

217

none of his things were there.

Finally everyone placed a large white cloth sack on his back. Sewn onto suspenders. And we stepped outside. We. The Wojs., the entire Wi. family. Down Piekna. To Marszalkowska. Here the crowd was already more dense. And in this crowd we stumbled along to the corner of Sniadeckich, Koszykowa and Marszalkowska with the above-mentioned bomb crater in the middle (where people had spent the night). Today it was somewhat easier to enter the stream. (It *was* a stream.) The Sniadeckich stream. The main stream of the departure. It seems to me that the weather was not completely sunny. But it was warm. Sniadeckich had walls on both sides, partly burned, somewhat destroyed, partly intact; at any rate, it looked like a street. We walked slowly. Because people were walking crowded together across the whole width of the street. In addition you had to take care not to step into a hole in the roadway or onto the stretchers with the wounded. We walked on and on. Although it's not a long street. At times to the left or right, or in front of us, a small uncrowded area opened up. Then people hurried to catch up. Or turned left. Or right. No one knew why. Something was said. People looked. To see what was up. But up ahead there were only people and more people. A single noise arose from all these people together. One was inside the noise, in its center. And one made noise oneself. With one's feet. By talking. The noise came in waves. Every so often a groan, a cry broke to the surface. Sometimes stretchers would pass us. The wave could be felt literally. Also a sense of floating. Which was actually an ebbing away.

The walls of Sniadeckich Street began coming to an end. Any minute now. Any minute. Then the turning off into Politechnic Square. Here the echoes changed. And one entered a whirlpool of sound. Stretcher after stretcher hurriedly left the crowd. The Germans were shouting. Carts were driving up. There were automobiles. The sick and wounded were being loaded. Green uniforms. Hitlerite uniforms. Worn out. Many of them. Everything against the background of barricades which lay across the square. A white sheet was draped over the barricades. The barricade only went halfway across. On its far side there was automobile traffic. And the Germans. Those who were receiving us. As we approached the barricade one of the German officers stared at us attentively. He stared at us one by one. One moment at me. He walked up to me. And quickly frisked me from head to toe. And already he was standing off to the side, watching and rushing up to the next people. But not so often. I was surprised then that he picked me out. As a suspicious person. Or rather one with a hidden weapon. After all, the partisans were supposed to leave at the last. And they were to lay down their arms here. At the barricade. And so it happened. Twenty-two thousand. October 9. Those who were leaving as civilians discarded everything that might smack of a uniform. And no one had any intention of carrying a weapon with him. What for? Now? Obviously, they didn't trust us. Now I am not surprised that he frisked me. They didn't trust the young. And I was twenty-two years old then. . . . The fact that I was dragging along with my family, in the crowd, with a sack on my back, didn't mean a thing. . . . In our own way we must have looked strange then. The civilians. And the partisans too. They weren't, after all, so very different from ourselves. All the people who were crawling out of Warsaw then were similar to each other and absolutely unlike all other people.

But perhaps that day it was cloudy and rainy? There was automobile traffic. Around the barricade and into Nowowiejska it sounded wet. As if the roadway were slightly wet. That's how I see it. And right after that, I think, a red brick hospital. On the left. Brick facing. Because it too was slippery... . . That's possible. But no. I see it too as wet. No one paid any attention to it. At all. We were too preoccupied with leaving. For the world. Whatever might come of it.

It was not so certain. That world. But it held out hope. And for the time being it wasn't so distant. But already—beyond the barricade—it seemed distant. No one wanted to go into the distant world. That's obvious. The Government General—that was the prize. Great. But people like me didn't have anything to count on. Unless we were to run away somewhere, near Pruszkow, along the road, from the train.

They were supposed to ship us off to the Reich. The Germans gave the impression of being knowledgeable, organized, sure of themselves. To the last. And besides that, they were shocked by our numbers. That so many of us were leaving. After all, so many had perished. So many had already been driven out before this. After an area had fallen. Or a street. From various parts of Warsaw. And yet so many still remained. We were amazed ourselves. That there were so many of us. Ahead of us—a line without end. And that line stretched the width of the street. Into infinity, because it

219

was difficult to speak of its beginning. Behind us—one couldn't speak of its end. The tail of the line departed on October 9. In that exodus which followed our total capitulation.

From where did we derive so much hope? After all, the transports from Warsaw had been bad. Transports from the ghetto in chlorine-gassed cars, in which people died. Transports to the camps. Transports to forced labor—now that was happiness. After all no one ever knew what or how. They transported my uncle from Bielanska, Aunt Olimpia-Limpcia's husband, to Auschwitz on August 31. That's why I said "that poor Stach." Limpcia received a tin with his ashes. Perhaps we thought we had a good chance because there was such a mass of us. Like those ants in the woods in Buchnik near Jablonna, which I saw before the war; we were near the highway then, the woods went off to the left and somewhere around there a good piece of land stretched to the Vistula; we woke up in the morning and there was a noise; we rushed out: the Vistula had come to us, a flood; we looked under our feet: a stream was flowing past, becoming wider and wider, near us and nearer; it grew wider by the minute; until suddenly a great ball of ants floated up, floated past; I don't know if they survived, or if only the ones on the bottom didn't, or if they all drowned gradually. They were counting on something, and must have formed a ball immediately; or perhaps they pushed by turns into the center? Like those people in *Miracle in Milan?** In one burst of sunshine very early in the morning they rush out from their freezing sleep, press together into a pile, each one wants to get into the center, and they're crushing towards the center all the time. Ludwik just shrugged his shoulders at that, for he had had it without the metaphor on Zieleniak—the first nights of the uprising were wet and cold and they were on the bare cobblestones.

The feeling that "since there are so many of us somehow we'll get through" can be misleading. Ever since the ghetto I couldn't believe in it.

Well, we were walking along Nowowiejska. There was no selection. The selection was done before Sniadeckich. We could have stayed with Kuba's family in the ruins. Under the hills of Sienna, Sliska, Panska. But we didn't stay. We walked on. Slowly. We got there. To the intersection of Aleje Niepodeglosci.

Here the line turned left. To Wawelska. Or rather, to Mokotow Field. And once more to the right. Along the edge of the field. On Wawelska. We could smell carrots in the breeze. Greenery. The sun broke through. The line ahead of us was dragging on and on. You could see far ahead. For there was a distant view. On the right, burnt-out villas and the elegance of the Staszic suburb, with its garden plots and terraces covered with flower gardens, and those smaller ones—everything empty, for a long time now. We were walking very slowly. We even stopped at times, because bottlenecks were created, jams. Every few yards an escort was dragging along beside us. I think they were. Or perhaps one escort passed us on to another? They definitely were walking in several groups. These men were from the Wehrmacht. Different from the ones at the barricade. They shouted without hostility. With humor. In gibberish. They picked carrots, tomatoes. They called to the women:

"Marijaa! Marijaa!"

And gave them what they had picked. The Warsaw "Marijas" accepted it and ate. Some of them answered in a kind of pidgin language.

At one bottleneck we tried to sit down. The Wehrmacht officers urged us on, very politely. As soon as we began moving they started calling out once more.

"Hey, Marijaa!" And something else, about our moving on.

Wawelska made people feel good. Because Mokotow Field smelled fresh and no bombs were falling.

Perhaps I ought to describe more fully how Warsaw looked as we bade it farewell from the outskirts. The outskirts were there at that time. Mokotow was invisible. It seemed to break off abruptly. And Mokotow Field, beyond the part that hooks around the projection of Grojecka by way of old Ochota (smaller now and shorter) went on and on, we didn't know where to, wide open, to Koluszki and Konstantynopol. So, Warsaw from its outskirts. Did we look around then? A little. But after all, we had just left from the center of what we could see from here, and the sight of it could not make an impression on us. I am exaggerating a little. Along one side of Mokotow Field there was abundant growth. And no people in sight. On the right there were distinct streets, houses, one after the other, in a row—and everything was dark and empty. But we were walking between them. We walked and walked. Sat a little. Moved on. And talked. We all were walking along the same street. Which was not so common. After Zwirki and Wigury, which at that time did not look very much like a street, we began to enter the center of Ochota. Between the destruction on the right and the destruction on the left. There should have been traffic on

Grojecka. But I don't remember any. Because—after Zawisza Square—there were no other Poles but us. And there was no movement of German troops. I remember our route. Cutting through Grojecka. I remember the cobblestones and trolley tracks under our feet. The ruins. The ashes. In our nostrils. In our eyes. I remember how we looked around. But I don't remember what we were looking at. We walked out into a small ruined area of Kopinska—several low buildings, wooden houses, carriage houses with stables. Kopinska had narrow cobblestones on a rounded slope. Two gutters with boards across them at each entranceway. Kopinska came to an end there. That is, it continued, but as a passageway to the Western Station, through a field with vegetable gardens, almost part of Mokotow still. One could see earthen mounds, platforms, cars. Freight cars. A lot of them. A curving line of people. And at the end against the background of the platforms, a scene of mass confusion. Past the end of the road, past the tracks, the platforms, the ruins of Wola, the rounded roofs and tanks of the Gas Works must have been visible. I don't know if I saw it then as my last view of Warsaw.

Sidings. Shouts. Traffic. Masses of people and things, crowded together. We are not far from the platforms. We push our way through very slowly. Suddenly, at the end of Kopinska, we can see a group of Poles. They are carrying shovels, sacks, bags, onions, tomatoes, potatoes. Those are Krauts in front of us. Railway workers. Platform attendants. Also Krauts. We draw close to the Poles, the ones who had been digging. Only one German is guarding them, and not very strictly at that. The Poles are carrying their sacks on their backs, their shovels in their right hands. I look: among them is an acquaintance of mine. I walk up to him. He steps back. Everywhere else there was excitement. But here—indifference. My acquaintance greets me. I ask him what they're doing here. They have been coming here from Pruszkow for several days already to work at digging; I ask if it would be possible to join them. He gives me his shovel immediately.

"Try it, perhaps you'll pass."

I take the shovel. After all, I had my own sack. I didn't think I was particularly conspicuous. My people, our people from Warsaw are fluttering and bustling about. Everything takes only a moment. We go on. The Germans check from memory. Everyone: Left march! *links*! . . . I see already. But I'm afraid. Halina. Zocha. With those white bags on their backs. Will I succeed? No-oo. What am I afraid of . . . a beating? . . . But the scent of a miracle is in my nostrils. Betrayal. But . . . in the first place . . . how could I leave my own people! Practically without discussion. Nothing. Just like that. Already. They've barely noticed. It's not important. I don't know. Suddenly I'm shoved to the right, something "fafluchter" and nothing else, no digging, back to the transport, I immediately give back the shovel, say goodbye to my Pruszkow freedom—Halina once more—the white sacks, Zocha, Dad. The herds. And already I'm among them. Who noticed? No one. And Halina? No. Then I was certain. But I felt myself a traitor. Disgusting. Here comes the punishment. We're moving on again. Nothing came of it. What else was there? Taking our places? We just got onto an open flatbed car. It began to drizzle. Gray. Long. Sad. A sudden letdown. Where to? What's it all about? Stupid tracks . . . tracks. . . . We're hungry! Wlochy—a stop. From the streets, from the windows, from platforms, from stairs, people throw large quantities of carrots, onions, radishes, beets at us. The Germans didn't do anything about it. We snatched it up. Father and I did too. An onion. Crunch. At once. Half of it. Raw. Father ate it up right away. I couldn't. We were moving. Very slowly. Very slowly. Past Warsaw. A sensation! What happened in Piastowa? In Ursus? It was drizzling. Vegetables were thrown from the platforms. Haze. Small crowds of observers-helpers.

We rode on and on. About ten miles. In those cars. Red. From under a Christmas tree. (When I was four, I got a freight train with four freight cars. I know that one was for coal and one, a very long one, for lumber. My family and I were riding now in the one for coal.) There was already a dense crowd in Pruszkow. Getting out. Full of jumping, crawling, shouting. Because there were not only a lot of us. But also many people who were waiting. Germans. And our Welfare Council—a council (The Central Guardian) whose job it was to make the wait easier by serving soup. And people from the Red Cross. We went immediately from the tracks to the right into the midst of the ranks. And we began to go deeper, into the Pruszkow railway yards, factories; now—camps. For those were originally cement areas with tracks underfoot, and then roundhouses, roundhouses and still more roundhouses. The camp was a terminal. That is, a number of terminals. The series of terminals had begun back in Ursus. Of similar ones; not these. It's correct that Ursus comes after Wlochy. Piastow after Ursus. And only after Piastow comes Pruszkow. I associated it with colored pencils. Because Pruszkow got its start from that industry and from those pencils. At least that was the source of its being a railroad town. The sector on the right, where our line—a transport—a conveyor—or rather, a constant flow, floods upon floods—stretched out. It was that part of town, the right side, lesser Pruszkow, with not as much pseudogothic ornamentation as on the left.

The Germans. Darkness. We, the transport, sent off to the roundhouse halls. An unwound ribbon. Was it raining? If so, it was just a fine drizzle. You couldn't see it. We walked on. We went in right away. To those figures standing there. Every yard, every half a yard. From the Red Cross, from the Welfare Council. On both sides. We walked as slowly as possible. Who knows what there was underfoot. They were standing in place. Wearing raincoats. To be recognized. More clearly. More clearly. And they shouted. Out loud. Addresses. Names. They searched. All the time. Left. Right. Left. Right. Left. Right. Addresses. Names. They kept announcing them. All the time. Those men in the raincoats, from the right and the left, by turns. The Germans walked back and forth carrying rifles. And we floundered on and on.

"35 Marszalkowska. Jadwiga Szamotulska."
"18 Chmielna. Andrzej Polkowski."
"5 Bracka. Zofia Wegrzyn."
"Malwina Kociela, 5 Mazowiecka."
"13 Grojecka, Pelagia Wachocka."
"Antoni Marzec. Artur Marzec."
"Malawski . . . 2 Chopin St."
"Kazimierz Czeladz."
"35 Hoza."
"Jadwiga Penetrowa, 12 Poznanska."
"Mieczyslawa Puchalowska."
"43 Wspolna."
"Zenon Kolodziej."
"94 Marszalkowska."
"Jerzy and Barbara Poroscy, 7 Zlota."
"Borowska Barbara. 5 Chmielna. . . ."

Why couldn't I stop thinking about All Souls' Day? Because we were walking in a crowd, just as one leaves the cemetery on All Souls' Day, between the statues of angels which were palely glimmering (because it was already dark) and the tombstones of ancestors laid out in rows. The strangest thing was that during that whole time no one, but no one, neither ahead of us nor behind us, answered the rollcall; no one stopped or even looked around. Total indifference.

My All Souls' Day metaphor was definitely not a metaphor at all. And if it was, then I've never experienced one more strongly.

We enter new terrain. If I say roundhouse No. 5 for steam locomotives but minus the locomotives, that will explain nothing. Exactly: a new terrain, without edges, without end, and not so much dark as filled with a crowd of people entering, separating and arranging things, crouching down with candles in separate plots. . . . Exactly as in Powazki, the sections divided by paths and each plot having as many graves as belonged together; on each grave candles and a family tidying things up or sitting there talking together and praying. . . . So, after leaving a cemetery (Brodno or Powazki) we entered a cemetery: a reversal in the natural order of things. For a long time I couldn't believe that this was not a cemetery and not All Souls' Day. Even when they had already settled us into a section covered with something, or maybe simply on the bare concrete; it seemed as if tombstones were being erected from bundles and suitcases. Halina and I began to look around right away for a board to sleep on.

"Just to stretch out," I say to her.

"I'm also looking forward to that, let's go find something."

We went into the recesses of the hall. We looked about to the left, to the right. Everywhere, crowds, gravestones, candles, bustle and a noise reverberating against the walls and the roof of the hall. Something like a wall was outlined in the same color as that space, perhaps I distinguished it by its shine or by some hardening of the shadow because otherwise the general darkness was pervasive. It was harder to make out the ceilings.

We came upon a strange wing with a railroad track under which was a pit (as it's called professionally) for repairing the undercarriage. At the end of the track was a booth. In the booth we found a long wide board.

"Ideal," said Halina.

We grabbed our treasure. What luxury! And completely happy we carried it back to our family gravestone, which we didn't find right away. We stretched out to sleep at once. It was marvelous. For the time being we didn't care about anything else. We also ate something which Zocha gave us, and so on haunting All Souls' Day, in a gigantic hall, the first unfinished day of the non-uprising slipped away from us.

In the morning it was completely different. Not at all like All Souls' Day. The smell of tracks, of the roundhouse; people. Bombs were not falling on our heads. For the time being no one was driving us out to work. Nor even to a transport. We found out that the Welfare Council was distributing soup, that there was a lot, that it was good, that it was made with tomatoes and potatoes. We ran over. The lines before the barrels of soup moved quickly. They poured out full bowls. Warm, fragrant, real tomato soup with potatoes. We ate it up. They offered seconds. Again we ate it up.

There was an awful lot of soup. Always good. Barrel wagons or cisterns would drive up. I don't know what they were exactly, and they would pour as much as you wanted. That's how it was throughout our entire stay. Until I developed diarrhea, and was running to the large, long latrine in which there was always a crowd.

They transferred us from hall No. 5 to another.

In addition to eating, running to the latrine, sleeping and talking there was also plain moving about from boredom. I saw on these occasions countless commotions with negotiations going on in small groups between the evacuees and the people from the Welfare Council and the Red Cross. There was endless traffic through the gate. Male and female nurses carried out some people on stretchers and led others outside. I concluded that there was a lot of pretense in front of the Germans. I was angry at my own people that they were so rich but were not sharing. Because it turned out that money was important. I was flabbergasted. It became obvious to me suddenly on the second day, I think. We went to a small building on the side. I didn't know why so many people were going there and why we were. Until I noticed an opening in the brick wall, or a small window, in front of which Zocha, Halina and Father were standing. I didn't know what they were looking at. I noticed vertically, just as at a shooting gallery, a part of the corner house, the roadway and the sidewalk. From behind the corner an elegantly dressed man in a hat walked out and turned in the sunshine. He was simply going for a walk. So, outside of Warsaw life and business went on in their normal Occupation way. . . .

At that moment a woman, one of "them," walked up to the little window from the street side. She and Zocha and Halina said something to each other through the opening. They gave her something. A moment later I noticed in their hands a slab of butter.

"So money's being used now?" I inquired of Halina.

"Naturally."

"And it's important?"

Father nodded.

Of course. Why should money have been unimportant outside of Warsaw? Here they hadn't had to build a stove from three bricks. Here there was no primitive cave communism.

We were able to stay on in Pruszkow. And the cleverest among us arranged things that way. After all, what was there to rush off to? Forced labor? But Halina infected Zocha and Stacha once again with the idea that "the sooner the better." My father agreed with them. He felt a great deal of affection for Halina; he was really attached to her; and even knowing her weak side—that she's an opportunist and doesn't take any risks (which she herself confirms) and that she and Zocha were always carrying suitcases because they had to have several changes of underwear—still he respected and even admired her.

We decided to report for selection on Thursday, October 6, in the afternoon. Selections were taking place continually. Between those who were fit for work and those who were suited only for distribution among the villages of the Government General. The Wi. family, with Jadzia, the aunt, the mother and the two children, stood beside us in a gigantic line. They told each other: "You take the little girl, I'll take him." And that's what they did; an only guardian of a child also wasn't fit for labor. The selection went rapidly. A number of Germans, two whole rows of these important men, shouted, questioned, selected and at the same time guarded us. To the left, the Government General; to the right, the Reich. Stacha held on tightly to Halina. A German wanted to send her to the Government General as too old. Stacha grabbed Halina's arm when she heard this.

"No-oo . . . together," and she was already in our line, and already we were moving toward the gate, past the gate, and to the cars.

Red freight cars, so-called pig pens. There were sixty of us in ours. They locked us in. The train moved. We were packed in. However, we gradually made some room for ourselves. Suddenly a problem arose: the need to piss. And what joy: there was a huge golden bucket. It was already being passed around. You had to piss in front of everyone. We were used to that. What was worse was that because of the shaking of the car I couldn't get started, although I really had to go. I just stood there with the bucket. I

227

became nervous. That I'd lose my turn if I gave it back with nothing added, but finally I had to give it back, for so many were waiting. A quarter of an hour later I succeeded. Happiness at last.

Then we lay down on our bundles and—when we began to wake up—dayling was entering from high above, through a narrow window. People climbed up and looked out through the window to see where we were. Halina also looked outside, dressed in her coat with the ash-gray collar.

"It seems we passed Lodz earlier" That's all that we knew for now.

So for the time being no one saw anything. Gradually we figured out that they were taking us to Lower Silesia.

The train stopped at last. It was morning. A time of urgent needs. Those near the door drummed on it. Until the bolts grated and we hurled ourselves out. Everyone leaped from all the cars. I squatted down beside Halina. Along the entire length of the train, lined up in four rows, we defecated in a squatting position, as if nothing were amiss. Then we leapt back into the cars for our things and were ordered to line up for a march. At a station with several tracks, with wooden beams stacked on one side, we read the sign: "Lammsdorf." Lambinowice today.

They led us out into the countryside. The first real landscape. Warm. Without explosions. Since the whole pre-August 1 epoch. After a while we were allowed to rest. Everyone collapsed, with bundles, suitcases, wherever they happened to drop, under the bushes, the trees, among the heather. It was in full bloom. People lay down, stretched, rejoiced, sniffed, breathed deeply.

Finally they led us in through a gate and down a long, wide avenue to the camp which was surrounded by barbed wire. In the camp grounds there were trees, grass, hillocks. It seemed peaceful here, and pleasant, exceptionally so for a camp. Along both sides of the avenue were earthworks, which were overgrown with greenery. A dozen or so years after the war those earthworks were opened accidentally. It turned out that there were corpses in them. That's why they were there.

The camp stretched far into the distance, for we turned into another avenue and walked to the areas reserved for POWs of various nationalities. I was seeing a prisoner of war camp for the first time. I hadn't imagined that there'd be such a small plot of land around each barracks for so many people, and then wires, and the next "run." They were like runs in a zoo. Cages.

From the train they led us into a wire-enclosed space without a barracks, without anything. Perhaps some zookeepers, or otherwise we wouldn't have fit in. (Or rather, we would have all fit, since the Hitlerites relied on literally jamming everyone together into a single mass.)

To the left we had Poles, from 1939. After them, Frenchmen. Farther on, Englishmen, Belgians and other nationalities. Russians too. We immediately became a sensation. The French threw colorful trifles over to us. Something to eat. Razor blades. The prisoners of war were sufficiently well cared for, shaved—at least, that's how it seemed on the surface and at that time. The Poles from 1939 said that now it was peaceful there. Father remembers that they mentioned something about a worse time, now past.

I asked one of the officers—they were officers only, I think—when they had learned about the uprising.

"The first day, in the evening."

"Right away?"

"The radio," he explained.

They began taking us to the baths in groups. People said about it then, "To the mikvah."

Once more we walked quite a long way, through meadows. Near the barracks with the "mikvah" there were plenty of Ukrainians, prisoners of war, moving about. They assisted us in bathing. Or rather—a locker room, showers, standing about—and we were led out.

The bath was like any other. Only one detail. Lice control. And compulsory advice. That on a pole in the center there is a gray ointment. Everyone must take some and smear it on his hair, in his armpits and in the third place. It's a little embarrassing but I will intruduce here a popular song from the occupation:

> Gray ointment is the greatest,
> You only use a little.
> Simply rub it everywhere,
> And your lice will shrivel. . . .

When we were united with the women again on the road Halina told me that they were also attended by Ukrainians, that is, by men only. They walked among the naked women in order to check the showers, laughed and chatted.

"Well? Do you think all the women were offended?"

"Were they?"

"Not in the least. They grinned too and made dates with them."

As we set out on the semicircular road a group of people in special khaki uniforms appeared beyond the bend, carrying knapsacks, rucksacks and haversacks. They were the partisans. Who had just arrived. We were walking with an armed guard. They were too. We were walking towards each other. Excitement rose. Noise. Well —we passed each other. Shouts. Orders. The Germans hurried us on, their lips shaking. They were conducting them to the "mikvah." We were halted by the side of the road for the time being. We waited in place for a while. It was late afternoon. Warm. The partisans were led out of the "mikvah" and lined up beside the road in the meadow, a long way from us. First they just stood there. But then they were ordered to take something, perhaps everything, out of their packs and knapsacks. Then—the sun was just going down—the partisans undressed at a command. Then it became fairly dark and we were sent down the road to our new quarters. We saw them standing there and standing there, stripped down to their underwear for the time being. Despite that, there was nothing ominous in the warm breeze. But yet, as is known, after it was dark they had to strip naked and wait. It is difficult to ascertain what happened later. Some of them were taken elsewhere. Some of them returned. Survived. But no one knows what happened to the others. They disappeared. Were they silently taken off somewhere that night? Or later? It's never been completely explained.

This time they led us into a spacious compound on a hill with greenery—grass and trees—which was separated from the rest of the camp and bordered by the highway and fields of turnips and potatoes along the sides of the valley.

Several spacious tents awaited us. When we entered our tent we found out that we had to sleep on a thick rough layer of shavings. They were arranged in two rows with an aisle between them. The shavings were warm. In fact, the night was warm too.

They gave us something to eat. But we added leftovers from our Warsaw supplies. We had juice, macaroni, sugar cubes. We ate some uncooked food and went to sleep. We began to cook only on the morning of the second day. On stoves made of three bricks, on real little stoves—I don't know where they came from—but perhaps those weren't really stoves, only whatever we'd taken along. Zocha and Stacha also cooked macaroni, although towards evening Zocha was standing in front of the kasha cauldron as server. After one portion of thick soup I brought my messkit over for seconds because Zocha had winked at me, and she poured me a brimming ladleful.

During the day we got a good look at the terrain. We liked it very much. It was good weather, warm all the time. Beyond the string of tents, or rather, as if beyond the courtyard of this new household, was a patch of heather. Whoever wasn't cooking or wasn't in the tents went off to sit there. Halina and I also sat and chatted there. We felt good, as if we were on a school outing.

Towards evening, as was my habit, I took a careful walk around. It was roomy and country-like in the tents. Outside, in the "yard," people either rushed or dragged around. On the edge of the yard opposite the tents was a ditch and a rise covered with bushes. Near the ditch was a row of steaming cookstoves; the Warsaw women were preparing individual suppers. Right behind the stoves children were playing. And behind the children, against the background of bushes above the ditch, on the long plank benches of a field latrine men sat in a row and shat. From the end of the courtyard, from the last, smallest tent came a pious song but not one such as we were accustomed to. I figured out that those were the Russians from Warsaw, our civilians. They always stuck together in a separate group. And always last in their line was a man pushing a cart with quilts, bundles and a sewing machine on the top. They had a separate tent. I looked in: in the corner of the tent, under an ikon and candles, stood a crowd gathered into a triangular mass, crossing themselves every now and then, bowing and singing orthodox vespers.

In the evening, when we had all lain down already on the reed mats and shavings in our tent, we got in the mood to organize a cultural evening. One man stood in the aisle between the shavings and recited Wiech;* another man, young, played a Wieniawski* concerto on his violin.

During the night a storm blew up and during the downpour several of the Warsawites stole past the wires to dig turnips.

Sunday we sat in the heather practically all day.

Transport selections took place almost daily. The Germans would come, the interpreter would make an announcement, ask, explain. It was announced to what destination a particular group was being sent now—and volunteers were called for. You could

231

choose not only whether you wanted to go to a Bauer or a factory but also how far. We immediately decided against a farm.

We were thinking of a city.

I insisted that it should be as near as possible to the borders of the Government General in order to escape to Czestochowa at the first opportunity. Halina was dreaming of Vienna. She liked to sing:

> *Give me back my heart*
> *Which someone stole in Vienna. . . .*

I said that that was frivolous at such a time, and it was also so far away. But she replied:

"But I want to go there and that's all; you're drawn to Czestochowa because of your love affairs."

And so one more separation was in the making. Father didn't want to part with me, or Stacha and Zocha with Halina. But Zocha didn't want to lose Father, and Father also depended on Zocha's and Halina's company—in fact, very much. So that later, in Opole, he ate practically nothing from grief at the separation.

On Monday before noon new groups kept leaving. Until the call came.

"Who wants to go to Opole?"

Father and I volunteered. Halina remained stubborn. Vienna —and that's all. And so we said goodbye hastily. And with our white knapsacks, with the rest of the macaroni and sugar, we got right into the train. That was October 9. November 11, after one month of work as bricklayers' assistants on the construction of a gasworks in Oppeln, Father and I escaped to Czestochowa. During the first snowstorm. Someone had come for us along the circuitous route through Berlin.

The first person from the uprising whom I suddenly saw one evening near a kiosk in Czestochowa was Swen's mother, and the second was Swen, who was holding her arm.

I set eyes on Warsaw again in February 1945.

NOTES

The Doll and his *Weekly Chronicles* include realistic portrayals of Warsaw life.

124 **Kochanowski**—Jan Kochanowski (1530-84), Poland's most important Renaissance poet; translated the Psalms.

133 **Lt. Radoslaw**—Pseudonym of Jan Mazurkiewicz, a career officer who served in the Polish Legions in World War I and as a Home Army leader during the Warsaw Uprising.

135 **Victor Hugo's Jean Valjean**—The ex-convict Jean Valjean is the hero of Hugo's famous novel on social outcasts, *Les Miserables* (1862).

148 **Wanda Wasilewska**—A writer and political activist, Wasilewska spent the war years in the Soviet Union working with various Polish communist propaganda organizations.

150 **Woytowicz**—Boleslaw Woytowicz was a 20th-century composer and pianist.

158 **Wojciech Bak**—A religious poet (1907-61).

185 **"With the smoke from the fires."**—The opening words of a popular patriotic "Chorale" from Kornel Ujejski's (1823-97) *Lamentations of Jeremiah* (1847).

Confederation of Bar—An armed confederation of Polish magnates in southeastern Poland and the Ukraine, 1768-72, which led to Russian intervention and eventually a bloody peasant uprising.

202 **Government General**—That area of occupied Poland, outside of Warsaw, which was not incorporated into the German Reich.

220 **Miracle in Milan**—Italian film directed by Vittorio de Sica, 1950.

231 **Wiech**—Pseudonym of Stefan Wiechecki, 20th-century author of feuilletons and humorous sketches of Warsaw life.

Wieniawski—Henryk Wieniawski (1835-80), violinist and composer.

MEMOIR OF THE WARSAW UPRISING